Praise for *Your Psychic* (

"This book is a responsible and positive approach to what can often be a scary subject for parents and children alike. *Your Psychic Child* might also be called a manual for reaching the Divine. Sara Wiseman has brought the reader a step-by-step introduction to the different aspects of reaching greater levels of consciousness and then takes it a step further with terrific how-to exercises."

—Meg Blackburn Losey, PhD, author of the internationally best-selling *The Children of Now*

"Children today are in touch with energy, intuition, and the inner worlds more than ever before. Sara Wiseman helps us learn to honor kids' wisdom and keep it alive so our young people can grow to be fully integrated human beings, inspired creators, and well-rounded leaders."

—Penney Peirce, intuition expert and author of *Frequency* and *The Intuitive Way*

"Sara Wiseman writes with extraordinary wisdom, clarity, and humor about how to recognize your sensitive children's special gifts, and how to help them avoid the pitfalls while developing their skills. She offers great insights on both parenting and developing intuition that would benefit any reader. Warmly recommended."

—Miriam Knight, founder of *New Consciousness Review*

"A must-have guide for helping children to hone their intuitive gifts and parents to become the conscious creators they long to be."

—Vicky Thompson, author of *Life-Changing Affirmations* and editor of *New Connexion Journal*

"Sara Wiseman is the Erma Bombeck of the psychic crowd . . . Her writing style and her personality offer us a break from the usual 'psychic kids' material. I recommend *Your Psychic Child*, not only to parents and the general public, but also to our children themselves. Kids could and should read this book, too."

—P. M. H. Atwater, author of *Beyond the Indigo Children*

"Finally, a book that answers all the age-old questions about spirit guides, soothsayers, mediums, channels, and more. This book will open the hearts and minds of parents whose children are trying to find their way through a maze of confusion caused by their gift of knowing, feeling, and seeing what others cannot."

—Shirley Enebrad, independent TV producer and author of *Over the Rainbow Bridge*

"This may be one of the most poignant books on parenting of the century. Sara speaks to us not just as an authority, but also as a balanced mom and friend."

—Debra Lynne Katz, author of *You Are Psychic*, *Extraordinary Psychic*, and *Freeing the Genie Within*

For *Writing the Divine*

"The lessons are reasonable, creative, and full of both insight and guidance. This is a good one."

—*New Age Retailer*

"Sassy and approachable, *Writing the Divine* is a great read filled with practical information on how to listen for the messages from the Divine. But take it seriously. There is wisdom in this work. Highly recommended."

—Sophy Burnham, author of the *New York Times* best-seller *A Book of Angels*

"Wiseman lovingly shares with us the treasures of Divine guidance entrusted her by spirit, while gracefully offering us wisdom culled from her own experience of spirit and of practicing *The 33 Lessons*. Wiseman shines in teaching us the true purpose of life: our soul growth."

—Michael J Tamura, visionary teacher, spiritual-healing pioneer, clairvoyant, and award-winning author of *You Are the Answer*

"In *Writing the Divine*, Wiseman demystifies the channeling process, making a sacred act simple. With wit and delightful humor, she shares practical tools for connecting with the Divine inner voice."

—Vicky Thompson, editor of *New Connexion Journal* and author of *Life-Changing Affirmations*

"A much-needed practical guide to safely opening your intuitive channels. The simple but powerful lessons provide a soul-focused approach to living, which is a breath of fresh air in a world obsessed with materialism."

—Susan Wisehart, author of *Soul Visioning*

"Wiseman's book is like no other. Her receiving is absolutely exquisite, and her narrative makes channeling understandable and accessible to anyone with an open heart and eager mind. It is the most concise, clear, and simple book on channeling I've seen since Sanaya Roman's *Opening to Channel* was published in 1987. I intend to make it required reading for my students."

—Terri Daniel, author of *A Swan in Heaven*

YOUR
psychic
C H I L D

About the Author

Sara Wiseman experienced a spiritual awakening in 2008, when she unexpectedly received *The 33 Lessons*, an intensive experience of channeled writing that begins "The purpose of life is soul growth." These *33 Lessons* are featured in her book, *Writing the Divine: How to Use Channeling for Soul Growth & Healing*. At that time, she also became fully psychic. Today, she teaches workshops and offers private intuitive counseling and intuitive training to clients worldwide. Prior to this, Wiseman was a journalist for national media, specializing in parenting and wellness. An award-winning musician living in Oregon, she has released three CDs with her band, Martyrs of Sound. For more information, please visit her websites, www.sarawiseman.com and http://yourpsychicchild.com.

— Sara Wiseman —

YOUR
psychic
CHILD

How to Raise

Intuitive

&

Spiritually Gifted

Kids

of All Ages

Llewellyn Publications
Woodbury, Minnesota

First Edition
First Printing, 2010

Cover art © Don Mason/Blend Images/PunchStock
Cover design by Ellen Lawson
Editing by Brett Fechheimer

Llewellyn is a registered trademark of Llewellyn Worldwide Ltd.

Library of Congress Cataloging-in-Publication Data

Wiseman, Sara, 1962–
  Your psychic child : how to raise intuitive & spiritually gifted kids of all ages / Sara Wiseman.
     p.   cm.
  Includes bibliographical references and index.
  ISBN 978-0-7387-2061-6
  1. Children—Psychic ability. I. Title.
  BF1045.C45W57 2010
  133.8083—dc22
                        2010032381

Llewellyn Worldwide Ltd. does not participate in, endorse, or have any authority or responsibility concerning private business transactions between our authors and the public.
  All mail addressed to the author is forwarded, but the publisher cannot, unless specifically instructed by the author, give out an address or phone number.
  Any Internet references contained in this work are current at publication time, but the publisher cannot guarantee that a specific location will continue to be maintained. Please refer to the publisher's website for links to authors' websites and other sources.
  Cover model used for illustrative purposes only and may not endorse or represent the book's subject matter.

Llewellyn Publications
A Division of Llewellyn Worldwide Ltd.
2143 Wooddale Drive
Woodbury, MN 55125-2989
www.llewellyn.com

Printed in the United States of America

Other books by Sara Wiseman

Writing the Divine:
How to Use Channeling for Soul Growth & Healing

Forthcoming books by Sara Wiseman

The Intuitive Path: 33 Steps to Clarity,
Inspiration & Joy

This book is dedicated to all the parents, stepparents, grandparents, teachers, and caregivers who have taken on the brave task of raising and mentoring this amazing new generation of children

Acknowledgments

First, love and thanks to my three amazing children and my step-son—my heart has been opened beyond measure by knowing you. Also to my mother, Sallye Knudson, who raised me intuitively during a time when intuition wasn't even on the radar. And, as always, love and gratitude to my partner, Dr. Steve Koc, for his saint-like patience and commitment.

Accolades to my literary agent, Krista Goering, who has a knack for knowing my next best step; acquisitions editor Carrie Obry, who's been savvy at every turn; publicity marvels Steven Pomije and Marissa Pederson; production editor Brett Fechheimer; cover designer Ellen Lawson; interior designer Donna Burch; and Dan Goodnow, my electronica guru, without whom I could not function. Thank you.

And, finally, thanks to all the colleagues, clients, and friends who have supported this work in which psychic development and spiritual awakening intertwine—it would not be possible without you.

Contents

Preface

I am four years old, standing in the living room, not doing anything in particular, when suddenly, inexplicably, the air around me shifts and I can see the energy of the Universe. The air appears particulate, as does everything around it: our plain-legged furniture, my baby brother's white playpen—everything moves both fast and slow at the same time, and I see a shimmer that is everywhere and everything.

Yet I am just a small child . . . I tell my mother I see "dust," and ask, does she see it too?

I am able to see this way for many years—this shifting, as if one dimension has suddenly overlapped another, and the essence of the Universe is revealed.

I am in fifth grade. I've just arrived home from the library with a stack of books so tall I can't carry them in one armload—thick tomes on religion, metaphysics, sacred texts. I want to determine what religion I will be, I tell my mother. She doesn't have any answers, but she takes me back to the library every week. Over time, I read all the books in these sections.

None of my questions are answered.

I am a child, perhaps eight, and we are at the coast for Thanksgiving. My brother and I wade in a small stream that flows from the forest to the Pacific, jeans rolled to our knees, feet red with cold. A breeze roars in over the ocean, and at that moment I hear God. I know this deeply—as completely as I've understood anything.

These mystic moments are just a small handful of what I now pull from my childhood memory bag. Looking back, reviewing this tiny sampling, makes it easier for me to understand how it is that today, as an adult, I'm psychic.

Of course, I didn't have the words for any of these mystic moments when I was a kid. My parents simply dubbed me "sensitive" or "creative." Most psychic and spiritually gifted children are similarly misnomered. It wasn't until decades later that I finally understood that my confusing ability to sense, see, and hear in a different dimension was the start of psychic and spiritual "opening." Back then, in the dark ages of my childhood, nobody knew how this stuff worked.

Luckily, we do now.

Introduction

Today I did a psychic reading for a client, had an enlightening discussion with my spirit guides, and scribed four pages of *The Messages*—spiritual teachings that I receive via channeled writing.

Oh, yes—I also transported three kids to school, whipped out five loads of laundry, and slammed together a family-sized lasagna for dinner.

I am a psychic—and I am a mother.

This unique commingling of the intuitive and the maternal in my life has given me extraordinary insight into the needs of today's psychic and spiritually gifted children. Another reason I understand what these kids need? I'm smack dab in the middle of raising three of them, currently ages nine, thirteen, and eighteen.

Over the past decades, there's been a lot of talk about Indigos, Crystals, Rainbows, Stars—just a few of the names given to the new breed of sensitive and intuitive kids who have begun showing up en masse on this earth. These names certainly opened our eyes early on, when these children were first being identified. But my belief, as a psychic and as a mother, is that such nomenclature isn't particularly useful anymore.

The truth is, we humans evolve—perhaps slowly, but we do move forward! Psychic development, the use of our "sixth sense," and our ability to do more with our brains not only intellectually but also psychically and spiritually—these abilities are all simply a natural part of human evolution. In other words, labels don't change that.

For reasons beyond our understanding, today's kids are more psychic than they've ever been. Technology is one certain catalyst—computers and smartphones are training our brains to work in new ways. But the biggest reason today's kids are starting to exhibit more intuitive gifts? In a nutshell, it's because *they've evolved to be that way*—they're a new generation, born with abilities that past generations simply didn't have.

If you're a parent, stepparent, grandparent, teacher, or caregiver for these amazing kids, this concept can be a bit disconcerting. A child more evolved than you? A kid with "superpowers" you don't comprehend? A child who naturally works with energies you don't understand? A little spoon-bender living right in your midst?

What's more, how do you support your little intuitive, especially if you don't have much psychic experience yourself? How do you respond if she sees visions clairvoyantly, or hears messages clairaudiently? What do you say when his spiritual knowing is deeper and more fully formed than that of any of the leaders at your church? What do you do when your child says there are spirits in his bedroom—and you realize he's telling the truth?

Luckily, help is at hand. In this book, you'll find everything you need to know about how to support, mentor, and raise this new generation of intuitive and spiritually advanced kids.

From communicating with spirit guides to picking up socks, working with energy to putting the toilet seat down, I'll share everything I know—gathered both from my experience as a psychic mom in the trenches and also as a journalist who has researched and reported on kids' issues for years.

You'll learn:

• The stages of intuitive "opening"

• What each specific psychic ability looks like

• How to help your child when she sees, hears, or feels with her psychic senses

• How your child may feel about being psychic or spiritually gifted

- How to maintain balance and humor in a mainstream life
- Age-appropriate development
- Problems and concerns to watch out for
- Exercises and practices to help your child's gifts open
- FAQs from parents, which address the most common situations you'll run into

Finally, this book contains the spiritual teachings that I received from my spirit guides via channeled writing. Dubbed *The Messages*, these Divine teachings offer support and guidance to those entrusted with these amazing new children.

part one

emergence

one

A New Shade of Indigo

Your world has changed. It has been changing since the beginning of time.

Your children are new. They are new to the world. They are not the same as you, or as the ones who came before you. Each generation brings forward its ability for that time. Your children bring with them the abilities of their Divine minds. —The Messages

————

Marissa, who is eight, first saw her grandparents (who died before she was born) when she was a toddler. Her mother chalked it up to an overactive imagination. But lately, Marissa has been seeing the spirits of departed people of all sorts—at the grocery store, the library, almost every time she's in public. Now, her mom is starting to think that Marissa might be a medium—and she's not sure what to do.

Juan is just six, but he understands how energy works. Not the kind of energy you get when you plug in a lamp, or turn on a stove. But the energy that streams forth from his hands when he's around people who are sick. His hands get hot and sometimes tingly, and he has the overwhelming feeling that he should put his hands on people—especially his uncle, who has been ill for the last year. Juan thinks if he can do this, his uncle will get better. But when Juan asks his father about it, his dad gets angry.

Olivia sees angels. She also talks to them, sings to them, draws them, and plays games with them. Her parents were so concerned that they had her tested last year, but the psychologist said she was one of the happiest, most well-adjusted ten-year-olds he'd ever seen. At this point, they're hoping she'll grow out of it.

Animals follow Brandon. Not just dogs and cats, but sometimes wild creatures. He already knows he's going to be a veterinarian when he grows up, "because we don't take care of animals right," he tells his mom. When asked how he knows this, he answers, "They tell me what they need."

Max has trouble at school. From the moment he walks into the building, his head hurts, he gets distracted, he's overwhelmed with stimulation. The school wants him tested for ADD/ADHD, but his mom doesn't think that's it—Max is fine when he's at home. "The energy isn't good there," he says about school, and after volunteering in the classroom last week, his mom agrees.

Jasmine sees things before they happen. She's been so accurate about her predictions that her parents have come to accept that she's got some kind of psychic ability. Yet they're not sure how to help her further. She's only seven—should she go somewhere for training?

Thomas has refused to be an altar boy this year. He's thirteen, and he's been a server since he was eleven. But now he says, what's the point? "God's always with us, not just in church on Sunday," he explained to the priest as he turned in his robe. His parents are upset, and so is the priest—but Thomas won't apologize.

Jake is off in dreamland so much, he might as well live there. He gets a distant look on his face and just sits there "with my thoughts," as he says. When his mom asks what he's thinking about, he says, "God, and just being," and can't explain anything more. She's decided not to push it, since he's popular at his middle school and his grades are fine . . .

Are you raising a little spoon-bender?

Do you know children like these? What's more, do you get the sneaking suspicion that they might be living at your house, disguised as your kids? If you're raising or mentoring a psychically or spiritually gifted child, you've probably already begun to suspect there's something "different" about him or her. For example:

- Is she "psychic" about certain people, situations, even places or objects?
- Does he communicate with dead people, such as your great-uncle Rudy on your paternal side?
- Does she see entities, orbs, other energies?
- Can he heal things and work with energy, without being able to explain how he does it?
- Does she tell you in great detail about places she has seen and traveled in, even though she's never been out of her home state?
- Does he talk to animals and/or commune with nature?
- Is he so "sensitive" that he can hardly deal with the stress of going to school each day?
- Does she have the calm presence of a little Buddha, even though you yourself are notoriously unable to meditate?
- Does your child "just know" about God and energy and time and the Universe, and you have no idea where this information came from?

These are all clear signs of having a psychic or spiritually advanced child.

A generation beyond Indigo

Of course, we've known about these new kids for years—and we've been inundated with labels for them!

The "Indigos" were the first group to be named—brought to our attention by Lee Carroll and Jan Tober, authors of the 1999 book *The*

Indigo Children, in which they defined this new type of child as "one who displays a new an unusual set of psychological attributes."

While most people think of Indigo as synonymous with intuitive, it's important to note that Indigos weren't primarily categorized this way. Instead, Indigos were categorized as being identifiable with ten common traits, a few of which included:

> *(1) They come into the world with a feeling of royalty (and often act like it). (2) They have a feeling of "deserving to be here," and are surprised when others don't share that. (3) Self-worth is not a big issue. They often tell their parents "who they are."*[1]

In other words, Carroll and Tober identified the Indigos as different—but their focus wasn't specifically on intuition.

Other experts soon came forward with their own names for this generation of unusual kids, and many focused on the needs of ADD/ADHD kids or children with autism—an epidemic that began to be noticed about the same time. Nowadays, some form of autism now presents in one out of 110 American children, according to a 2009 study by the Centers for Disease Control and Prevention.[2]

Author Doreen Virtue dubbed them the *Rainbows* (the group who arrived immediately after Indigo) and the *Crystals* (those born after 1995, often with pale blue eyes and a knack for telepathy, energy work, and healing). Other authors offered ways of determining which category of child you had, based on year of birth or physical characteristics or behaviors.

Adding to the mix, Sonia Choquette wrote elegantly (and sans label) about the intuitive kids in her book *The Wise Child*. And James Twyman traveled to Bulgaria in 2001, where he wrote about kids with spiritual gifts in his book *Emissary of Love*.

---

1. Carroll and Tober, *The Indigo Children: The New Kids Have Arrived*, 1–2.
2. The findings are described in more detail online, at www.cdc.gov/ncbddd/features/counting-autism.html.

In fact, so many experts had so much to say, and so many terms were used, that many parents didn't quite know how to categorize their kids. Were they living with an Indigo—or a Star? A Crystal—or a Rainbow?

In 2005, P. M. H. Atwater confronted the label confusion in her book *Beyond the Indigo Children*, stating that this new generation had been variously described "as Indigos (because of the supposed color of their auras), Star Kids (because of their purported origination from other worlds), Crystal children (because some say they are highly developed), and so forth."[3]

More recently, author Meg Blackburn Losey added a few more categories (Angels on Earth, Transitional Children) in her book *The Children of Now*, which looks especially at the autism/intuition connection. For parents with children challenged by ADD/ADHD or autism, books like these are a compassionate cry for new ways of helping these kids.

But for parents with questions about mainstream kids who don't have these particular challenges, this long history of "Indigo" and subsequent labels can be confusing!

My own feeling is that as today's psychic kids continue to be born into this world at an accelerated rate—well, the time for categories is over. The tipping point for these new kids? It's been reached. These kids are here. They're our kids. And they're very much more evolved than we are. Yes, they're still children. Yes, they still play too much Nintendo/fight with their siblings/forget to feed the dog. But their minds are far more nimble in understanding and working with psychic and spiritual concepts than ours.

That said, how can you help your own child?

Fortunately, crystal-ball gazing lessons are not required. In fact, as you read on, you'll discover that the most important thing parents can do for their psychic or spiritually advanced child is to teach him how to have a *direct connection* to the Divine, and then to provide an

---

3. Atwater, *Beyond the Indigo Children: The New Children and the Coming of the Fifth World*, 51.

environment that supports this. I'll show you how to do this, as well as how to work directly with your child in all aspects of his gifts, including:

- Clairvoyance—the art of psychic seeing
- Clairaudience—the art of psychic hearing
- Clairsentience—gut feelings, instinct, "vibe"
- Channeling—moving aside so other entities can communicate
- Mediumship—communicating with those who have departed
- Energy healing—the ability to work with energy for hands-on and distance healing
- Spiritual knowing—a deep understanding of spiritual and meta-physical concepts
- Other abilities—abilities that emerge as we continue to evolve

How understanding psychic gifts helps your child

First, if your child has been confused by some of the psychic or spiritual experiences she's had lately, then understanding more about these gifts will definitely help. She (and you) will learn that what she's experiencing is normal—part and parcel of what's happening to many kids in the world today. She'll also learn which gifts come easiest to her, and what to expect from each particular ability.

Second, psychic gifts and spiritual abilities aren't mere parlor tricks; they're exciting tools your child can use in her everyday life. In fact, understanding how to work with these abilities—these "extra" or "sixth" senses—can help your child create a more enjoyable, more directed life that's in tune with Divine Flow. Living this way is the most blissful, effortless way to live that's available to us as humans!

That's a pretty handy tool for your child to learn.

Furthermore, these skills aren't particularly hard to teach or learn, and I'll walk you through them step by step, with plenty of room for questions. Yes, there's a certain paradigm shift involved—you'll need to move from "I can work with energy?" to "I can work with energy!" But besides that, you certainly don't have to have any psychic skills to help your Divine child . . . although there's a very good chance that simply by reading this book, your own intuitive abilities may "open."

That said, how do you feel? Are you curious? Excited? Uncertain? Worried you won't know what to do—or worse, that you might become psychic along the way?

Take another deep breath, and get ready.

You're a parent.

You can do anything.

two

Your Child Has Chosen You

The terms you have used: Indigo, Crystal. We do not require these terms.
Each generation of children, even the generation you have been born
into, is an evolution in consciousness. The human collective in first-
world countries is evolving. Partly this is due to better state of the body.
Partly this is due to the fact that beings in a safe state are able to evolve.
For humans in war, disease, poverty—evolution goes more slowly for this
group as a whole.

In order to elevate the human race, all humans must be elevated. We
are all One. Surely this is known to you?—The Messages

———

It happens to every parent eventually.

You wake up one morning, slap some milk and cereal on the counter in preparation for another race-the-clock routine of getting the
kids to school, and you realize amidst the clamor of "Where's my
backpack?" and "I need the bathroom, now!" that you—yes, you!—
have become The Person in Charge.

Somehow, unwittingly, by some sly trick of the Universe, you became Head Honcho (or Honchoette). Fearless Family Leader. Go-To
Gal or Guy. Somehow, you have become The Parent.

It's not an easy task for anyone—and especially not for those of
you who have found yourself suddenly faced with the challenge of
raising psychic or spiritually advanced children (whom I call *SAKs*).

How in the heck did this happen, you might ask? How is it that you've been chosen to direct, mentor, and guide this child who is so obviously different, gifted, advanced . . .especially when you don't have a single speck of psychic ability yourself, or if you do, you don't really know how to use it? What's more, with all the advice out there from parenting pundits, development experts, and mothers-in-law about what's "best" for kids, how are you supposed to know if you're doing it right?

Well, I'd like to let you in on a little secret.

You don't have to do it right.

Perfection is not the goal

I have a confession to make.

I'm a B-minus mom.

Twenty-six years ago, when I first started this commitment or life-style or whatever you want to call this Perilous Path of Parenting, I most definitely rated an A-plus.

I was stepmother to one bright, lively little boy at the time, and I did it all: sewed elaborate Halloween costumes, cheered from the sidelines, joined every school committee, gathered materials for arts-and-crafts projects, agonized over which kindergarten was best, and screened play dates for "bad" influences.

Super Stepmom? I was front of the pack, racing to the finish line of overachievement as fast as I could.

Today, with four kids under my belt, I can barely hear the starting gun.

I shamelessly check "No, can't make it" on the school forms requesting field-trip drivers. I'll sit on the sidelines in my fold-up chair for a soccer game—but only if that particular child insists I attend. I avoid sewing (and ironing and pie-making) like the Black Death. I accept my children's friends differently than I used to, looking deeper instead of only seeing what's on the surface.

I don't love my kids any less than when I was Super Mom.

It's just that over the years I've learned that many of the things I thought were Immutable Laws of Parenting just don't matter.

Permanent residency on the pee-wee soccer sideline?

On call 24/7 as a classroom volunteer?

Sandwiches cut in star shapes?

I've done it all for my kids—and nowadays, I don't do very much of it. In fact, as a parent, I no longer follow many of the parenting "rules."

Who's in charge here, anyway?

What happened?

Simply put, the Divine had other plans for me.

One day I was a soccer mom, cheering from the sidelines, fully enmeshed in the team, the tournaments—everything to make sure my child would have an enriched life brimming with possibilities. I was PTA volunteer, homework coach, head chauffeur—you name it, I was doing it "right" for my kids.

The next day, out of the blue, I became a channel, receiving *The 33 Lessons* via channeled writing—profound spiritual teachings that became the starting point for my book *Writing the Divine*. During this same time, my psychic abilities "opened." Boom. No warning signs. It just happened. And this "awakening," which was both unexpected and not entirely welcome, changed my life forever.

Those "rules" that I was such a stickler for? They didn't make much sense anymore. Those parenting pundits I listened to? I stopped caring what they said. The game of parenthood I was playing so fiercely to win? It became clear that "winning" wasn't the point—and probably not even possible.

My opening as an adult-emergent psychic shifted my perspective from "I am in charge of my life, and ergo I am in charge of my child's life" to something along the lines of . . .

I'm not in charge.

The Divine's in charge.

And with the Divine in charge . . . well, it's a whole new ball game.

Of course, the basic tenets of child development still apply: roll before crawl, crawl before walk, kindergarten before first grade, driver's permit before car keys! But as I began to build my life upon a direct connection to the Divine—the source of my psychic abilities—I also began to turn off the voices that compelled me to live in fear of "doing something wrong" or "missing an opportunity" or "not keeping up." I stopped getting unnerved when I heard other parents talking about the "best" preschools, early specializing to get into the best college, the importance of enrichment activities every day of the week, and how to pump up SAT scores. I opted out of many mainstream parenting "must dos," and instead began to listen to the Divine instructions that would provide me with new ways to live my life and raise my children.

Yes, it can be quite scary to quit, bow out, or excuse yourself from all the things that everyone—from the media to your mother-in-law—tells you are necessary for raising a "successful" child.

But at a certain point, when you are raising a child with psychic and spiritual gifts, there is no other option.

But what if I mess up?

The Path of Parenthood is fraught with peril.

For parents of psychic and spiritually advanced kids (SAKs), it's even more challenging. Not only do you need the patience of a saint and the stamina of a triathlete, but you also need perseverance to continually steer your child toward the end goal of becoming a responsible, well-adjusted, and productive adult.

Even more challenging, you often have to raise your child with someone else, which even in the best marriages or partnerships means copious differences of opinion on child rearing: *SpongeBob* or *Sesame Street*? Christmas or Hanukkah? Strawberry jam or grape jelly? And so on, ad infinitum.

Of course, if you're a single parent, then you do have the luxury of setting up your home the way you want it with no interference from grape-jelly aficionados—but you also have to deal with being overextended, exhausted, and not having the support of a partner when the going gets tough.

Plus, even if you're an A-plus parent who does everything "right," your child might still grow up to be a thief, slacker, cheat, liar, addict, abuser . . . all these things we stay awake at night worrying about. Yep, it's entirely true; you can do everything absolutely right, and your children still might not turn out the way you planned! If you're a CEO, they're sure to become hippies. If you're a hippie, CEOs you'll breed. Genetics, environment, destiny, free will—with a mix like that, anything can happen!

Fortunately, the Universe is not random.

This means only one thing: *your child has chosen you.*

Your child has chosen you

You know those old-time cartoons where the baby is left on the doorstep of some unsuspecting couple? The stork or angel or whoever is delivering the baby rings the doorbell, flees, and out step the unsuspecting new parents-to-be, cooing and oohing, and they take the baby inside for a life of comfort and bliss?

Energetically, apart from the business with the stork, this actually *is* what happens.

Your child chooses you.

You and your child have a karmic contract written in the time before time.

You are destined to be with your exact, specific, particular child, on this earth, in this lifetime.

Now, you may not see this clearly at the moment your little squeezer pours the contents of his sippy cup into your computer keyboard. You may not see it when your preteen shouts "I hate you" and storms from the room, slamming her bedroom door so hard the windows shake. You may not *want* to see it when your older teenager goes Goth right before your eyes (and yes, that is your black eyeliner he's wearing).

But so it is.

In the Divine messages I've received, it's crystal clear that children choose their parents long before they're born, long before they're even a twinkle in their parents' eyes.

Your particular child—that tiny bundle of gooey mouth, dirty diaper, and irresistible dimples—whether he arrived to you via birth, adoption, or in any of the myriad ways that true families are formed, has chosen you.

You have a karmic contract, signed by both of you before you even set foot in this particular lifetime on Earth. Even though this time around, you're the parent and this new being is the child, in reality you are both simply souls on your path of soul growth.

It can be very hard to remember this—especially with your first child. You feel so responsible! But whether you're the parent of your first or your fifth, it's true—your job is to protect each and every one from wild creatures who might carry them off into the forest; you must slather the appropriate SPF on their bodies every twenty minutes; you must demand they eat their broccoli. It's all part of your Parental Job Description.

Yet no matter how hard you try to protect and prepare your child for this amazing journey called Life, she must follow her own path. She is responsible, even from babyhood, for her own soul growth.

Every soul knows this. Especially psychic kids and SAKs.

Your child has chosen you means that you have agreed to work with this soul. This soul has agreed to work with you. Your child may be a soul you have known for a long time, and you may recognize him at birth, as in "Oh, of course, I know this kid." Or, your child may seem like an alien to you, as in "How could this possibly be the fruit of my loins?" Or, your child may be someone you recognize—i.e., your ex-husband's deceased aunt.

Regardless of you and your child's previous relationship, you're in for the duration. In this life, on this planet, you and your child are here to teach each other. And all of this teaching, learning, and growing? This soul growth? Well, it goes both ways, regardless of who's holding the parenting rudder this time around.

So don't think you can mess up. Don't worry that you're going to do it all wrong. Your child has chosen you, so that the two of you may experience your soul growth together.

Karmic contracts and more

How do karmic contracts, soul clusters, and primary soulmates work?

In most cases, your child will arrive to you via what Dr. Michael Newton, author of *Life Between Lives*, calls a "soul cluster": a group of souls who have agreed to go through many lives together. Newton's research into past-life regression shows that most people are able to recall the place they existed before their life on this earth—not their past life, but a life between their past life and this one. It's here, in this holding tank for souls, that people review their life choices, and work to decide what will happen for them in their next life.

Remember: the purpose of life is soul growth. Souls who, during their *life between lives*, are reviewing mistakes made and progress achieved aren't hankering to acquire the biggest McMansion on the block in their next life, or to be the star pitcher for the Yankees (okay, maybe some of them are). No, these souls are hoping to experience soul growth in their next life, and to work on specific soul lessons that perhaps, shall we say, eluded them the last time around.

I find Newton's work to be especially interesting, because as I have worked in deep trance, I've had amazingly similar experiences to what Newton's subjects report. In his book *Destiny of Souls*, he reports specific places and teachings that I've experienced during my own psychic journeys; seeing diagrams of these places in his book was a shock to me—déjà vu! I've been there already!

From my psychic experiences, I also know this: the spirit realm is alive and well. We have all lived on the spiritual plane, as spiritual beings existing within many dimensions, layers, or realms. But the human experience is, quite simply, the cherry on top!

This particular life on Earth is a fantastic place for us to learn more complex soul lessons, as spiritual beings inhabiting Earth bodies, bound to each other not only through our collective soul but also through the emotions of our tender, human hearts.

Newton's concept of soul clusters means that your child is very likely to be someone you knew before in another lifetime. He or she may be from your soul cluster or from a neighboring soul cluster. What this means, again, is that your child has chosen you (and you've chosen your child). Birth, adoption, stepchild, met later in life—doesn't matter. Karmically, family is family is family across all dimensions, no matter what the blood tests show.

The fine print

About that karmic contract you and your child signed? Well, if you look at the fine print, the areas where your child continually challenges you, tests you, and makes you crazy—hmm, this may be where you'll find the soul-growth lesson you're here to learn.

Master psychic and spiritual teacher Michael Tamura puts it nicely in his book *You Are the Answer*: If you ask for patience, you can bet that events and incidents are suddenly going to pop up that try your patience! You don't just say, "Hey, I want more patience" and suddenly, boom, there you are, Ms. or Mr. Serenity! No, you get to *practice* patience. You get to try it on, until that aspect of your personality eventually begins to fit you as easily as a favorite jacket.

For example, if you're a neatnik and your child is a total slob—we're talking wet towels left on the bed until both towel and bedspread have bonded together in a mildewed funk, dirty socks left to stiffen like dead mice on the floor, half-finished mugs of cocoa breeding a fuzzy substance on the surface—the choice eventually becomes one of response: will you try to control the issue or will you try to let go? It's not that one response is wrong or right. It's just that deciding how you'll act is one of the soul lessons that you face with this child.

Or, let's say you're a parent with a very open, compassionate heart, and for whatever reason, your child is consistently mean-spirited. To your mind, your child does not show a proper amount of compassion. Will you battle and rage against your child so that he or she will become more openhearted? Will you show by example? Will you suffer deeply? How will you respond to your child? How will you teach your child? How will you learn this lesson?

Pretty fertile ground for soul growth, here.

Karma runs in families, too

The above examples, of course, are minor problems. Unfortunately, most families experience the gamut of ugly, huge, life-altering issues: divorce, death, poverty, abuse, molestation, abandonment, illness, addiction.

Wow.

Some theories point to the idea that these issues don't just present in this family—that they're deeply imbedded in the karma of our ancestors. In Systemic, or Family, Constellation, a process created by German psychotherapist Bert Hellinger, participants are taught to explore the "constellation" of their family: mother, father, siblings, grandparents, and so forth.

Working with a facilitator skilled in this process, these patterns are psychically revealed. For example, if you have a grandparent who was interned in a concentration camp during World War II; if your mother was abused by a family member; if your great-aunt died of tuberculosis; if your father had an addiction—these kinds of issues can play forward energetically now, in your own family. In other words, sometimes we aren't just working with our own karma. We're working with karma inherited from our ancestors.

Forgiveness is the watchword when reviewing your ancestral "constellation," according to Hellinger, even if those from the past may have caused harm to others in the family: "We then realize that all of us are just the same. No differences, especially in front of that which carries us, all of us together, all of us are just the same."[4]

---

4. Bert Hellinger, "New Development in Family Constellations." From a talk in Santa Barbara, California, on July 28, 2002. See www.systemicfamilysolutions .com/articles_newdevelopments.html.

As a parent, as a human being, it's rare to be perfect. Most of us stumble along with our kids, messing up a lot, yelling when we wish we hadn't. (Just the other day, I yelled at my son for not doing his homework. Turns out he had the flu, and he promptly vomited his dinner and missed two days of school. Nice going, Mom!) As parents, we'll make bad decisions sometimes, good decisions other times, and this happens continually and constantly as we move through yet another life with this particular other soul.

It may be that in this particular Earth life, with this particular child, you'll make some progress.

Or maybe you won't.

Our Earth reality is that we have a limited, finite number of years, days, hours, and minutes to spend with our beautiful, lovely, maddening, fantastic children, in these bodies, in this life.

But from a soul perspective, you've got time. In fact, the process of soul growth takes as long as is required. You and your child, both souls who have agreed to hunker down in this life on this earth this time around and get through it as best as you both can, have got all the time you need.

three
Evolution Happens

We say again: your children are different from you. They are moving further along in the area of connection to the One. It is not that one generation of children is better than another. It is simply that each generation brings with it what is needed for your Earth life now. These children understand how to use energy. They understand time and space. They see what is unseen, and what has been shrouded by belief, religion, custom, training, education—all the ways in which you create your view of the world. —The Messages

———

You know those "You Are Here" maps at the mall? You know, the ones with the big orange arrow that points to right where you are?

Same goes for life.

For whatever reason, You Are Here on this earth, and one of your tasks is to raise a child with psychic or spiritual gifts. When faced with a challenge like this, it can be tempting to scurry around, searching for a label or category to use—the way we used "Indigo" or other names in the past.

Instead, I'd suggest that you simply *recognize that your child belongs to a new generation*—a generation of kids that is more evolved, more gifted, and more able to delve into the realm of "sixth sense" than we've ever seen before. Labels not required.

Another reason to skip the labels? The truth is, we're all souls; we're all brimming infinite beings. Labeling, even the positive kind, can limit us all.

I mean, imagine you had two identical little marigold sproutlings, the kind your kid brings home from preschool around Mother's Day in a little paper Dixie cup (unless you will be getting a macaroni necklace this year). Your child's chubby hands have carefully planted these seeds in the dirt, and he's diligently watered them for the past two weeks with the rest of his preschool class, proud that his seeds have survived the first treacherous days of life, and now, *voilà*! He presents you with two little tender sproutlings, and you're so touched that you hug him and reach for the Kleenex and secretly pray, "Please God don't let me kill these plants."

Now, each of these two little marigolds are brimming with possibility—tender new shoots with a lifetime of growth potential before them, their whole bright futures ahead of them! But what if you decided to label one the "good" marigold, and the other the "bad" marigold?

As we've seen from countless research over the years—including the studies in Dr. Masaru Emoto's *Messages from Water* books on how emotions and intent affect water's vibration—what we expect, what we project, and what we manifest is what will in fact happen.

You'd expect that the "good" marigold will grow to be a sturdy, blossoming plant, entirely suitable for repotting outside—and it likely will. You'd guess that the "bad" marigold will wither to a sad little shrivel and be tossed on the compost heap—and it's pretty much a given that this is what will come to pass.

What we expect to happen, will.

Yet—what if the "bad" marigold was really, secretly, of sturdier stock than the "good" one? What if the "bad" marigold actually *had more potential to thrive*, but because it was labeled "bad," it satisfied expectations, manifestations—and didn't?

In the same way, *when we label people, we disconnect from the fact that they are souls, and that all souls are inherently perfect and inherently equal.* We lose sight of each person's innate beauty and Divinity.

It's bad enough when we label an adult ("loser," "deadbeat," "neurotic"), who may have made his or her share of mistakes, bad decisions, and so forth over his or her decades on this planet. But when we label a growing, developing child as "bad" or "good," we effectively set expectations that the child can't help but fulfill.

Even the most basic research on academic performance shows that kids who are told in elementary school that they're "smart" consistently perform better than kids who are told they're "dumb." It doesn't matter which kids actually have higher IQs—kid perform as they're labeled.

What we expect is what comes into being. In other words, if your kids hear you saying they're "this" or "that," they'll believe it—and they'll become it. This is true of academics, sports, music, and so forth.

It's also true of psychic and spiritual development.

Saints and mystics and SAKs, oh my!

Age of Aquarius! Year 2012! Global shifts in awareness! Yes, the world is changing—and fast. Yet it's also important to remember that at their core, psychic abilities are nothing new.

As human beings, we've been psychic for eons—not en masse, as is happening now with our kids. But people having visions, visitations, and revelations from the Divine? It's one of the most common stories in ancient cultures worldwide.

For example, as anyone who has been raised Judeo-Christian knows, the Bible is brimming with saints and mystics, starting with Moses who saw the burning bush and who also hauled himself all the way up a mountain to get the Ten Commandments. When he got there—wind howling, sun beating down, his legs aching from the climb and his mouth parched with thirst—God simply told him what to write, and Moses scribed in stone.

If this isn't early channeled writing, I don't know what is!

And let's not forget Joan of Arc, who as a young peasant girl in eastern France was said to have heard the voice of God. In this saint's particular psychic opening, she channeled Divine guidance in order to lead the French army to victory during the Hundred Years' War.

Clearly, clairaudience!

And these are just the stories from Christianity!

The same stuff happened to Buddha and all the other numerous enlightened beings and spiritual masters who have existed or now exist on this planet.

In fact, I'd be hard-pressed to think of any religious tradition in which the masters and leaders did *not* converse directly with God. All we have to do is look back in the ancient sacred texts, and we see that every culture on the planet hails spiritual leaders who received Divine guidance via their psychic abilities—they saw, heard, or were fully directed by the higher presence of the Divine through clairvoyance, clairaudience, channeled writing, and more.

What's more, even non-religious literature is full of psychic stuff! Myths, legends, and fairy tales the world over tell stories of a young man (or maiden) who sets off on a journey of discovery, then comes across some type of Divine guidance in the guise of an old wise woman, a talking fish, a magic table, or some aspect of the natural world.

An old wise woman who provides the secrets to how to get into the castle? A spirit guide, pure and simple.

A talking fish that tells you what to do next? Clairaudience, for sure.

A magic table that fills with food every time you set it out? Divine manifesting, no doubt.

Even hundreds of generations before us, folks the world over understood that this was how the Universe worked.

Of course, this is nothing new; all these tales of saints and mystics and fair maidens speak to our common understanding that *it is possible to connect and communicate directly with the Divine.*

What is new, and what your child already knows without being told, is that you don't have to climb a mountain like Moses, or lead an army into war like Joan of Arc, or meet a talking fish on your particular hero's journey through this life. This kind of Divine guidance is available immediately to all of us, at any time, simply by asking. Again, this is nothing new to your psychic or spiritually advanced child.

They've been waiting for us to catch on, since the day they were born.

Evolution through technology

Did you really think we wouldn't evolve? That we'd never emerge upright from our knuckle-dragging days as Cro-Magnon men and women? That we'd never lose our full-body fur and protruding jawline?

Well, change is constant.

Evolution happens.

And it is happening now.

As human begins, we've experienced major shifts over the past centuries in how we live and think. Moving forward has required us to adapt, change, transition, and, yes, evolve. Your children, born into this new time, have arrived ready to go, with new abilities we never dreamed of.

Take cell phones, for example.

Maybe your child has one. Maybe she doesn't. Is a cell phone useful or harmful to kids? We've all read the statistics on teen driving accidents while texting, and worried over the potential risks of radiation.

But regardless of the dangers, cell phones are here, they're reality, and it's pretty clear that if we adults can't keep our own hands off our iPhones or whatever the Hot New Thing is, we'll be hard-pressed to keep our kids from getting addicted, too.

Is this a good thing? The jury's still out.

But one thing is definitely clear: in terms of psychic development, cell phones are important. That's because electronic technology, especially the cell phone and the Internet, *is changing the way kids use energy to communicate.*

In other words, electronic technology is helping to make kids psychic.

This is because technology trains kids *how to work with energy.* When your child (or anyone) uses a cell phone, he or she is making a connection with another being by sending messages "through the air"—the cell phone is just the intermediary. We can do this from anywhere on the planet, even into space.

In a nutshell:

a) Messages are transmitted via energy

b) We once needed wires and cables to transmit this energy

c) They aren't necessary now

d) Electronic devices (cell phones, computers) are currently acting as intermediaries in this energy communication

e) In time, we won't need these devices anymore

It's odd to think about now, before we've seen it happen. But it's the direction we're clearly heading, and a lot faster than we think. Soon, we'll be able to send and receive messages with telepathy or some other mode of communicating through energy transmission—*no cell phone, Internet, texting, or other electronica required.*

Maybe not this year. Maybe not in a decade. Maybe not in fifty years. But sooner, really, than any of us thinks.

Your Divine kids are at the forefront of this evolution!

Already, we communicate soul to soul—we do this countless times a day, whenever we are with others. Our One collective soul, housed as many souls in Earth bodies, understands itself to be One. We can sense each other's emotions, read the "vibe" of a group, and more.

But at some point, somebody (likely T-Mobile or Verizon!) will figure out a way to make brain-to-brain telepathy a practical reality. We'll be able to communicate psychically, just with our minds: mother to daughter, friend to friend, with no minutes plan required.

And remember, this kind of brain-to-brain communication training isn't just happening with cell phones. It's also happening with:

• The Internet, within all aspects of e-mail, forums, chat rooms, and so forth

• Facebook, MySpace, and all the rest, letting us communicate simultaneously, via energy

- Google, which works sort of like energetic manifesting—seek and you will find

- Electronica that you might think of as entertainment, such as Wii, which teaches kids how to respond physically to something that is happening energetically

- Computer games like *Wild Divine*,[5] which teaches the mind to do simple energetic tasks (raise a ball, open a door) by controlling the metabolic rate—the same method ancient yogis used to enter mystic states

- Other computer games of all kinds, which create a virtual reality that we experience as real or near-real

- iPods and MP3 players that teach kids that music is energy—not just the vibration in every song, but in the way it is stored, transferred, and played

- Digital photos and art, which work the same way

- Movies and television, which teach kids that they can use their minds to transport to other realities. For example, when you watch a movie, your mind actually travels with Jackie Chan to *The Forbidden Kingdom*. This kind of electronica takes us out of our body energetically, and lets our mind enter another realm. Of course, this is exactly what we do when we are clairvoyant or when we astrally project—we travel to other realms! *To the brain, there is no difference between physically doing it and psychically doing it!*

In other words, your kids are communicating with energy, no matter what medium they use. Right now they need a middleman: the cellphone, the computer, the iPod.

But in the future, they won't.

Like it or not, believe it or not: technology is training their brains for the next step.

---

5. See the *Wild Divine* website, www.wilddivine.com.

four

Is Your Child Psychic or Spiritually Gifted?

Psychic development and spiritual awakening are one and the same, engendered from the same Source, which is the Divine, God, the One, the All of which we are intrinsically a part, without separation or divide. For children, for adults, it is the same: when there is spiritual awakening, all psychic abilities become available. The converse of this is also true. When your minds become awakened, all things are possible. —The Messages

———

How can you tell if your child is psychic? How do you know if you've got a SAK (spiritually advanced kid) in your home? What do psychic abilities look like? How can you support your child?

I'm going to answer those questions, in detail. But before we delve deep into the *what*s and *when*s and *how*s of intuitive abilities, there's something that you need to know first.

It's a concept that's difficult for many people to understand or even believe at first, and even as a psychic myself, it took me a long time to figure it out. Basically, what you need to know is this: *psychic development and spiritual giftedness are the same thing.*

In other words, if you head down the path of psychic development long enough, you're going to become spiritually aware. And if you head down the path of spiritual practice long enough, you're going to become psychic.

They're two peas in the same pod.

A tandem bike headed in one direction.

That's because both abilities stem from the same source—the Divine. You access them through God/Source/The One/The All—whichever name you choose to use. As you learn about your child's psychic and spiritually gifted abilities—what I often call Divine abilities—please keep this in mind. If you head down one road, you'll eventually reach the other.

This applies to your child. And also to you.

What do psychic abilities look like?

Eager to know if your child has psychic or spiritual gifts? Ready to determine which gifts she has—where she falls on the spectrum? It's customary at this time to provide a quiz with questions and answers–a, b, c—for you to take. You know, something along the lines of:

1. Is your child sensitive?

    a. Yes. Even his clothing labels itch him. 30 points.

    b. Somewhat. He gets overwhelmed by the crowd when we go to World Wide Wrestling. 15 points.

    c. No. He is entirely unflappable, lives on a diet of M&Ms and Red Bull, and is never, ever affected by his environment. 0 points.

You see where I'm going with this. I don't want you to answer a lot of questions, guessing on some or fudging on others to get a higher score (don't tell me you won't!), and then frantically adding up the total and tossing your kid into a little box labeled "Lotsa Psychic Abilities" or "Kinda Psychic" or "Not Particularly Psychic at All, I'm Afraid."

I just hate those quizzes!

There is more to our beautiful, glorious souls and the souls of our beautiful, glorious children than tallying points on how psychic or spiritual they are!

Whew! Don't get me started.

Especially for children, who are growing so quickly—right before our eyes they are growing out of clothes that fit them perfectly well last season, and their brains are developing lickety split, so that the joke you told them last summer and they didn't get, they now understand and repeat to their own friends—well, we don't need to label these marvelous evolving beings.

Kids' skills are developing as they grow. They might have one kind of psychic ability now, and a new ability next year. From what I've seen, once a child begins to open to intuitive abilities or spiritual knowingness, their abilities continue to open (and open, and open!). So where they are now may not be where they're going to end up.

For example, one month ago, Margaret might have shown no clairvoyant ability at all, and now she might be easily able to see "movies in her head." At Christmastime, Trina may have been obsessed with Santa, but by February she might have received a message from her grandmother, who died four years earlier.

Opening, awakening, emergence—it happens quickly.

I'm also, for the same reasons stated above, not going to break down your children into categories determined by their year of birth. As I've already mentioned, there's no point in labeling. It's just too simple to look up your child's birth year and them firmly nod your head and say, "Oh, Gabe's an Indigo," or "Jesse's a Crystalline," or whatever the category du jour is.

I know, I'm stubborn.

I know, it makes it harder for you.

But we've evolved past that.

My point is, your children are whole beings, and even if they score off the charts on some imaginary PQ (Psychic IQ test), it's just as important that they have Earth skills for this very earthy life, such as how to make themselves a bowl of cereal, play nice with others, and get their science project turned in on time.

What are the ten core psychic abilities?

That said, your child is likely to develop in some key ways. Here's an overview of what I call the core abilities (in Part Four, we'll discuss each in detail, so you don't need to take notes now).

Remember, there are no points to tally here, no grades to hand out, no birth years to consider. It's just a list of psychic abilities that your child may or may not have. She may have one of them strongly or a few of them moderately. Or, it might be hard to tell which abilities she's using most.

In other words, don't worry about it too much. Just take a look, and see if any of these abilities matches up to what you've noticed about your child.

1. **Clairsentience** is the art of psychic feeling. Basically, a clairsentient child feels everything. He feels the energy in the room when people are arguing. He picks up energy from a crowd, at the grocery store, in a hectic classroom. He may feel energy over distance (if Grandma's got the flu, he might have a stomachache—even if Grandma lives two thousand miles away). He may "just know" stuff, such as "That's not a nice man," "That dog is lost," or "That lady is sad because her husband died."

   It's tough being a clairsentient, because kids aren't equipped to deal with heavy emotions. In later chapters, you'll learn how to teach your child to clear himself from emotions and energies he doesn't own. Clairsentients may also have the ability to hold objects in their hand, and to tell you about the owner or history of that object (officially known as *psychometry*).

2. **Clairaudience** is the art of psychic hearing. If your child is clairaudient, she will hear things—unfortunately, this does not mean she will hear you calling her for dinner! She may hear via spirit guides, angels, or other entities. For younger kids, this may show up as an imaginary playmate. She may hear words as if they're coming through the radio. She may hear in her "mind's ear," but she also might hear a voice outside her ear

(usually in one ear or another). Your clairaudient child may also hear music.

3. **Clairvoyance** is the art of psychic seeing. If your child is clairvoyant, he will be able to easily see what he might call "pictures in his head" or "movies in his mind." He might see images in his mind's eye or that are symbolic—for example, seeing an image of the metal bars of a jail if someone is trapped or imprisoned. Basically, a clairvoyant child will receive the bulk of his information visually. Visions, premonitions, going to a place and saying he's already "seen" it before may fall within the purview of kids who are clairvoyant.

4. **Mediumship** is the ability to communicate with those who have died. For kids, this can either be really cool (I saw Aunt Martha yesterday) or really awkward (there's a ghost in my room). If your child is a medium, she'll need support—it can be tricky when you are constantly being contacted by spirits from other realms. Your child will need to know how to deal with unwanted and pesky energies, while being able to keep the connections and communications that are useful to him.

   It may also be socially awkward for a child who is a medium, in terms of what other people think. There's a certain fascination with mediums—both positive and the "ewww factor." Your child will have to deal with this.

5. **Channeling** is the art of receiving via another entity, usually an ascended being or spiritual master. Channels *move themselves aside* in order to receive from the collective consciousness of the Divine, which may show up as a spirit guide, angel, or other teacher. Channeling may be verbal or whole body, as Esther Hicks does with Abraham. Or, it may be the channeling of spiritual messages, which is what I do; I receive messages from spirit guides in writing. In some cases, your child may channel music, art, other creative expressions.

6. **Remote viewing** is the ability to see things that are far away, as if you were there in person. Kids who are good at this can

have a career working for detective agencies! You might also think of them as your little "finders"—they're the ones family members ask, "Where did I leave my glasses?" Remote viewing is a highly specialized kind of psychic viewing that has been qualified and quantified by researchers, who are attempting to learn more about it.

7. **Astral projection.** If your child tells you she went to Mars last night, you might as well believe her. Kids who astrally project are able to move their consciousness to different places, while their bodies stay put. It's not the same as dreaming, which is subconscious. Astral projection is a different, deeper state, and many kids can do it at will. If your child says she can see her body on the bed because she's floating on the ceiling, or tells you about transporting herself to other lands, distant galaxies, and more, she's probably astral projecting.

    On another note: astral projection can also be related to shifting or traveling across time—such as seeing or visiting the future or the past. This may include *past-life regression*, which is the ability to see the life you lived before you lived this one, or dealing with alternate dimensions of time, space, and matter.

8. **Energy healing** is the ability to use energy to heal via hands or distance. If your child is an energy healer, she will want to rub your neck when it hurts (she'll just "know") and can find the exact area that aches without being told. She'll be able to sense illness in the body—for example, to scan the body as a *medical intuitive*. She may run energy in her hands—her hands might get "itchy" or "hot" or "feel like they need to heal something." Energy healers can be any age—some are younger than you'd imagine. Like all energy work, healing can be transdimensional, across layers of time, space, and matter.

9. **Spiritual advancement** is the gift of deep spiritual knowing. You'll find this in the child who can tell you about where we go when we die, what spirit guides are, what Jesus or the other great spiritual masters really meant, why forgiveness is impor-

tant. Your spiritually advanced kid will astound you with his deep knowing of things he hasn't studied or hasn't had access to in his upbringing.

A Divine child with these gifts can understand spiritual concepts on a deep level, and can discuss them clearly with adults. It's as if he's been born with this "knowing" of how the Universe, the Divine, God works. If you have a child like this, listen to him—he's got plenty to teach you!

10. **Other abilities**. If you can't determine your child's abilities in the above categories, consider the idea that our children are evolving beyond the abilities we've had in the past, and that new abilities are evolving. Who knows what we are capable of?

Overlapping abilities

One last thing—lots of these abilities overlap. You might have a child who is clairvoyant plus a channel, or a kid who does astral projection and is clairsentient. Some kids will have many abilities. Some kids will have one aptitude that's much stronger than another.

Another last thing? Your child may be better at some of these skills than others. He might be a top-notch clairsentient, yet entirely unable to do remote viewing. A superb energy healer, but terrible at clairvoyance. For example, a few minutes ago I took an online "psychic test" that involved guessing the shape of the next on-screen card to be shown (square, circle, star and so forth).

Well, guess what? I flunked. I got every single one wrong. Not even a little bit wrong, like I "thought it might between A and B, but I guessed B." I wasn't even close!

Ah, well. So I can't do the "guess the card" exercise. Does this mean I'm not psychic? No. It simply means that my gifts are in other areas, such as channeled writing, clairvoyance, and energy work. "Guess the card" is not in my particular repertoire. That's all.

Your child may have some gifts, but not others.

No big deal.

A little dab will do you when it comes to the Divine.

five

How Will Your Child "Open"?

The spiritual and energetic mind may open very early; a child may manifest, a child may move matter, a child may heal. All the energy techniques available to the more developed human are available to the child. However, the child does not always have the experience to understand what the purpose of these techniques are: Love. To exist as One with the Divine. To become infused in the creation of a positive and sustaining Earth life.—The Messages

———

It's late afternoon, and I'm doing my usual after-school routine: heading downstairs to where I have a collection of old jazz records. I "stack" these old albums on our stereo, so they'll play one after another, then let myself dance to the music for hours. I'm in fourth grade. I do this every afternoon.

I think everyone does.

As I dance, I find myself entering trance very quickly. Of course, I didn't know what trance is yet. Yet as I dance, I release and transport myself in ways that I don't yet understand. These sessions will act as early training for the work I will do as an adult, exploring trance.

It's 7:15 a.m. on a Tuesday, and I'm wiggling on the piano bench, attempting to finish my "practice time" before breakfast. I'm in fifth grade. My teacher, a brilliant pianist who has taught students at the highest level, has been saddled with me.

I am not a student at the highest level.

It's not that I'm opposed to playing the piano. It's that I want to play what's in my head: songs with every layer of instrumentation and voice, received from an unknown source. I'm a kid, receiving music clairaudiently—I hear it loud and clear, entire compositions of magnificent sound, yet I can't make the notes play through my fingers. I squirm on the bench, waiting for "practice" time to be done.

It will take over thirty-five years until the music that I hear in my head gains expression in song, and even then I will only be able to translate the smallest fragments of what I hear.

Some people say music is the voice of God. When I am sitting quietly, listening to the music that plays in my head, I am certain this is true.

As a child, I wasn't a channel, I wasn't a clairvoyant, I couldn't see the future. In fact, I didn't really have any psychic skills at all.

Or did I?

That creepy feeling I got when I had to be driven to school by an adult who did not have a "good vibe"? Clairsentience.

The times when I had to come home and "recover" from a particularly intense school day? Clairsentience again.

The numerous times I heard voices that gave me guidance and direction? Clairaudience.

The times I heard "my" music, regardless of my ability to play it? More clairaudience.

Yet, tons of psychic abilities were unfathomable to me. I could never do any of those slumber-party games like "What card am I holding?" or "What color am I thinking of?"

I spent numerous afternoons holding private séances in my bedroom—and not a single spirit ever showed up! Ever!

I sat cross-legged for hours attempting to self-levitate like the ancient yogis—and remained with derrière firmly planted on terra firma.

The rest of it I never even tried, because I hadn't heard of it yet: astral projection, past-life regression—oh yeah, and spoon-bending. I would have had a field day (of failure!) with that one.

The point is, I *opened* in different areas at different times.

Your child will open in stages, too.

I didn't have all the abilities all at once.

Your child probably won't either.

He or she instead will probably have a *psychic opening.*

What is psychic opening?

Basically, psychic opening is the act of going from one level of awareness to a higher level of awareness. It may happen very gradually, or it may happen quickly (in which case some folks might call it a spiritual awakening), or it may happen as the result of sudden incident or experience, such as a near-death experience (NDE).

I know about openings, because I've seen them happen many times to adults I've worked with—for some folks, once you teach them the ground rule, then—whoosh!—they're off and running, with abilities opening so fast they can't keep up!

The difference for your child is . . . they're open from the start.

If you can approach your Divine child with tools of psychic development before they hit the teenage years (and then all bets are off for a while, mostly because they won't want to do anything you tell them until they're over twenty-five), you can keep your kids open from the beginning.

This means they won't ever have to be "shut."

This is an amazing gift.

And what if you just found this book, and your child is already thirteen? No worries. There's plenty of time. Even the simple act of teaching a few basic skills will result in lifelong benefits for your children.

That said, what's the most important thing to know?

Kids open in stages.

How kids open

As adults, we're grown-ups (at least in theory!). We understand how the world works, how to wend our way through it; in other words, we've mastered the basics.

But our kids are still newbies. They're learning every day, navigating crucial stages of development and growth from birth through adolescence, from the simpler stuff (burp, smile, roll over, sit, stand, walk, talk, get potty trained), all the way up to reading, writing, using a computer, driving a car, getting a job at the local ice cream store, and going on a first date. Development happens over time.

That's how your child will develop psychically, too. In stages.

That means your child will not pop out of your womb and remark, "Hey, Mom, my clairvoyance is telling me you'll have a new career as a businesswoman" or "Say, Dad, my spirit guide told me that screwdriver you lost is behind the refrigerator."

He still has to learn to talk, for goodness sake!

Psychic development arrives alongside, *in tandem with*, your child's other developmental skills. This means that even if your four-year-old daughter is a fantastic medium, it's not in her best interest for you to drag her out and display her abilities. At age four, she's not emotionally developed enough to handle that kind of pressure. Children need to be respected as whole beings, for all the aspects of their selves—not just the ones that are most interesting to adults.

A word about kids with challenges

A great deal has been written about kids with autism and ADD—and many folks believe these kids have special intuitive abilities.

Meg Blackburn Losey, author of *The Children of Now*, has called kids with autism the "Beautiful Silent Ones," and notes they have telepathic and spiritual abilities. Many parents of these kids have told me they believe their autistic children are so far advanced, we can't even begin to keep up. Doreen Virtue posited many of the same opinions in her earlier book *Crystal Children*, and in other writings.

With kids who have ADD/ADHD, the issues are different. They're so awake to the world, it's boggling! They're sensitive to *everything*, all the time. These kids have lickety-split brains that may be exceptionally able to grasp how energy works, to use energy, to understand how time and space overlap. My belief is that the problem with most kids who have ADD/ADHD isn't the kids, or the condition. It's the situations they are being put into, such as being forced to sit at tiny school desks for hours on end, with no release for physical energy. It's hard to fathom that massive prescriptions of drugs like Ritalin are the answer for most kids with these conditions.

Some experts say that specific gender needs contribute to ADD/ADHD problems. According to author and educator Abigail Norfleet James, a pioneer in the field of gender-based teaching, movement is so necessary for boys that they "may actually learn better standing than sitting."[6]

That's probably a far cry from how your son, ADD/ADHD or not, spends his day.

Overcrowding of schools is also a likely culprit. In recent years, school budgets have been stretched to their limit, often resulting in increased class sizes—with many more students per classroom than we experienced in our own childhoods. If you had to spend thirteen years of your life in a classroom of thirty kids all day, would you be happy? Not even your own little cubicle to hide in, but just crammed in a room and told to sit still, be quiet, and learn? How well would you do?

Still not convinced? Try spending a day being herded along at your local middle school or high school. The crowding, the intensity, the energy of the kids—it's a lot to handle for anyone, and I would argue that most kids don't handle it very well, even the ones who appear to be "succeeding." For psychic kids and SAKs, who are by nature sensitive, this type of environment can be overwhelming.

Common stages of opening

That said, let's next take a look at some of the common developmental stages your child will experience, in terms of his or her psychic and spiritual development.

Why is this important?

---

6. James, *Teaching the Male Brain: How Boys Think, Feel, and Learn in School*, 50.

Because timing is everything.

There's nothing worse or more harmful than a parent trying to push a child into a situation she's not developmentally ready for, no matter how gifted she is.

If you've got a dynamo spoon-bender who has turned your entire silverware collection into bracelets for his friends, that's great. But if you push too hard and make that kid focus only on spoon-bending, as opposed to say skateboarding with friends, by the time your child is eleven, he will either be (a) a prodigy (but he won't like you very much) or (b) a burnout.

Pushing too hard is a mistake. Don't go there.

Remember, your child is here on this planet for his or her soul growth. Your kid is not here to appear on the local morning show doing readings for people in the audience!

You may consider your child as an extension of yourself, and yes—he may have your nose, your chin, the same color hair and eyes. But your child is unique. Her soul has her own path. Thus, the more you can help your child find his or her own way, not yours, the better.

part two

connection

six

Prayer—Teaching Your Child Direct Connection with the Divine

When you understand how to create a direct connection with the Divine, nothing else matters. When you, forever, are able to receive in this way, you know clearly that the Divine exists, and all your plans in life, all your insecurity and the way your heart skips and leaps through your life, are settled. This direct connection grounds you. The Divine grounds you, and makes you better able to live your Earth life.—The Messages

———

You've heard me yammer about *direct connection* a few times already, and you're probably wondering what the big deal is.

First off, let's clarify what direct connection is.

Direct connection is a way in which your child can talk to God, the Divine, the Universe—and get a clear answer back. It's *two-way communication* between your child and the Divine. It's the most simple, foolproof, consistent way to have clear, direct, back-and-forth communication between human and Divine.

Best of all—it's remarkably easy to do.

As I've said before, teaching your child the technique of direct connection is one of the biggest gifts you can offer.

I mean, think about it! Having a hotline into Source? Having the top-secret, never-to-be-given-out number for the private cell phone of the Divine? When you teach your child how to do this, you are teaching your child a spiritual skill he or she can rely on for an entire lifetime.

In fact, I would say that all those "extras" that we strive to provide our children with—those must-have material items such as computer games, My Little Pony collections, private schooling, and piano lessons? These pale besides your child knowing how to create a direct connection with the Divine.

I mean, God—or a Wii?

Hmmm. Which would you choose for your child?

"But . . . I don't know how," you say.

That's the nifty part, isn't it? As you discover how to teach your child the technique of direct connection, you'll naturally learn how yourself.

I'd say that's a win-win.

The three layers of direct connection

There are three layers of direct connection, each slightly different from the next. These three layers are:

- Prayer
- Meditation
- Trance

No one layer is better than another—each is simply different. *Layer*, which is the word given to me by my guides, seems a little confusing to me—it might imply that one state of direct connection is deeper or lighter than the next. However, each state is complete and perfect on its own.

Another example? Think of each state—prayer, meditation, trance— as a different color. Let's say red, blue, green, for purposes of illustration. Or pink, orange, yellow. The colors don't matter. What matters is that you know that each color is intrinsically whole; it isn't any better or worse than another. You might have a preference for a certain color, but that's just personal choice. All of the colors are good.

Now, your child can experience direct connection within any or all of these layers—prayer, meditation, trance. However, what's important to know is that psychic abilities *are most often enabled within the energetic layer of trance,* so it's very useful to teach your child how to access that state.

Again, he can access the Divine in all three layers. But for easiest access to psychic information, trance is where he'll want to go.

Direct connection through prayer

Prayer is a tricky thing—so shrouded in the mysteries of religion and church, so tightly held in the hands of priests/pastors/rabbis. For many who have been damaged by traditional religions, or for those for whom religion no longer quite works, prayer doesn't always appeal.

And yet, prayer is a marvelous way to connect with the Divine!

To teach prayer *on your own terms* and to use it as a spiritual practice can be one of the greatest gifts you give your child.

So, what does this kind of personal prayer look like?

Well, we all know what traditional prayer looks like—and it's not that!

You've seen it in movies—Sister Mary Margaret kneeling on the cement floor of her nun's cell, slashing herself with branches and trembling with ecstasy. You've seen it in PBS documentaries—people on their knees in holy places all over the world. And, if you've been raised in a religious tradition, you've had your own experiences of churchgoing and church praying.

As a child I attended Catholic school, and I remember all too well the allure of the padded kneelers, the waft of incense in the air, the coolness of the marble floor, the way the light gleamed through the stained glass, the hush of holiness that descended on everything. I was eager; I wanted to be absolved of all my ten-year-old sins! I flung myself on those padded kneelers and prayed with my heart so big it roamed outside my body. Next to me knelt my schoolmates— I could only assume they were in the throes of the same passion!

Later, I prayed in Presbyterian churches, where we didn't kneel but sat stiff-backed on pews or metal chairs. Still later, I prayed in temples and holy houses, with people of every nationality, race, and religion. I prayed at festivals and ceremonies, at 24/7 perpetual adorations. I prayed in nature, under the canopy of generous, graceful trees. I prayed rote prayers that I'd memorized or read out of a book. I prayed the usual Catholic suspects: the Our Father, the Hail Mary, the Act of Contrition, memorized for so many years and from such an early age that if I slow down I can't remember the words. I prayed prayers that I didn't even understand the meaning of—ancient Sanskrit mantras, recitations from old Christian prayer books, prayers in other languages. I prayed in song—old hymns, even older mantras, all those voices rising in song and mine not separate.

Today, with all that praying under my belt but no religion that fully satisfies all that I am searching for, I still pray incessantly. It is an act as normal and as necessary as breathing, and I hope that I am teaching my children to do the same.

My prayers are not fancy. "Help me, God!" or "Give me patience, please—and hurry!" are common prayers in my daily routine.

And this, really, is the purpose of prayer: to provide comfort, sustenance, and Divine guidance to the average person going about his or her average life.

After all, when do we pray? Well, most of us pray when we need help or are afraid. We pray when there is no one left to turn to except God, the Divine, the Universe. We pray when we have reached our limit. We pray at all times when we need help, comfort, support, grace.

Also, we pray when we are so touched by the extraordinary beauty of this life on Earth, that we have nothing left to say but "Thank you."

You might say that (a) asking for help and (b) saying thank you are the two methods of prayer. We ask God for intervention, for help, for action on our behalf. Or we say thank you for the blessings we've already received—and if you're like most people, these gifts in our life are so numerous, so enormous, so beyond measure that you could spend your whole day, every single day, praying in thanks.

Kids' prayer 101

Teaching kids to pray is easy.

There's no special way to do it—your child can pray on her knees in a church, in bed at the end of the day, right before the pop quiz in math class, or strapped in precariously to the front seat of the roller coaster at the State Fair—all are good places to pray!

In my opinion, there are no special words she needs to say—you do not need to find a prayer in the Bible, or in a prayer book, or on the Internet. She can pray with whatever words are on her mind.

There is no time when your child is too young to pray, either. Even the littlest toddler will appreciate some quiet time with you, where he can sink back into your arms, you can rub his back, and he can close his eyes if he wants. Then, simply suggest that he talks to God privately. Prompters such as "Ask God to help you," "Ask God for what you want," or "Say thank you for what you're happy about" are okay, but he doesn't really need these.

Even when he is very small, your child knows what is on his mind and what he wants to talk to God about!

Explaining prayer to your child

"Who's God?" your child might ask as you begin teaching and modeling this practice of prayer, and the key is to keep it very simple, as in:

"God is the love in your heart" or

"God is Jesus' Father," if you practice Christianity, or

"God is everything in the Universe," if you don't.

Whatever you want to say that fits with your own particular religious beliefs or non-beliefs is fine—the Divine is not picky.

However you choose to pray, you will discover benefits from the practice, including:

- Relief
- Tenderness
- Compassion
- Courage

- Love
- Gratitude
- Peace
- An opened heart
- A sense that all is well
- Comfort as only the Divine can provide

Teaching kids to pray

With kids, simpler is always better.

If you have a religious practice, teach your child in that tradition. If you don't, make up something that works for you.

Prayer is personal—there's no right or wrong way. What's more, you can't pray for your child. Your child has to pray for herself. All you can really do is get her started—she has to figure out the rest.

I often tell my kids to "tell God what's in your heart," and then I give them some private space—I might leave the room, or just sit there and rub their backs at bedtime. It doesn't take long for a child and God to have a clear, perfect communion—a minute may be all that's needed for younger kids. Older kids often need to be reminded to take time to pray—with all the distractions in their lives, it's easy for them to forget.

Sometimes kids will get God confused with other all-powerful entities, such as Santa Claus or the Easter Bunny or whoever is currently popular on the Disney Channel. If this happens, don't worry about it. They'll catch on to the Infinite, Universal, All, One part as they grow.

As your child matures and her brain becomes able to think at a more complex level, you can start teaching her your version of theology, your own version of who, what, where, when, or how God is. If you don't know or can't put it into words, you can just tell her, "I don't know."

For your child to understand that you have a prayer practice, even if you can't put it fully into words and even if it doesn't slot neatly into a traditional religion, is inordinately useful.

Respecting differences

There are many roads to the Divine—and it is quite possible and perhaps even probable that your child may take a different path than yours.

This is okay.

In my family, spiritual practices are diverse. Our little tribe contains a former Sikh, a lapsed Catholic, and three young Catholics who have been exposed to spiritual and religious ideas from all over the world. We have close friends who are Buddhist, Christian, Hindu, Jewish, agnostic, atheist, New Age, followers of Osho, followers of Amma, "not sure," and "I don't know." Thus, one of the core values at our house is respect for all belief systems. We recognize that differences exist, and they are to be valued.

As you and your children travel toward the Divine in prayer, I might suggest that it doesn't matter which religion or belief system you use.

This is because all roads, all paths, eventually lead to the same place.

Eventually, everyone ends up moving from "go" to God, regardless of which traditions you do or don't keep.

This is how the Universe works.

With this in mind, you can relax and trust that whichever method your children seem to be most attracted to is likely to be the correct path for them.

How young is too young?

Prayer can be taught at the youngest age. Your kids, as toddlers, can watch you close your eyes when they're fighting over the Legos, and ask, "What are you doing, Mom?"

"Praying for patience," you might tell them.

Let's see—if Mom the All-Powerful is praying for help from someone Bigger, Better, Stronger, and Faster, does this means this Divine is more powerful than Mom?

The little brains churn—what is this prayer, and who is this God anyhow?

One simple way to introduce prayer to your kids? Praying at meals.

At my house, we've prayed before meals since before I can remember. As a kid growing up, we bowed our heads and folded our hands in front of us, and prayed something short and snappy such as:

God is good.

God is great.

And we thank Him for our food. Amen.

Wow! Now that's some powerful praying!

My brother, now a full-grown adult, still insists it is *God is great, God is good*, not the other way around. It boggles the mind that we have somehow reached our current ages (not to be disclosed here, but the word "fully mature" comes to mind) and will still say this simple prayer when we celebrate a holiday with my mom.

The rote learning instilled at age three still beats strong.

Nowadays, our tradition is different. For one thing, we reach around the table and hold hands with whomever is nearby. When siblings are in arguing mode and then are called to dinner, this can get interesting! Since punching is not allowed at prayer time, sometimes even the tip of a brother's finger touching the wrist of a little sister is likely to ignite World War III! I myself hang on to my partner's hand for dear life, so happy we're all there together, and wanting to savor every minute of it.

We don't say "God is good" either. Instead, whoever is moved to speak, from the oldest to the littlest, says their piece. It's usually something like "Help this person get home safely" or "Thank you for letting us all be here together" or "Thanks for such an amazing life."

Other times, we say long prayers—the Lord's Prayer mumbled at variant speed as the kids try to go faster and faster, the adults trying to slow things down. Prayers someone has learned at the local Catholic school. Prayers from different religions, in different languages. All kinds of prayers, said by anyone at the table who feels the need—and sometimes, we hold the space with simple silence.

Asking for help. Saying thank you.

This is what praying at a meal looks like in our house.

What's more, we even pray in restaurants! I used to think my kids would find this really weird, but in fact they seem to like it. If we're in a restaurant, we're faster, more casual—a quick hand squeeze all around and a few heartfelt words and we're good to go. Yet even in those few seconds, we're recognizing the fact that our own family is together, eating a meal together—and we're grateful.

Prayer and religion

Does it matter if you pray in church?

I don't think it does.

I used to think regular church attendance was crucial for my kids. But after I unexpectedly received *The 33 Lessons* in 2008 (spiritual teachings that affected me profoundly and are in my book *Writing the Divine*), this belief has dropped away. Receiving messages such as "The purpose of life is soul growth," and that I was God, and everyone was God, and All was One, no exceptions . . . well, a lot of what I heard in church just didn't make sense anymore. It was like waking up out of a huge dream where everything you believed turned out to be false, a mirage.

So you might say, during spiritual awakening, I lost something— the ability to embrace a church or religion of any kind, as a power in which I could believe.

You may be different.

You may not agree.

This is what happened to me.

I still miss the community of church—hundreds of good people in community. But the dogma won't sit; I can't settle with it. This is the place I am at, and I know that I am not alone. According to the Pew Forum on Religion & Public Life, Americans who are unaffiliated with any particular religion have seen the greatest growth in recent years.

It's confusing—losing your religion because you have grown into a person who requires a more relevant spiritual practice? That's both good, and sad. It's similar to inheriting a religious practice from your parents, grandparents, or great-grandparents—and finding that this family tradition no longer fits for you.

I don't have a good answer on this one.

Going to church may or may not be useful to your child and your family for many reasons. That's for you to decide.

Prayer as direct connection

I can't make the decision on whether your child should go to church every Sunday, but I do know one thing—doing so won't help your child to make a direct connection.

Direct connection through prayer is private. It doesn't belong to any religious tradition, and it is not based on church attendance or a belief system.

Yes, you can keep a religious tradition and have direct connection.

But religion is not required.

That's because direct connection is your child and the Divine, one on one, on their own terms. Direct connection is personal, and solely belongs to each person and the Divine. Direct connection is your child one on one with God, saying what's on his mind, speaking from his heart—and hearing the answers that the Divine will bring.

Christianity speaks of this concept as the "still, small voice." Many other religions share the concept.

It's one way to describe it, although the Divine also answers in other ways.

Remember—psychic and spiritual abilities stem from the same source, the Divine. A child seeking psychic information and a child in prayer will receive answers in much the same way. Thus, ways of receiving Divine guidance include:

- The "still, small voice," like an inner voice in his mind's ear
- Signs and symbols
- Synchronicities

- Having a sense of deep knowing
- Enjoying a sense of deep peace

Once your child understands how Divine guidance can be accessed through the direct connection of prayer, this practice becomes a constant, infallible source of Divine information.

seven

Meditation: Teaching Your Child How to "Lock into the Hum"

To know oneself as a part of the Universe is the simplest task. To feel particulate as energy, to feel energy as self, to understand that there is no distinction between the Divine, the self, the other—this is effortless. In meditation, the journey is fast. Here is the place where the mind can rest. Here is the place where the Divine can present itself fully, as complete understanding.

Children are meditation, up to a certain age. Later, they learn separation from the culture. In pure meditation, you can return to the state of a child. In pure meditation, you may enter a state that is One Soul— the collective hum of All. —The Messages

———

Meditation is another way of having a direct connection with the Divine.

Many Westerners still think of meditation as being this tricky process that involves forcing your body into the lotus position for three hours at a time, mumbling mantras while alternately breathing in through the left nostril, out the right.

That's one way.

But if you haven't figured it out already, meditation's gone mainstream—and the lotus position is no longer required. You can meditate anywhere: while lying in bed, in an airplane, on the bus, at your kid's soccer game, at the park . . .

How is meditation different from prayer? Mostly, it doesn't involve asking for help or saying thank you for blessings. Instead, meditation is based on what I call *locking into the hum* of the Universe.

What is "hum"?

Well, once you reach a certain level of awareness, you understand that all of us, every piece of matter, and yes, every thought and emotion, all vibrate with a certain frequency, and when you listen very closely to how we are energetically vibrating together, you can sense the "hum" of the Universe.

An example of this might be the way a hummingbird moves its wings so quickly—it's a blur of movement and sound. We know a hummingbird has "hum"—we can see it shimmer and hear its drone. Yet a rock, which really doesn't move very much, also has "hum"—it's just a cooler, slower, more dense vibration. All things, all thoughts, everything has a vibrational hum. This is how the Universe is.

In meditation, you are simply allowing yourself to hear and see and exist as this hum, to feel it with your whole body. You "lock in" to this hum. And it is one of the most wonderful feelings you'll ever have.

Mantra, and why it works

In ancient meditation traditions, such as those begun in India thousands of years ago, people often used *mantra*. They might say mantra as a phrase in their heads, or repeat mantra aloud, or sing mantra as a call-and-response chant in the practice of *kirtan*.

So, what is mantra?

It could be a phrase of words in Sanskrit, such as:

• *Om Namah Shivay*

• *Om Hari Om*

• *Om Namah Shivaya*

• *Sita Ram*

• *Eck On Kar*

Or, it might be a part of a traditional prayer or holy scripture, said or sung, such as the Anand Sahib of the Sikh tradition, which goes something along the lines of:

Ik oa'nkaar sat gur prasaad,
Ana'nd bhe-a meri maa-e,
Satguroo mai paa-e-a.

This is the start of the very famous Anand mantra, which was written thousands of years ago. It translates, roughly, to:

There is but One God. By True Guru's grace, he is Obtained.
Joy has welled up, O my mothers
For I have obtained my True Guru.

This mantra is one of the most celebrated mantras ever written (and I love it so much I recorded the percussive, up-tempo song "Ananda" with my band, Martyrs of Sound!)

Why is mantra so useful in meditation, yoga, trance dance, and more? There are a number of reasons.

First, mantra isn't in English. This is helpful for English speakers, because it allows us to repeat words that have been considered sacred, holy, spiritual for thousands of years by millions of people—and yet our mind does not hang around freaking out at any particular meaning of a word. For example, most mantra translates into words such as *Divine One Love* or *Infinite Love God or God is Love* or *I have obtained my True Guru,* and so on.

For many of us raised in traditional religious backgrounds, the idea of sitting around chanting *I have obtained my True Guru* doesn't sit right. It makes us feel squirmy and cultish. But to say instead some beautiful phrase such as *Satguroo mai paa-e-a,* which translates to the same thing, sounds exotic and cool.

Try it.

Satguroo mai paa-e-a. (Sat-eh guru may pie-ah.)

Wow! Very fancy!

Which leads us to the other reason that mantra is useful—because it has been created and developed to sound beautiful rolling off the tongue.

Try another one.

Ommmmmmmmmmmmm.

Yes. That feels incredible.

Each of the words in mantra, at least in Sanskrit mantra which is one of the most common, sounds simply, perfectly marvelous—the resonance, the mix of consonant to vowel, the way these words can be spoken or sung slowly or quickly, mumbled or sustained, with so much emotional resonance. These sacred words are brimming with "hum." They put us in touch with the Divine quickly, effortlessly, and in a way that allows us to lock into the hum without effort.

Another reason mantra is useful is that when repeated, mantra gives your mind something to hook on to. Here in America, we have so much busyness and distraction—the idea of sitting still and breathing (what, no texting, no e-mail—just breathing and being?) is more frightening than anything we could imagine.

The repetition of mantra gives our wanna-stay-busy minds purpose. It effectively gives the mind a job or task; while doing the job of repeating mantra, the mind can effectively rest from its own thoughts.

A trick, perhaps. But one that works brilliantly.

Finally, many people believe that the words used in mantra are in themselves so sacred, that simply by repeating them you allow the vibrational aspect of that word, that sound, to resonate through your body; this opens your chakras and allows you to heal.

Although I can't say that in my experience that I've felt my chakras open from mantra, I know many people who would argue vehemently that they have and do. I'm also not convinced that the words themselves matter; I don't know if saying the mantra *Ommmm* forty times heals in a different way from saying the mantra *Shanti* forty times.

However, what I do know is that saying *Ommmm* or *Shanti* can get you to a very blissful meditative state very quickly, and this will allow you to have direct connection with the Divine. Any tool or technique that does this is of tremendous value.

Kids and meditation

Your child meditates all day long, without even trying. You see him sitting there absorbed in an art project, and this is meditation. You see her fully entranced watching an ant cross the sidewalk, and this is meditation. You notice he's sitting outside on the back porch, listening to the sound of the grass rustled by the wind, feeling the breeze on his cheek, hearing his heart beating—it's very easy to see that your child is locked into the hum; he's in full meditative mode!

In other words, you do not have to drag your child down to the local ashram in order to meditate!

Yes, you could do that. But in a normal day that contains a fair amount of time and space, your child will be meditating all on his own, thank you very much.

Meditation let kids lock into the hum by (a) allowing their minds to relax and (b) allowing their minds to reach a state of bliss. Both of these states, relaxation and bliss, are places the mind can't get to very quickly in normal life—i.e., during the pop quiz that your child, um, forgot to study for, and now the teacher is saying, "Take out your pencils, class."

The goal of kids meditating is not to spend hours in the lotus position either. Instead, the goal is simply to provide your child with a method of accessing the meditative state easily. Once your child has the ability to meditate at will, in any situation or setup, she will have the ability to lock into the hum of the Universe, any time she needs to. This is another method of direct connection.

Turning in—and blissing out

Once they understand that meditation can take them to a very lovely state of being, a lot of kids become little bliss addicts—and it's not a bad thing!

What is bliss? Simply stated, it's a tiny little bit of Divine energy that feels really, really good. Bliss happens in the mind, but it also gets noticed in the body—and it's a very nice, floaty, happy feeling to have.

Part of how bliss happens is due to changes in the body's chemistry when the breathing is slowed. "The glands release, the muscles relax, and the parasympathetic nervous system becomes dominant, as opposed to the sympathetic system," says Dr. Steve Koc, my partner, who is also a chiropractor, healer, and longtime practitioner of Kundalini yoga and breathwork.[7]

"The sympathetic is our fight-or-flight system, the adrenal-based system of our body chemistry," he says. "This rules nervous excitability." Conversely, "the parasympathetic system is the at-ease state, the relaxed state in which your body does self-healing and rejuvenation. It's the way you feel right before you drift off to sleep, the feeling of peace and calm you get when you are in nature, or when you are daydreaming," he notes.

Your kids won't understand that they're altering their body's chemistry by changing their breathing in meditation, but they will notice they start to feel great—blissful, in fact.

You'll know your kids have reached bliss if:

• They can't stop smiling; they literally can't get their mouths to turn down

• They're giggling, laughing, falling-on-the-floor goofy

• They have a sense of being larger, more expansive

• They perceive everything—the breath of air on their skin, the smallest sound in the room, every particulate of energy, all of it, all at once

• They are in a state of complete relaxation—everything is as right as it can be

• They feel fearless, loved, protected, calm, well, happy in this moment

Bliss can last for a few minutes, but in some cases, with some kids, bliss will last for hours; it's like they've entered an altered state and just

---

7. Quoted in Sara Wiseman, "Use Kundalini Breathing for Self-Healing," Suite101.com, April 28, 2009. See http://newage.suite101.com/article.cfm/use_kundalini_breathing_for_selfhealing.

walk around "blissing out." In very young children, this bliss state is common. Kids who are spiritually gifted may reach this bliss state and stay in it for days—if this kind of transcendence is happening, you'll know it. Bliss is one of the characteristics of spiritual awakening, and it can be life-changing.

Meditation 101 for kids

First off, it's just meditation—you're not trying to teach your kid brain surgery, rocket science, or even fifth-grade math. It's more like teaching kids how to eat an ice cream cone.

Only easier.

I take a no-rules approach to meditation for kids—basically, if it feels okay, keep going. Here's how:

1. Sit your child down with legs crisscrossed. Or not. Some kids can't do crisscrossed legs. If she can't, have her sit comfortably, or lie down—on her bed, the ground, on a patch of grass.

2. Have her close her eyes.

3. Ask her to let her thoughts and body relax.

4. Have her listen to every sound in the room, and after she's listened to every sound in the room, ask her to listen to her own breathing. When she can, ask her to listen to her own heart beating.

5. Have her stay there, in this place, for as long as it feels good. Two minutes. Five minutes. Whatever works. If she can go longer, that's fine, but ten minutes is more than plenty to start with. If she falls asleep, simply note this and let her rest—she probably isn't getting enough sleep.

6. After a while (and in the beginning, ten minutes is max) ask her to come out of the meditation, back to present reality. You can touch her arm gently, or tell her she'll be coming out of the meditation at the count of ten, then count aloud backward from ten to one.

Another option is to use music.

1. Sit your child down, or let him lie on the ground, and turn on some repetitive mantra music designed for inducing a state of bliss or trance. Some CD suggestions include Jai Uttal's *Loveland*[8] or my CD, *Mantra Chill,* by Martyrs of Sound,[9] which takes kids (and adults) quickly into states of relaxation and bliss.

2. Ask him to close his eyes, and simply listen to the music.

3. Have him stay in this state for as long as he likes—with music, it's easy for your child to stay in this state longer than ten minutes.

4. If you do this at bedtime and your child falls asleep, let him sleep!

Direct connection through meditation

With meditation, a child achieves direct connection in a more floaty, less concrete way than with prayer. For example, when using direct connection in prayer, your child might ask God for the answer to a specific problem, and then expect to hear an answer as "the small, still voice" or in the other ways we've discussed.

With direct connection in meditation, it's more as if your child is infused with the Divine. If your child meditates on a particular question, the answer will arrive—but it may arrive as imagery or symbolism, more similar to receiving clairvoyantly.

For example, receiving Divine guidance during meditation might look like:

• Bliss. Simply the experience of bliss may open a new awareness or way of looking at a question that reveals a new answer or brings clarity.

• Seeing images in the "third eye" such as movies in your mind, or symbolic images—the same way we receive clairvoyantly.

---

8. More information is online, at http://jaiuttal.com/.

9. See www.martyrsofsound.com.

• A sense of deep knowing.

• A sense of clarity.

In other words, the direct connection in meditation brings Divine guidance that's a little more diffuse and little more expansive, a slightly different way of receiving than in prayer.

What will work best for your child? It's a matter of preference. Some people find it easier to have a direct connection in prayer, others in meditation. Many folks (like me) take advantage of both methods. One thing is true—no matter which way you choose to experience direct connection, in prayer or meditation, the Divine is always the result.

eight

Trance: Your Child's Psychic "Sweet Spot"

You may reach us in the place that is easiest to find us. We are not hard to find—we arrive immediately upon calling, we arrive even before calling. In a few breaths, simply by asking and with the longing of your heart, you will find us. We are here for you now; we are here at all times. Our windows are always open, waiting for you. When your window is open, we are able to converse with you in the ways that you can understand.

For children it is even easier. It simpler even than for you, for their windows are often open, usually open, mostly open. In one breath they have arrived to the place where they may connect with the Divine, and remember what it is they have already known forever. —The Messages

——

By now, you've got two methods of teaching your child direct connection: (a) prayer and (b) meditation. The third method or tool, which many folks find the most useful for accessing psychic information, is psychic trance.

I know—trance has gotten a bad rap!

It sounds spooky and mysterious, like throwing yourself down the shaft of one of those endless *Twilight Zone*-style tunnels where the lights flash psychedelic and you think you'll never stop falling—but it's really not. It's just a slightly different layer of consciousness that can be extraordinarily helpful when you're gathering psychic information.

Some folks find the word *trance* to be really loaded, and prefer to use terms such as *altered consciousness* or *altered state* or *zone*. No problem! I've simply found that when I teach workshops, the term that most people understand fastest is *trance*.

In any case, trance isn't any better than prayer or meditation; it's not any trickier to do; it doesn't take any special skills. It's just another tool on the old psychic tool belt—another layer of consciousness that you can teach your kids to use.

Why is psychic trance important? Basically, because it's really easy to work with—especially for kids. Kids "get" trance, the same way they "get" Froot Loops necklaces, pepperoni pizza, and those sneakers with wheels in the soles that turn into instant roller skates—after the first time, they've caught on for life.

We adults—muddled and mixed-up creatures—are often baffled by trance. ("Am I doing this right?" "What if I don't come back to reality?" "Is this self-hypnosis?" "Is this against my religion?") But kids jump in as eagerly and as carefree as they'd hop into the kiddie pool on a scorching summer day.

That said, let's dispel some of those creepy, freaky myths about trance, and talk about what it is—and isn't.

First off, the way I'm using the word *trance* (and others may have other definitions, but for purposes of us getting on the same page, this is mine) is this: *trance is a state of altered consciousness.* It's a turning inward through breath and intent that takes you a place of connection with the Divine.

It's not prayer, because when you go into trance you don't do the same things you do in prayer—i.e., asking for help, or showing gratitude.

It's not meditation, because when you go into trance you don't do the same things you do in meditation—i.e., lock into the hum, become one with the universal energy, and experience bliss.

Trance is a *particular layer* of consciousness—a deep, Divine layer that is the "go to" spot for psychic receiving. When you go into trance in this way, you go in with a mission—to gather psychic information.

That means, if your kids are working to gather information clairvoyantly or clairaudiently, or communicating with spirit guides, angels, or other entities to get information, trance is the place they'll want to be.

Yes, you can get psychic information through prayer. You can get it through meditation. But for whatever reason, if you head first toward the layer of consciousness known as trance, you'll get there faster.

What trance feels like

Some people think of trance as "zoning out." When you're driving on the highway, and you suddenly realize you don't remember the last three miles you've driven, it's not because you've been in prayer or meditation—it's because you've been entranced, in trance, zoned out.

When you dance to music in a free, ecstatic way, you easily go into trance—you suddenly experience a sense of timelessness and non-being.

When you are in a place of nature that is so beautiful that you forget for a moment that you have a body at all—you just become pure soul. Yep, that's trance, too.

When you are so deeply in the flow of project that you forget anything else you are doing—you're in trance.

For your child, trance is the place where he can have his *window* open to the Divine, and the Divine of course has its window open to your child, so communication back and forth is very clear and easy in this state.

Again, now's as good at time as any to forget what you've seen on late-night movies; there's nothing weird about trance. It's simple to do, and there's no head-spinning required! In fact, it's so simple that most adults have this funny *uh-oh* feeling when they enter it, as in "Is that all there is?" or "Could I possibly be doing this right?"

Yes, you are.

It's that easy.

The third layer

Trance is the third layer of experiencing the Divine—and *layer* isn't even the right word for it. I use the word *layer*, because it makes me think of this etheric bean dip: cheddar cheese on top, sour cream in the middle, refried beans on the bottom. Prayer is where you dip in first (the cheese), meditation is the blissfully decadent sour cream, and then the third layer—the beans—is trance. Hearty. Sustaining. Mesmerizing.

But that's just me.

Now, I could go ahead and call the trance state something tricky or uber scientific, such as "alpha vibration," "beta matrix," "theta stratum," or anything else that came to mind. But giving it a fancy name doesn't matter.

Although brilliant researchers are measuring brain-wave activity on the subject of trance as we speak, nobody's actually cracked the code. Many agree that the brain-wave activity changes dramatically when people are in these three different states of Divine direct connection: prayer, meditation, trance. But aside from that, nobody really knows how it works.

Does this mean we can't try it and experience it for ourselves?

Heck no!

With a little bit of practice, you'll understand how to reach your own personal "sweet spot"—that exact layer of trance that you'll need for direct communication with the Divine—and you'll find it's very easy to return to that place, or layer, time and time again.

Once you know how, you'll be able to show your child in about thirty seconds.

Really. Kids are that fast.

Help, I've fallen into trance and I can't get out!

Adults and kids naturally experience trance all the time. For kids, it usually presents as behaviors we often consider negative: daydreaming, zoning out, not paying attention, etc. For adults, we may momentarily lose our train of thought, or be so involved in some other fantasy that we don't remember what's happening around us.

This is normal, everyday trance.

But stuff gets really interesting when you go just a tiny bit deeper. Music, mantra, breathing, and sometimes *simply asking to go deeper* all make deep trance happen with ease.

My first experience with deep trance was at a Krishna Das concert years ago. A world-famous kirtan leader, Krishna Das works with the call-and-response of ancient mantra—he sings the first line, and the audience echoes the second line. This back and forth of music and voices can go on for hours, and one of its purposes is to create the lovely blissful state of transcendent trance.

Well, there I was, singing away, when suddenly I felt myself in-voluntarily sinking in, in, in, down, down, down—and, yep, before I knew it I was slumped over as if hypnotized. This was really nice—for a while. I had definitely transcended! I was definitely tranced! But after twenty or thirty minutes of this state of "trance paralysis," in which I was unable to tell my body to move, sit up, get organized, and so forth—well, somewhere in the back of my brain I realized I was "in" pretty deep, and perhaps might have a bit of trouble getting "out."

Luckily, my partner eventually noticed that the slumped-over body next to him in the audience could use a little help, and he touched my shoulder. That little bit of "reality" was all I needed to give my tranced brain enough information to start coming back to the state of consciousness that we call reality—it was like ascending from a deep, dark, luscious hole where you climb and climb and climb and only finally are you back in the light of Here and Now.

I was shaken when I finally arrived in the present moment—the first time you go deeply into trance, it's quite an experience. However, from that I learned something very important—no matter what hap-pened or how deep I went, I had complete control over my trance. I could go in as deep as I wanted, stay in as long as I wanted, and come out with no trouble, when I was ready. Even in deep trance, you are in charge.

I "went in" a few more times that night, and chose to stay "in" for long periods of time. But during those experiences, I was able to enjoy the depths of trance and consciously come out at will, simply by suggesting it to my mind.

The psychic "sweet spot"

In trance, you're working in a slightly deeper layer or realm than when you are praying or meditating. Again, it's a matter of finding that "sweet spot."

Consider a seagull swooping on ocean breezes. As you might imagine, hanging out in a wind current at a certain elevation takes a certain finesse and no small amount of wing adjustment.

Now, if said seagull (for fun, let's call him Jonathan) wants to fly over to another current at a higher elevation, he has to navigate a certain kind of "wake" in the breeze—a little rumbling between wind currents, as he moves from loft to soar. If he wants to go up further, where there's more turbulence, he needs to shift again—spread his wings and scope up, so he can navigate that next level. It's never *better*. It's just different. It's the wind, with all its channels and streams and rumbles. It isn't harder to change current levels; he just needs to *choose* where he's going to go, and then adjust accordingly.

Let's say you're Jonathan.

When your heading for that psychic sweet spot, you're not going to choose prayer, even though that's a nice place to be. You're not going to choose meditation, even though that's also lovely. Your intent, your choice, will be to enter trance, where you can have a direct connection with the Divine, and where your intent is to gather psychic information.

Is one state better than another? No.

Is one state more difficult to experience than another? No.

But if you want to experience this back-and-forth communication, this psychic gathering from the Divine, then trance is the place, the layer, the "sweet spot" where you will find this happens most easily.

Direct connection happens in prayer. It happens in meditation.

It just happens *most easily* in the state of trance.

That's all.

Teaching kids trance

The most important thing to remember if you are helping your kids learn how to go into trance is . . . none of the above!

They're kids; they don't need to get bogged down with the details!

Kids are hands-on beings, they learn by doing. So while it's important that you understand a bit about trance as an adult, when you're working with kids, all you need to tell them is this—they have a job to do when they get there.

That job is gathering information.

One more thing? You're not going to send your child into, or teach your child how to go into, *deep* trance. It's good to know about it, in case it happens inadvertently (and sometimes it will). But really, there's no sense having your child slumped over in trance for an hour if, when he comes back to reality, he doesn't remember a thing.

I mean, he might as well take a nap instead!

How trance works for kids

Basically, to take a child into a light trance, you simply suggest to the child that he will go "in," and stay "in" for a while. Then ask him to close his eyes, take a few deep breaths, and hang out in that state for a while. Basically, it's the same first steps as meditation, with the difference being that your child is going to look around for psychic information while he's there (you'll learn how in the next chapters).

Before you start, you might have a little discussion of what going "in" feels like, including:

- His body might feel heavy
- He can control the level of trance he enters—light to deep
- If he's sitting and he goes into deep trance, he might slump over
- If he goes deep, he might feel like he can't "come back" to reality

- If he goes deep, he might want to talk or move, but won't be able to do so easily
- He can control the level of deep or light, just by thinking of whatever level of trance he wants
- In light trance, he'll feel deeply calm in a very nice way
- In light trance, he may experience bliss
- In light trance, he may see things, hear things, or meet spirit guides who have messages for him
- He can come out of trance at any time, simply by saying in his mind, "I'm ready to come out now"
- In light or deep trance, he'll feel a little funny or floaty (but good) when he comes out of trance

Psychic gathering for kids

What understanding trance does is give you a starting spot for your child. Now, when she begins to work with the psychic ability she's best or most natural at (again, we'll cover that in the next section), you know where to start.

It's like the "You Are Here" arrow on a map at the mall. Yep, you're starting here, at the entrance, every time. The main mall entrance is trance—it's the best door to walk through, and it gets you to your destination fastest.

For example, if your child is a gifted clairaudient, and most easily gathers psychic information through hearing, you'll want to proceed like this: (a) have her go into trance, and (b) ask her to listen to what she hears there, and then take her through the process of clairaudience. If your child is really good at remote viewing, you'll want to proceed the same way: (a) have her go into trance, and (b) ask her to do the process of remote viewing.

Your child is always starting from trance. That's his "go" point. He's always walking right through the main entrance, right through the front door, because that's the way that's fastest and easiest. Yes, he could get the same information through prayer and meditation, but those are side doors. It takes longer to reach the information you need, with those doors. But if he walks right in the front door that is trance, he can march right up to the information he sees, hears, or senses psychically, and grab it easily.

Steps of trance

Again, going into light trance is about as basic as you can get for kids. Adults may need a slower, more careful process, but for kids, it's easy:

1. Ask her to close her eyes.

2. Have her breathe deeply a few times.

3. Tell her she's going to hang out in trance for a little while, and that the only "layer" she's going to visit is the highest, most Divine layer.

4. Remind her that she is fully protected by the Divine at all times—that on the journey she is taking, no other possibility is present.

5. Remind her she's got a job to do when she gets there—to gather the information she sees, hears, or senses psychically.

6. Remind her that she only wants to go into light trance—and she's in charge of her level.

7. Remind her that she can come out of trance at any moment—and that she will always return safe and happy.

8. When she finishes exploring the information, have her come out of trance.

9. If she goes in too deep, touch her arm or shoulder gently, or remind her to come out.

10. When she returns, remind her she is safe and protected.

How does psychic gathering work? In some ways (and I find this both fascinating and maddening), going into trance and doing clairvoyant work (psychic seeing) is very similar to what happens when your kids play those computer games where they have to go through all those doors and mazes to gather the "keys" or "treasures" or "points" they need. When your child is in trance, working clairvoyantly, the same process happens. He'll find a bit of information, look deeper for more, go deeper still as more information presents itself—he can go as far as he wants, gathering info. Just like racking up points on a computer game!

Don't expect to understand "how"

Spiritual teacher Osho writes that with intuition, there is no process. It just happens. The information simply presents itself, with no explanation being possible for how it works. In other words, your child can get the most precise, detailed psychic information—and he won't be able to explain how he did it. He can't tell you how he got from point A to point B, but he did.

Also, because psychic receiving is Divine, it is presented in Divine time (if there even is such a thing!). Because of this, you can ask your child to explore a psychic question and as quickly as the question is spoken or thought, the answer has already appeared. Sometimes even beforehand!

With this kind of warp-speed, I-don't-know-how-I-did-it-but-I-did-it response time, there may not even be time to use trance.

Sometimes, a child's mind is so open, the "windows" between the Divine and your child are flung so wide, that your child won't even need trance. If this is the case, he or she can just skip this step.

And this is lovely. It's like being able to fly without putting on any wings first. Or winning the lottery, and you didn't even buy a ticket.

If you notice this happening with your child, let it happen.

Don't demand that they use trance if they don't need it.

Just let them soar.

As an adult-emergent psychic, this is now happening for me. Whereas in the beginning of my "opening" I had to work carefully, slowly, always starting from trance and taking all the steps, this isn't required anymore. But mostly, the information comes so fast, it's

scary—I just try to keep up. I can go back to trance if I need it, but it isn't always required.

If you notice this happening for your child, respect that she is receiving in her own way, and that she may be receiving with such speed and clarity that this "prep" or "setup" stage may not be required.

It's like those first times on a bike without training wheels—you'll hold the seat and run alongside, until your child is moving on his own and you can let go. If your child gets stuck, can't remember how to begin, or otherwise needs a helpful hand, trance is there. If she is riding along fine without it though, get out of the way—and let 'er ride!

part three

abilities

nine

What to Expect: Stages of Psychic and Spiritual Development

You have asked if you can find a way to help children, to teach them how to develop their skills. We say: it is not a matter of helping them to develop these skills, but to affirm that having these skills is valued by you, the mother; you, the father.

Children will do anything to please the parent. If you would like your child to enjoy the full nature of his psychic development, you may encourage and support these practices. And, you may love your child.
—The Messages

———

Before we get into specific abilities in the next chapter, I want you to have a realistic idea of what your child can—or can't—do.

Psychically speaking, every stage of childhood brings with it new abilities. By now, you've had a chance to mull over whether your child has *emergent* abilities, which means her skills are readily identifiable, she's able to use them at some level, and they're a part of her life already. Or, if your child has *latent* skills—where you suspect she's intuitive, but either she's too young to determine this yet, or it's not clear to you what specific abilities your child has.

I also want you to understand that while abilities are nifty, what's most important is your relationship to your child.

Respect the whole child

You are the most important influence on your child.

Yikes!

Remember all those tear-jerking movie scenes where the boy (now a grown man) returns to his father's deathbed to tell him he loves him, even though they've been estranged for thirty years and the father has disowned him from the family estate (although by movie's end there's always time for someone to find a pen and reinstate). Get out your hankies! Everyone's crying! Father and son reunited!

The reason we cry is because it is true.

Your parents, love 'em or hate 'em, remain huge influences in your life—even after you've become an adult yourself.

You, as a parent, are the most important influence on your child.

Knowing this, it's important to put psychic development in perspective. Not sure your daughter can do clairvoyance? *That's okay.* Pretty sure your son isn't a medium? *It doesn't matter.*

Your kids are Divine, whether they have emergent intuitive abilities or not. Your kids aren't show dogs, trick ponies, or prize pumpkins. They're whole children, unique souls, and they are yours for this lifetime. Love them. Give them your attention and understand your importance to them. Nobody matters more right now.

That said, let's take a look at how abilities commonly present at each age.

Ages three to five

At this age, your child is fully open and naturally intuitive. In most cases (until she reaches eighteen months, which is really when those terrible twos begin), your child will be mellow or cranky depending on stimulus—dirty diaper, hungry tummy, too hot or cold, tired out, Mom's mood, too many hours in the car seat, and so on. Later on, it's still stimulus, just different kinds: long day at daycare, hungry tummy, needs cuddling, overtired—you get the idea.

This age is a great time to introduce intuitive concepts easily and naturally, the same way you'd teach her how to put on her jacket or use scissors. The reason for early introduction is basically *to give your child a vocabulary* to work with. For example, if your child is seeing deceased people, you can casually talk about spirits—no big deal, no stress, just reality. You can say, "Oh, you saw a spirit guide" and continue whatever else you're doing.

At this age, teaching intuition is interwoven with all the other learning they'll do in these years—potty training, language acquisition, small motor skills, color recognition, letters and numbers, shoe tying, etc. It's all important. At this age, your Divine child:

- **Can't concentrate for long periods of time.** Don't bother teaching meditation to your little wiggle worm—a moment of quiet at bedtime while you rub his back will be fine.

- **May be fearful of ghosts, monsters, etc.** These may be early flashes of clairvoyance, early mediumship. It could also be that your kid doesn't want to go to bed yet! My advice: if your child says he saw a ghost/monster/entity, believe him. Do active, physical clearing of the place with a problem (get a broom and sweep the ghost/monster/entity out from under the bed), and let him watch you do it. If the monster's still there, move the bed, ground the room energetically. Let him sleep with the lights on and the door open. If it helps, let him bunk with a sibling.

  My own bedtime trick for this age? Playing music designed for trance or meditation. My youngest daughter has been falling asleep to Jai Uttal's *Loveland* CD for three years now. Thank you, Jai! Find something that is designed to produce trance, and play the same music every night—that's right, the same music. Within a matter of days, your child will be conditioned to drop into slumber the minute you press *play*.

- **Can sense energy.** The best thing to do in this case is to acknowledge it. You can talk about vibe or energy or whatever word works for you. If your child senses a shift in vibe, tune in—chances are good you'll pick up on it, too.

- Telepathy, mediumship, healing may become apparent. These are abilities your child will present during everyday life. For example, once while shopping with my daughter, who was three at the time, I walked past an item hanging from the ceiling, and glanced up at the price. It was one hundred dollars.

One hundred dollars! I thought, in shock, thinking it was way overpriced. Immediately, my daughter, who was much too young to read and much too short to see the price tag, bellowed, "One hundred dollars! That's waaaaaay too much!" loudly enough for the shopkeeper to glare! Telepathy in shopping!

In terms of mediumship, if your child says that Grandpa has visited her (and he died ten years earlier), I say, believe her! Grandparents are one of the most common visitations that children have, likely because these spirits are interested in supporting their young descendants. Encourage your child to talk about these visitations, and to enjoy them; they can be a wonderful comfort for the whole family.

If you have a little healer on your hands, you may notice him spending a lot of time with family pets, or telling you what's wrong with them. A psychic friend of mine has a psychic son, who was about five when the following happened. One day while visiting, I noticed he was spending a lot of time with our dog, Buddy. A little while later, he came up to me. "Your dog had something wrong with his ear," he said, pointing to Buddy's right ear.

While I hadn't suspected anything was wrong with our dog, I took him to the vet a few days later. Sure enough, a tiny seed had lodged itself deep into his ear canal and was in danger of causing permanent damage. There was no way it could have been physically seen or felt by this intuitive boy; the vet had to use a flashlight. We were able to catch a health problem for Buddy quickly, before it became severe.

Ages six to eight

All of the above skills, plus more! These are prime years for gentle teaching. Kids are open and interested; they've got the intellectual development to master most tasks, and they can concentrate for longer periods of time.

Kids this age will have more awareness of (and possibly more interaction with) spirit guides and entities, and can easily work with energy. It's very simple for you to teach your child to have a direct connection with the Divine—show him how once or twice, and he'll know how for a lifetime. Children this age can work with energy with the same intensity (just not for the same duration) as an adult—ask them to heal you! Other abilities may also emerge now.

Ages nine to twelve

Kids this age have all the abilities of younger kids, along with these emerging traits:

- Can concentrate for longer
- May have *direct connection* with Divine
- Emerging spirituality
- Books and media have influence
- Can use psychic skills in daily life
- Can do healing
- Can work with energy
- May hide abilities from peers or others

As I've mentioned before, psychic training (at least from parents) gets trickier the older your child gets. Even now, as your child approaches the preteen stages, it may be harder to see what skills are emerging. It's not that your child isn't open at this age or isn't in the midst of developing new skills—she's just not as open to *you*!

Don't worry. This is normal. Remember, our goal as parents is to teach our kids how to be independent, whole beings who can survive on their own in the wilds of the world. The beginning of separation from parents and identification with peers is normal, natural, and to be desired.

The good news is that kids at this stage have a really strong ability to concentrate. The bad news is that this is the time your child will start wanting to spend time with his peers! Usually, this means same-sex

PARENTS ASK

My ten-year-old daughter has amazing psychic abilities, and I'd like to get her on a radio show. Can you recommend any?

No. Whether your child is two or twenty, I don't recommend putting her in the "psychic spotlight." Divine kids have very real, very sacred abilities, and they have these abilities for their own clarity, understanding, and soul growth. Commercializing these abilities or exposing your daughter to folks who don't understand that these abilities are Divine is not in her best interest. If your Divine child wishes to help others with her gifts, such as locating missing people or objects or predicting natural disasters, look with great scrutiny at any organizations that work in this way. If you have even the smallest doubt in their integrity, say no.

peers—your daughter will want to hang out with her Girl Scout friends, or you son will want to hang out with his baseball buddies. That means, if your child is psychic and her friends aren't particularly in the psychic loop (or may even have been taught to fear or shun it), then your child is not going to want appear any different.

Yes, your dearly beloved, amazingly gifted, totally psychic kid is going to want to sit for hours playing Barbie computer or Wii or whatever the trendy thing is, with nary a psychic thought in her head.

Don't worry. This is normal.

All it means is that your child's growing psychic abilities will need to be handled with extraordinary deftness by you, the parent. If you've already set up the concept that intuition and spirituality are welcome in your home, and that these abilities are welcome and useful in your child's daily life, he'll use these skills naturally as they occur (but he probably won't call his friends to tell them what he's doing).

Ages thirteen to fifteen

In general, Divine kids this age:

- Are peer based
- Don't want to be different
- Have a strong ability to concentrate
- Have a direct connection with the Divine
- Have independent spirituality
- Can do many psychic skills without strain
- Have the psychic abilities of adults—just not the experience
- Can do healing
- May delve into darker energies

At this age, your child is no longer a child. He or she is either a preteen or a teen, depending on physical maturity, which can range wildly: your fifteen-year-old boy may be four feet tall or six feet two, still a soprano or already a deep bass, with nary a facial hair or growing a moustache—it's all the luck of the genes.

Kids of this age are both more worldly and more sheltered than kids decades ago. They've got cell phones and are exposed to alcohol, drugs, sex, and violence as a matter of course in music and the media—but they're probably also still being chauffeured by their parents to their activities, for fear they'll be kidnapped.

Overly exposed—yet overly protected.

Go figure.

Age sixteen and older

My oldest daughter is one of the best psychics I know, and she doesn't even use her skills! At least, she doesn't admit to using them. However, abilities like this can't be masked forever. I find it extremely funny when I wonder where she is, and then the phone will ring. Of course, it will be her, checking in on her cell. "Did you call me?" she'll ask. Yes. I did. With my mind.

I'm not concerned that she acknowledges her psychic abilities right now. The Divine works in its own time, and when she's ready, she'll be ready. Besides, it's her life, her soul growth, her soul path—not mine.

At this age, your child can benefit from training from outsiders. If he expresses an interest, send him to meditation class, take him to hear speakers, accompany him to workshops or expos. Not just on psychic abilities, but on spirituality and metaphysics in general. Allow him to go to the church of his own choosing sometimes, even if you insist he goes to the family church most often.

You'll want to watch out for cults, people who want to get them to join a group in an aggressive way, and teachers who appear powerful but are in fact weak (you'll know, because you'll get an "ewww" feeling). If you notice signs of dark energy, get your child out of there, pronto.

At this age, kids in our culture are adult in terms of what they can do psychically, but they don't have the emotional maturity to deal with it all. In general, they:

- Are peer based
- Desire to be independent from parents
- Have concentration skills that can be intense
- Have distractibility levels that are high!
- Can easily have direct connection with Divine—but don't always want it
- Have independent spirituality
- Can do all psychic skills, including healing
- May explore smoking, drinking, drugs, and sex
- May delve into darker energies

By the time they enter high school, your kids are no longer your kids anymore. You might even think of them as "adults in training" rather than teens. Most teens will drive by sixteen, or soon after. Most will experiment with, avoid, or dive deep into smoking, drinking, drugs, and sex—and they'll do what they're going to do, no matter what you've told them. They're adults in training, remember? They're starting to learn their soul lessons—even if they're still in high school.

At this time, many kids will have psychic skills that are equal to or better than adults. However, they may choose to pretend they don't have these skills, or they may use them in a haphazard, distracted, non-focused way. If they dabble in drugs or alcohol, this will affect their psychic abilities in different ways.

The time for parental control is basically over, even if you or your child hasn't figured this out yet. However, the time for parental support is still ongoing—it's a subtle difference, but it's important.

Psychic parenting

As you can see, this psychic stuff requires a certain level of responsibility. If your child is working in these energies, then it just makes sense—it's time for you to get the training you need as a parent, so you can help your kid out.

"But, but . . . I'm not psychic," you mumble, backing away in terror.

Oh, come on—of course you are!

"No, I'm not!" you say stubbornly, crossing your arms.

All right—I'll be patient. Especially since I've noticed that a few of you are already starting to lean forward and raise your hand.

"I might be a tiny bit psychic," you say, shyly.

Or, "I've always been intuitive—is that the same as psychic?"

Or, my favorite "My grandmother was Native American/Albanian/Pennsylvania Dutch/Irish/Romanian/insert your nationality here, so I'm very in tune with this stuff."

Great! Superb! Perfect!

"No, I can't," the stubborn ones still say.

"Show me how," the eager ones plead.

Okay. You can admit to being psychic or not—that part's up to you. But you still have to help your kid—fair enough?

Everyone nods. Of course you're going to help your child. You're the parent!

That said, I'm going to take you on a crash course of what you'll need to know to help your psychic kid, and to understand how energy, the Divine, all that psychic stuff works. If you end up picking up a few psychic tricks by reading this section, hats off! I knew you could do it!

Don't worry. I'm gonna go really easy—extra light on the "woo woo."

Besides . . .

If you can go through eighteen hours of labor (or help someone else go through it while rubbing her back and feeding her ice chips), you can do this stuff.

If you can change a diaper, you can do this stuff.

If you can watch a three-hour elementary school concert in which your child portrays a banana, you can do this stuff.

If you can sit with teeth clenched as your child slides behind the wheel for his first driving lesson, you can do this stuff.

And as you turn the page, and begin to learn about specific psychic and spiritual abilities and ways to help your child "open," remember—you can do this stuff!

PARENTS ASK

My kids (I have three) are psychic, and the experiences we have at our house are a lot to deal with. I'm not psychic myself, so I don't know how to help.

Well, you probably are psychic. Allow yourself to believe simply in the possibility that this is true—"I might possibly, at some time, be psychic"—and see what happens. In the meantime, whatever time you can spend in prayer (asking the Divine for help, and showing gratitude for your great kids) or meditation (locking into the hum or energy of the Universe) will be useful to you. Both of these practices awaken the latent psychic abilities in all of us.

ten

Clairsentience: Gut Feelings, Vibe, and Energy

Every child is psychic. Yet most children are sent into the world with the knowledge of all things, then have a loss of remembering. This loss takes place in the very early years, before a child is five. As much loss of remembering takes place in the process of being born as it does in the transition from death to life. For a child, this loss of remembering is similar to the loss of remembering at the moment of death, when a being makes transition.

Much of the loss of remembering has been protection for children, in order that they may assimilate the culture of the family, place, and time in which they are born. —The Messages

─────

We're in the car. It is Tuesday, 7:40 a.m., the sky is ominous with rain, and it is not the best morning of my life. Coffee swirls precariously as I drive one-handed to school. I clench the cup, gun the gas; we're already six minutes late.

Those 360 seconds, to the teenager riding shotgun and the preteen in the backseat, are everything.

"If you hadn't slept in, we'd be on time!"

"It's your fault—you wasted time using the hair dryer!"

"Guys, does it really matter?" I ask in my Parental Voice of Reason as I swerve along the winding country roads. "In five years from now, do you think you'll care?"

No dice.

Wailing ensues from the back seat. "If I'm late, it goes on my permanent recooooord!"

"You don't have a permanent record in third grade."

"I doooooo soooooo!"

"If you're late more that three times, they don't let you into college," *the teen rebuts.*

"Your hair looks stupid. You should shave yourself bald."

"I hate you."

"I hate yoooooou!"

Being the parent, and thus the adult in charge, I do not chime in, "This morning, I hate you both!" but instead hold steadily to the wheel. Breathing in, breathing out, I assess the situation.

These kids need some energy.

I begin by building a ball of yellow energy for my son—I don't know why he needs yellow, but after a quick body scan, that's clearly what he's missing. I send it over, poof, like a big envelope of smoke that emerges from me and descends on him. Instantly, he's succumbed—he's helpless against energy like this.

In the backseat, my daughter needs blue—fast! I send her a volley of tiny balls of vibrating blue energy, ping-ponging her with little zaps of calm.

"I just sent you guys energy," I announce, once I've released these secret weapons.

"Mom! No!" the teen says in disgust, but it's too late. He's already shifted—his vibe is just slightly lighter, more positive, as if something missing has been supplied.

"What color did you send?" my daughter asks, perking up. She's very interested in energy right now.

"Blue."

"I think I need purple."

"Okay, here it comes.'

"This is insane," the teen grumbles, but it's a slightly less grumbly grumble than before.

"You need orange, I can see it," the preteen says to her brother cheer-fully. "I'll send you some."

"Mom, make her stop!" He pulls his sweatshirt hood over his face, but I've already caught sight of a grin.

In the backseat, my daughter has her cheeks puffed out like a blow-fish, concentrating on making balls of energy for her brother. And . . . the car is humming. In just a few seconds, we're back on track, from "I hate you" to harmony. We're still late for school. But with the vibration raised, nobody seems to care.

Clairsentience: what it is, how to use it

It sounds complicated: *clairsentience* (pronounced "clare-sent-eee-ence"). But it's not. Remember, learning psychic lingo is no different or harder than, say, learning basketball lingo (*foul, dribble, three-point shot*), or cell-phone lingo (*texting, ringtone, voicemail*), or coffee lingo (*double mocha with whip, puh-leese!*). It's all lingo, it's all verbiage—you learn it as you go.

Clairsentience is the first of the three "clairs," as psychics like to call them (the others are *clairaudience* and *clairvoyance*). It's a big mouthful

---

PARENTS ASK

My child is only seven, yet she does healing on our pets. She gets very quiet and moves her hands over their bodies. Is this normal?

The ability to work with energy comes very easily to many kids, even when they're young. Check in with her to see if she's able to identify illness or problems in the body, using her abilities of medical intuition. If she shows interest, introduce her to energy work such as Reiki, and other forms of energy healing when she gets older.

of a word, a complicated, hard-to-spell word. A word that can slow you down or get in your way if you aren't careful.

That's why my advice is, use it if you want to. But when I am teaching kids about how it works, I usually don't.

Instead, I say, "gut feelings." Or "vibe." Or "how your body feels." Or "energy."

Kids get these informal, slangy terms much faster, and with kids, you want to move as fast as they can go. They're leaps and bounds ahead of us most of the time, anyway—so the sooner you can get them doing and exploring and enjoying rather than listening to you drone on, the better!

So, what do I mean by "gut feelings"? Basically, clairsentience is energy felt in the body. It is the ability to perceive the energy that surrounds us, whether this comes from other people, places, situations, or even other realms.

What's more, having strong clairsentience ability is quite possibly the most important of the psychic skills your child can develop. This is because "gut feelings" or vibes are the most protective form of intuition for any human.

What does clairsentience feel like?

It's the queasy stomach before a difficult encounter. The way our heart races when danger is present. It is that "uh-oh" feeling when something creepy is happening, has happened, or is going to happen. It's the chill up the spine, the hair rising on your arms or the back of your neck. Sometimes, we feel clairsentience as emotion—anger, fear, nerves, irritation, hesitation, and so on. Other times, we just feel crummy or out of sorts, and we don't quite know why.

All humans—children, teens, and adults—are clairsentient. What's more, we are all clairsentient from birth; it's the one psychic skill that arrives first, is doled out equally to everyone, and can be utilized most quickly by humans as young as babies.

Other skills may be latent (for example, a child may be able to hear clairaudiently, but may not be able to tell you about it because he can't talk yet!), but clairsentience, or gut sense, is there from the get-go.

Unlike other psychic senses that can be hidden, blocked, or repressed later on in life, our clairsentient gut feelings don't desert us, ever. I'll say it again: our body does not, will not, cannot lie. If there's anything you can depend on in this world, it's your innate clairsentient gut feelings or vibe.

How kids sense vibe

Children live in their bodies. Even before they are born, they are rolling and punching and kicking—and the minute they are birthed out into this earth world, they are flailing their arms and legs, and within a few months they're rolling over! After that, the progression ensues: sitting, crawling, standing, walking, running.

Later still, the coordination increases: skipping, dancing, throwing a ball, kicking a ball, until, eventually, the pinnacle of teen coordination is achieved: maneuvering four thousand pounds of steel (plus the body weight of a knuckle-biting parent sitting in the passenger seat) at sixty-five miles per hour on freeway "test drives," even though one week previously, the same child could not yet properly operate a dishwasher.

Let alone take out the garbage or make the bed.

Once your child reaches adulthood, it's all over—he or she is a coach potato like the rest of us: in a car, in a cubicle, in front of a computer for hours, living so much out of tune with our body that the only stimulation we get is our next e-mail hit, our next cell-phone call, our next text.

Yuck!

As a culture, we're so in our mind, and so much in the world of cyber addiction, that we don't have any idea what our body feels.

If you don't believe me, try this now. Set down this book for thirty seconds. Resist the urge to check your e-mail or phone during this time. Instead, close your eyes and breathe deeply in through your

PARENTS ASK

Are the specific practices for being grounded?

Yes, you can ground yourself and/or your child energetically. Simply go into trance, and attach an energetic "grounding cord" to your lower back. Send this grounding cord deep into the core of the earth, and plug it in! This grounding cord works by tethering you to the earth, similarly to how astronauts are tethered to their spacecraft. If your child is all floaty and flittery, go ahead and ground 'em in this way; you'll be amazed what a difference it makes.

nose, and let the air come out slowly and peacefully through your mouth. Do this five times. Now, take a little body scan and notice what hurts—what's tight, what feels numb, what aches, what feels sluggish instead of active, passive instead of involved. If you would really like to feel different, after you have found an area that feels "yucky," stand up, stretch that area in whatever way feels good, and breathe into this stretch. It might take you a total of two minutes to do a small amount of stretching, more if you get into and start feeling how great it feels.

Now, sit back down, and head right back to where you were—breathing shallowly, or perhaps even holding your breath. Drinking coffee or soda while you read, maybe eating a snack. Your mind racing, racing, racing to get to the next word, all the while trying to block your own private thoughts that come up unbidden—thoughts about what I'm writing, thoughts about your own experiences, anxieties, anger, emotion, and so forth.

This is you living in your head.

It's not the nicest place to live!

Don't feel too bad—most everyone else on the planet is living right there in their own private mental mansion, too.

You can live there if you want. However, *the body is where you will find truth.* How the body feels, and what stories it has to tell you. What your gut feelings are. The vibe you sense about people, places, situations.

If you can tune into your body, even for just thirty seconds, your clairsentience will always tell you the truth.

When we begin our Earth lives as children, we fully live in our body. Later, we discover we've somehow moved into our mind, and the struggle to get back to the body is immense. But right now, your child is still there, actively inhabiting her body. She still knows how to listen to the truth of her body. Encourage this.

What vibe feels like

How does clairsentience present itself for your child? Clearly, easily, and in ways that she can understand. Such as:

- Stomachache
- Neckache
- Backache
- Nervousness
- Tiredness
- Avoidance
- Fear
- The sensation of a difference in energy: color, denseness, vibration. Some kids can see this. Some kids feel it. Some kids just have a *deep knowing* that it is there.

What's deep knowing?

It's the way you feel when you understand you are hearing, seeing, or perceiving truth. For some people, it's just that unshakable sense of "yep, that's it." They can't be persuaded any differently—nor should they. Their body, their clairsentience, simply tells them All systems go, and this is correct, true information. In my own body, I experience chills or shuddering if someone tells me something that is a truth. My back will become on fire with chills. Usually, this happens when

I am working with a client, and he or she is discovering something new about themselves, or saying a truth they didn't understand before. When my body reacts in this way, with chills or shuddering, it's my "aha!" moment; I know that what I am hearing is true on a soul level, and I'm able to pass this on to my client.

Everybody's hooked in

Unlike other psychic skills that are inherent but may need to be nudged and trained and taught in order to use them easily, clairsentience or vibe does not have to be developed. It's the only sixth-sense skill that requires no learning curve, no training manual, no step-by-step instruction.

It's a freebie, a gimme, a bonus point—you and your kids just have it.

Pretty nifty, huh?

However, if you read the small print, you'll find that one thing is required: you have to bring attention to it.

Your child's stomach hurts? Instead of tossing him some Tums, perhaps a quick check-in with Divine guidance about what that stomachache's about may help more.

Your child always tries to avoid a certain teacher/coach/pastor? Instead of saying, "Oh that's silly," or worst of all, forcing your child to spend time with this person, perhaps a quick check-in with Divine guidance may reveal that this person is not safe, trustworthy, or someone you want hanging around your child!

Trust your gut feelings!

Trust your child's gut feelings!

The body never, ever lies. Please, teach your child this.

The more your child trusts her clairsentience, and the more she understands how to pay attention to what her body is telling her, the safer your child can be.

Clairsentience and child abuse

One of my friends, author Shannon Riggs, has devoted her career to writing and teaching about childhood sexual abuse. Abused herself as a girl, she wrote the children's book *Not in Room 204* for kids facing similar situations—and she won an Oregon Book Award for her efforts.

The facts are grim: one in four girls will be molested, usually by someone she knows quite well, before she is eighteen. The numbers are just slightly lower for boys. This means that if you have taught your child to trust her gut feelings, and then she says, "I don't like Mr. Smith," it is your job to pay attention to this information!

Riggs teaches why "stranger danger" is a lie—why a sexual abuser isn't that person on the park bench; it's the popular coach who gives your son a ride home after practice. It's the friendly pastor who sponsors Youth Night. It's your child's grandparent, father, stepfather, or other male living in the house. It's tragic, but these are common scenarios.

Please. If your child says that he or she feels a certain person is "creepy," or you yourself just have a bad vibe about that person, *even if there is no "reason" for it*, please trust your and your child's clairsentience, and keep your child away from that person.

You're the parent. Your job first and foremost is to protect your child.

Exercises

1. The next time your child complains about a stomachache or another body discomfort, check into it psychically. Find a moment that you can sit down together privately. Then, both of you close your eyes and take a few deep breaths. After a few breaths, ask your child to identify where the pain or problem is in her body. Sometimes I ask a child to look for "a different color energy" or "where the energy is thicker." After a few more breaths, ask your child to tell you what is causing the pain or problem. Believe what your child says! If your child is unable

to come up with an answer to what is causing the pain, or the answer just doesn't make sense to you, open your mind to all possibilities, and ask to receive Divine guidance on the issue. Believe what you receive!

2. If you receive guidance that your child is in danger or needs protection, believe it! This may present itself as a vision, a voice, or just a sense of deep knowing.

   However, if you receive guidance that your child is simply nervous or anxious or cranky—in other words not in any danger but just dealing with emotions—you can begin to work with your child on healing this anxiety or tension.

   One of the fastest ways to do this is to send energy to your child. First, picture in your mind the color of energy your child needs. A color will pop into your mind, and this color will be right (so don't worry about getting it wrong—you won't!). Say your child urgently requires green. Build a big ball of green energy with your mind, and then send this gigantic ball of energy to your child. You can have this energy be as big as a beach ball, a house, or even the world, or as tiny as a little ping pong ball. Even if you can't believe you are doing this, do it. Send the energy to your child. Watch him get calm and happy, fast.

3. Teaching young kids this technique is as simple as saying something like "Let's make a ball of energy with your mind." "What color would you like it to be?" "How big is your ball?" "Who would you like to send it to?" "What other color does Grandma/the dog/your brother need?" You'll find your child can make and send energy easily, and will be able to intuit exactly what color energy every person you know needs—including yourself.

4. For older kids, present it this way: "Energy is everything—everything is energy. Your mind can work with this energy, just as your mind can work with other concepts. When you work with the concept of energy as a color, you attach a certain vibrational level to this energy. Energy works via distance. Send-

ing someone positive energy in the color that you sense they need is healing and useful to them." Clear. Direct. Simple. Remember: your child is innately psychic and spiritually aware. More so even than you. She can use this as she needs it.

PARENTS ASK

My daughter (she's six) always gets a stomachache before school. Is this clairsentience?

It might be—or it might be she's having trouble adjusting to school. With younger Divine kids, you'll need to use both your parenting and your psychic knowledge to get to the bottom of a situation. Remember that clairsentient kids pick up everything in their body; it may be that the energy in the classroom is too noisy, or the room is too hectic. You can help clear her by having her imagine she's a sponge creature who has absorbed everyone's energy at school, and now she's going to give that energy back by putting it in an imaginary bucket where it will be taken away forever. It sounds too simple—but it works!

eleven

Clairaudience: Can You Hear Me Now?

Now, at this time, many children hear us. While you hear us continually and constantly, they do also—but they do not have the vocabulary to express what they hear. Furthermore, it would not occur to most children to mention what they have seen or heard, because it is natural. When you see a bird flying, you do not particularly remark to your neighbor, "There is a bird flying." Yes, it is a miracle, but because you see this so often, there is no need to mention it. In this way, children see miracles at all times, but they do not remark. —The Messages

———

You know how you tell your kids to "get dressed, make your bed, brush your teeth, and, by the way, that car in the driveway is your ride to school, and it is leaving in four minutes?" and they gaze at you with the stunned awareness of a rhino shot with a tranquilizer that has started to take effect, and then mumble something along the lines of "glemyckdafoshobit?" as they pull the covers over their heads?

Well, let's hope their psychic hearing is in better shape!

Clairaudience is the art of psychic hearing, and it is a psychic ability that may show up in your child around elementary-school age—it may emerge earlier, but if your child is very young, she may not have the words to tell you what is happening. Also, so many kids are used to hearing this way, they don't even know that it's "extra" sensory—they think it's the norm.

Clairaudience can be trained and developed in kids (or anyone), and this can be extraordinarily useful to your child. Taken to one of its highest skills, clairaudience can be utilized as channeled writing—writing down the Divine messages or guidance you hear as words. Clairaudience can also emerge as channeling—verbally reporting the guidance you hear, in words. Or, moving aside to become, in essence, a "channel" for Divine guidance to move through.

As a channel and as a person who receives channeled writing, I've found that clairaudience is often misunderstood by people until they start to experience it themselves. Thus, before we begin talking about how to help your child develop her talents, let's talk about what clairaudience is—or isn't.

What does clairaudience sound like?

Clairaudience arrives as words, language, sound, or music, *via your ears.*

The Bible makes frequent mention of clairaudience. Whenever people received messages from angels or other messengers of God, they "heard" or received clairaudiently. Moses, perhaps one of the first to receive channeled writing, received clairaudiently when he scribed the Ten Commandments into stone!

In old-time cartoons, clairvoyance was often depicted as the tiny "angel" and "devil" who sat on either side of person's shoulders at all moments, trying to convince their charge to do a good deed—or a bad one. Walt Disney gave credence to clairaudience, too, when he animated Jiminy Cricket and let him sing his sage advice to "let your conscience be your guide."

In many modern-day religions, the concept of listening to that "still, small voice" you hear inside your head, and understanding it to be the voice of God or the Divine, is a common belief.

One of the reasons it's common is because it's true.

That said, let's take a look at ways in which everyday people (including people who don't think of themselves as psychic) can receive clairaudiently without even trying.

Clairaudience from outside channels

Have you ever had the experience of having a burning question in your mind, or prayed or meditated for help in making a decision, and then you jump in the car to pick up the kids from school and flip on the radio . . . and there it is—a message, song, or newscast that seems as if it were tailor-made just for you?

Well, it probably was.

Because the Divine works energetically, a lot of clairaudience comes to us via energy or vibration—such as the vibratory energy of sound waves, such as what you might hear on your favorite radio station.

Your kids, who are likely to be using newer technologies like cell phones, the Internet, or texting, may receive messages with this modern technology.

All technology that is energy-based can be used as a "channel" of clairaudient information.

What about spirit guides, angels, and Divine messengers?

Ah, spirit guides. Those much-misunderstood, oft-maligned creatures from other realms! Some people believe in them, some people don't—but take it from me: spirit guides are real.

I didn't believe in them myself until I came face to face with them, when I first I began to "open." Now, they hang out all the time! These Divine entities actually come in, sit down (or hover), and tell me stuff to write down or give me advice for my clients.

Heck, Divine advice is way better advice than I could give anyone myself!

The spirit guides I'm currently receiving from, Ashkar and Ragnar, are two very tall, luminous beings who seem to be some kind of advanced twin entity. Some folks have told me they're "Nordics," but I really don't know. And, yes, I do wish they didn't have such *Star Trek*-sounding names, but they do. Who am I to say what a spirit guide's name should be?

As far as I can tell, these spirit guides accompany me everywhere, and are instantly available to me whenever I call on them. They protect me both in my Earth life and in other realms, 24/7. That they are good, of God, and messengers of the Divine, I have no doubt.

But what's important is, I didn't believe in them—in any spirit guides, angels, or Divine messengers—until they actually began appearing to me.

You can believe in them or not.

They exist anyway.

And if you're a stickler for the rational, logical, and proof-laden, consider this: does your ego really believe that we are the only entities in this Universe? Do you really, honestly think that humans and animals are the only conscious, sentient beings on this planet? In this galaxy? That there are no other realms or dimensions or worlds that exist—no other beings, save our own puny Earth selves?

I mean, c'mon!

Of course we're not the only ones here! There are many energies, many entities, many aspects of consciousness that are always coexisting at all times. It's just that we've gotten so used to not seeing or hearing from them (because we are too busy Tweeting or watching Netflix movies) that we don't.

PARENTS ASK

When it comes to clairaudience, how do I know that the messages my son hears are real, and that he isn't just making things up?

We live our whole life accepting the reality of just three dimensions, but in fact there are many dimensions that are just as real as anything else! When your son tells you he hears sounds and messages in his "mind's ear," relax your judgment and pay attention. The more you accept the possibility of the fourth dimension, the "sixth sense," the more you will begin to understand how useful and how pertinent the information he receives is.

Luckily, our kids are much more open.

Kids receive clairaudient messages from spirit guides, angels, and Divine messengers all the time. Many kids also hear from spirits and other entities.

This isn't particularly unusual, and it isn't particularly worrisome.

It's just part of life, as a conscious being, in this Universe.

How kids hear clairaudiently

First, most clairaudience isn't a loud booming voice like a megaphone from the other room—although it can be.

Most often, kids are aware of that "still, small voice," or what I call the voice in the *mind's ear*.

That's right. The mind's ear. In other words, an interior voice. Again, some people hear an exterior voice, and this is fine. But most people hear a voice that seems to come from inside their own head. It's not their own voice; it's different, separated, characterized by a higher level of consciousness. It's not ego-based either; it's soul-based.

This voice may be heard:

- In your child's native language
- In another language (though this is uncommon)
- In another language that is understood telepathically—i.e., understanding meaning without words
- As thought, without any language at all
- As music or sound

Many children hear music, song, and sound clairaudiently. Musicians and songwriters often hear music this way, with compositions arriving fully formed in their heads.

Clairaudience protects your child

Imagine if your child was in danger, and suddenly a warning boomed into his ear:

"Move now!"

"Run!"

"Stop!"

"No!"

"Watch out!"

Clear commands and warning such as these are common in clairaudience.

In my own case, I've discovered that if you receive a warning such as "No!" or "Don't'!" or "Go now!" or whatever it is, there is absolutely no point in hanging around disagreeing with the Divine. They say jump—you say how high!

Yes, you can avoid their advice. But why? They're on your side!

If you teach your child that clairaudient information can be trusted and acted on with faith, this will be of great use to her—this advice via her mind's ear is provided for her safety and benefit.

Longer messages and specific instructions

Sometimes your child will receive longer clairaudient messages that are quite specific. These include warnings, such as:

"Stay away from Mr. Jones; he's not a nice man."

"Don't eat that potato salad; it will make you sick."

"Get out of the water now! Sharks are coming!"

"Don't take the shortcut today; you'll find trouble there."

These are specific kinds of communication that are also meant for your child's protection. Perhaps the potato salad has reached a dangerous core temperature, and the bacteria have gone viral. Perhaps there's a *Jaws* remake at the beach. Perhaps a bully lurks on the shortcut trail.

Your child doesn't know. But if he hears Divine guidance like this, he'll benefit by following it.

You can teach your child to understand that listening to this "voice in her inner ear" is in her best interest—even if she's not sure why.

This is also a nice time to explain to your child that he has *free will*. No, not *Free Willy*, which is a whale movie you may have in your family video library. But free will, which is the ability to make one's own decisions, right or wrong, regardless of what Divine guidance tells you.

At my house, we call this "you're in charge of your own life" or "you make your own decisions." Even though it is tempting as the parent to rush in (where angels fear to tread!) when your child gets stuck, doing so is not advisable.

It's a fine line—your kids do need help; they're kids! But the more you can teach them that they are their own souls in the process of their own soul growth, the better they'll learn.

My own experience as a human on this planet has been that free will sucks if you're not aligned with the Divine. In other words, making decisions that are not in flow with Divine guidance always backfires— sometimes in huge, catastrophic ways, and always in small, annoying, miserable ways.

Yet fortunately, because "the purpose of life is soul growth" instead of "the purpose of life is getting it right, every time," your child (and you) have plenty of time to make mistakes and learn from them.

What about receiving from ghosts and spirits?

If your child is a medium, he may receive clairaudiently from ghosts and the spirits of the deceased. As a parent, this can be unsettling, to say the least. "Grandma says you should paint the living room blue, not brown." "Aunt Maeve says that moving to California is a big mistake." Not the kind of information you especially want to hear when the U-Haul is already packed.

However, most kids who are mediums will know very early, earlier even than you do, that they are to pass on messages from the deceased in order to help and heal. For example, they may see a spirit hovering near a woman in the grocery story, and then clairaudiently hear the message this spirit would like to relay to the woman.

If this sounds like your child's ability, remember that Freaking Out is not your best option. Remember what we just talked about—that the Universe is a big place, we are small beings, and there are many beings coexisting with us in many realms and on many planes.

This is just reality—not reality as you've perceived it, perhaps. But reality just the same. If your child can hear these beings, please support her in this truth.

What about information from Divine messengers?

What happens if your child receives messages "meant for the world" such as the messages I received with *The 33 Lessons*—about 120 pages of spiritual teachings included in my book *Writing the Divine*? This may happen to kids who are spiritually advanced—they'll have a direct connection to a particular spirit guide or teacher, who will impart messages for teaching.

Your child may impart these messages by speaking them to you or others. She may also receive them in channeled writing. It sounds a bit overwhelming, but, in general, most kids who are receiving genuine "messages for the world" don't go on the tour circuit, so you can relax—you can still sign him up for softball this spring.

However, if your child starts coming to you with spiritual information that's well beyond the scope of his exposure or experience, pay attention. Again, if he's old enough to write it down as channeled writing, give that a try. Or, you can try taping him, or writing it down yourself. If none of that works, don't worry: this gift isn't going to disappear, but will only increase as your child matures and is more able to work with this ability.

Using clairaudience for Divine guidance

Chocolate or vanilla?

Basketball or football?

Girl Scouts or choir?

These are examples of personal, everyday, mundane yet highly important questions that can be answered via clairaudience by your child via the Divine. It is a method of having direct connection that your child can use and trust to make every single decision in her life.

PARENTS ASK

My daughter is terrified of what's under her bed. She says there are monsters who talk to her every night. She's four, and still wants to sleep with me every night.

With young kids, the hard part is figuring out what's at the core: is she clairaudient—or does she just want to snuggle up with you? Assume the first, and take action. Clear everything out from under the bed, and move the bed to another place in the room. After you've cleaned, simply look or "sense" the energy in the room, and clear it as you need. It sounds confusing, but working with energy this way is very simple, and remember: you aren't doing the clearing, the Divine is. You should notice an immediate shift in the energy of the room. If your daughter still resists, have her sleep with a sibling, or with the light on, until she can relax into the new energy you've created.

Your child can do this through simple clairaudience, such as asking a question and waiting to hear the answer. Or, your child can do this via channeled writing—writing down a question, and waiting for the answer to be provided in writing.

Because kids sometimes have ego-interference when they are receiving, it's useful to teach your child what it *feels* like to hear Divine guidance, as opposed to his own ego voice. Remember, the body never lies! Thus, when your child is receiving Divine guidance, he might feel:

- Good
- Patient
- Calm
- Kind
- Nice
- Happy

- Encouraged
- Relaxed
- Expansive
- Safe
- Comforted
- Peaceful
- Upbeat
- Supported
- Loved
- Loving
- Blissful
- Healed

If your child has tendency to brush off the Divine and listen to his ego voice, don't worry. We're all just learning. However, you may remind him that he'll know it's ego if whatever answers he gets make him feel:

- Impatient
- Mean
- Jealous
- Angry
- Petty
- Guilty
- Rotten, or
- Get him into trouble

If you can explain that Divine guidance is always good, and the ego is usually confused even if it sounds convincing, your child will understand the difference.

Exercises

1. **Asking for Divine guidance.** Have your child ask a question aloud, or write a question down. This should be a question he is having trouble figuring out for himself, such as "Should I hang around Nate, or will he get me in trouble?" or "Should I join Band?" Then, ask for Divine guidance on the question, and have your child pay attention to what he hears in his mind's ear—either immediately, or later that day. Also, what he hears via electronica such as the radio, etc.

   For example, if your child is wondering if he should sign up for baseball, and, five minutes after asking for Divine guidance, you hop in the car and that old song "Take Me Out to the Ball Game" is playing on the radio, you can pretty much count on the fact that, yes, your child should sign up. But if the newscaster does a report on a "Three Strikes" law that mandates prison time, then skip the signups. The Divine is that clear—and is often funny in the bargain.

2. **Notice the receiving.** Have your child try the same thing—asking or writing questions for Divine guidance. Have her notice *how* the answer arrives: does she hear words outside her head, in her mind's ear, or does she just "know" the answer telepathically? Many kids are so quick that they hear the answer before they even finish asking the question.

3. **Practice.** Practice clairaudience—make a game of it! Tell the Divine a riddle, and ask to hear the answer. The Divine has a great sense of humor! For example, I once asked the Divine if I should book a trip to Hawaii with my partner, and the answer arrived ten minutes later, in a phone call from a psychic friend. "I'm not sure why I'm supposed to tell you this," she said, "but the answer is 'kiwi.'" Joke's on me—"Kiwi" is my partner's name in Hawaiian! Book those tickets, please!

twelve

Clairvoyance: The Art
of Psychic Seeing

*It is important to understand what a child's brain can do. In some ways,
it is faster than yours. In other ways, it cannot manage certain concepts;
these take time, as the child grows and develops.*

*In educating children, we do not care about tricks and techniques. We
are interested in giving you information that will help children become
more spiritual beings, one with the One. The clearest way is for you to
model this.*

*Teach your children, and yourself, to remember the Source from
which you came, of which you are.* —The Messages

———

When it comes to clairvoyance, kids are quick studies. In fact, when
teaching kids psychic skills, clairvoyance is often the easiest tool to
teach. They pick it up so fast, it can be a little unnerving.

Kids don't have any of the hesitancies that adults have, such as "Am
I really seeing this? "Is what I'm seeing real?" "I can't see anything!" or
"I see something, but I think I'm making it up!" Kids simply see the
information—they see it clearly, and they report it without hesitation
or second-guessing.

On the downside, kids don't have quite the same stamina (or interest) in exploring clairvoyance the same way an adult might. As a
child, you might be presented with extraordinary information about
the struggles of a person you are reading—but because you're a child,

you won't have the experience to identify with or fully understand what you're seeing. And, you may not care! You're a kid, and it's loads more fun to go out and skateboard with your friends than to rehash someone's unhappy experiences on a deep psychological level.

It's like a kid who's watching a very adult movie—one directed by, say, Ingmar Bergman, or one that's sad and desolate and confusing. A child can watch the movie, and describe the action, but he can't interpret the deep psychological meaning of what's happening on the screen—it's beyond his emotional development. He might say, "It's sad" or "There's a lot of snow" or "People die" or whatever it is, and that's what he gets. Whereas, an adult watching the same movie might be able to immediately relate deep emotional issues of the scene, such as "She feels guilty because she doesn't love her husband and now he's ill, and she feels hopeless and alone." You know—the *Sturm und Drang* of life!

Kids are kids. Even older teens haven't had the life experiences that you've had by age twenty-eight or forty-two or sixty-three or however old you are. So, don't except the same kind of analysis from them—they simply haven't had enough growing time.

What is clairvoyance?

We've already discussed some of your child's psychic abilities, such as clairsentience (gut feelings) and clairaudience (psychic hearing). But what exactly is *clairvoyance*?

Clairvoyance is the art of psychic seeing. People who are clairvoyant see in their mind's eye, or what's sometimes called "the third eye." Folks who are clairvoyant see "movies in their head." They may see visions. They may also see spirit guides, deceased people, "imaginary" friends, and other messengers who aren't exactly "real" but, then again, aren't not "real" either.

When kids are very young (pre-kindergarten age) they may have trouble communicating what they see—they aren't old enough to have the vocabulary. However, by elementary school, they'll be able to tell you easily.

What does clairvoyance look like?

Think it's hard to see psychically, in your mind's eye? It's not. I travel the West Coast teaching everyday folks how to see clairvoyantly and use their psychic skills, and I also teach people, by distance, in private phone sessions. Over the years, I've found that most people can learn clairvoyance in a few sessions—and, again, kids learn even faster. Extra training sessions are useful, because they build confidence and add experience, but it's sort of like learning to ride a bike—once you're up and rolling, wheeeeeee! You'll be able to ride a bike from then on. That's because psychic abilities are latent. We all have them. We just have to help them emerge.

There are lots of ways to learn clairvoyance, but knowing a few general concepts can be useful. These concepts, widely used by many clairvoyants today, and which are discussed in much greater detail in Debra Lynne Katz's book *You Are Psychic*, include:

PARENTS ASK

My son, who is ten, has been having nightmares about tsunamis—and yesterday, there was a terrible tsunami in the news. What can I do?

Prophetic dreams are common for Divine kids; however, they often confuse *receiving* information about a disaster with *causing* it. Sit down with your son, and explain to him that he is receiving information via clairvoyance during his dreams. Explain to him that it's like turning on a TV program—he doesn't cause the program to happen, he just watches it. If he's afraid to sleep because he might have more dreams, have him go into prayer and ask the Divine for relief—he can simply say, "Let me be comforted" or "Let me have a guide in my dreams to protect me." Keep him away from news coverage. Remember, seeing something on film is energetically the same as experiencing it, and your sensitive son doesn't need this exposure.

- **A viewing screen.** This is a screen that you put up in front of your mind's eye, a short distance in front of your face. It's here, on this energetic screen, that you'll see images and "movies in your head" via clairvoyance.

- **A rose.** The rose can be the most confusing aspect of clairvoyant training at first. Basically, you use a clear, crystalline rose as a barometer or symbol during a clairvoyant viewing—you put it up on your viewing screen, and it acts as a growing, changing, and often-moving symbol that helps you interpret what you are receiving. Why a rose? It's certainly got its share of symbolic meanings. But mostly, it's just a common technique that psychics use.

When I teach psychic development and start explaining how to use the rose, most folks think it's really weird at first, and then catch on right away, especially people used to thinking symbolically. People who are more left brain—practical, logical, math-and-science oriented—take a little longer.

Of course, some terrific clairvoyants never use a viewing screen or a rose—they just go straight into seeing "movies in their head" and this is great! Others use the rose with brilliance and aplomb, and are able to delve deeply into multiple layers of clairvoyance thanks to this handy symbolic tool. This is fine, too.

An example of the clairvoyant process

Viewing screens? Roses? Huh? It all sounds pretty weird, doesn't it! Don't worry—I'll walk you through how the process works for adults, and then we'll get to the kid version next. The more you understand the basics, the better you can help your own clairvoyant kids!

Here's how to do it:

1. Go into a light trance (simply close your eyes and breathe deeply a few times)

2. Run some Divine energy in your body. You might imagine celestial energy pouring down through your "crown chakra," or the top of your head.

3. Put up a viewing screen about six inches in front your fore-head—this is where you will "see" the images clairvoyantly. Yes, it's energetic, not physical!

4. Write your name in big letters on your viewing screen, then use an imaginary eraser to erase it. Or put up the alphabet on your screen, erasing each letter before you put up the next.

5. Once you get the hang of putting things up on your viewing screen and then erasing them, put up a clear, crystalline rose. What does it look like? What color is it? Does it have a lot of leaves? A lot of flowers? Is it big, small, healthy, unhealthy? Is it changing? Is it moving?

6. Ask the rose a question, and see what happens. For example, if your question is about your financial future, and you put up a rose that immediately starts shriveling up and walking around with a hand stretched out like a beggar—tough times may be ahead. But if your rose appears flush, firm, and fully petaled, and dollar bills start filling your screen—it's fat city, my friend!

7. Keep asking the rose to show you more. At this point, if you start to see full-blown "movies in your head," great! Keep asking the rose to "show you more"—if there's an open door, go through it. If an object beckons, check it out. If you get stuck or can't go any further, return to your rose and ask it again—sort of like a reset button.

8. Don't stay in too long when you're getting started; ten minutes is plenty of time to gather good clairvoyant info. With practice, you'll be able to receive for longer.

9. When you're done, do a little energy clearing by mentally gathering any yucky or unwanted energies you find in your body, then send these into outer space.

Clairvoyance process for kids

First, the younger your kids are, the slower you'll want to go. You may find that before the age of eight or so, kids aren't developmentally able to concentrate on the process for very long. Even if they're seeing clairvoyantly on their own already, training might be too intense for them.

Use your judgment; but if the process isn't working, stop. No big deal. Try it again in a few months or next year. Keep it fun and light, and if you hit a roadblock, just quit. No worries.

For kids, I don't use a rose—I use a *psychic buddy*. Why? Because kids think in kid terms. Finding ways to make psychic tools more kid-friendly just makes sense.

As we've discussed, kids work faster than adults. They go faster into trance, they read so fast it's scary, and they come out of trance very quickly, and are immediately ready to go to the next thing: "Can we have popsicles?" "Can I watch a movie?" "Can I have a cell phone?"

Yes. Yes. No!

For younger kids, I don't bother with an energy clearing at the end. It's not that it's not useful; it's more that they get bored, frustrated, or edgy, and this defeats the purpose of making a practice session fun. Thus, if I think a clearing is needed for them, I'll do it for them. Keeping the session short, fun, and easy is best for young kids.

A sample clairvoyant reading
from a nine-year-old

Sometimes, an example provides clarity faster than any explanation.

I'm in the car, driving my younger daughter back from swimming lessons. I've had some funny feelings about my mother's health, and I decide that I will check them out with one of the most powerful clairvoyants I know—my nine-year-old.

Now, I'm a not just a clairvoyant looking for confirmation from another clairvoyant, but I'm also a parent. That said, I've very aware of the need to proceed carefully, age-appropriately, and with respect for my daughter's emotions. Light and easy is my mantra.

It goes something like this:

Me, driving: "Wanna do a reading?"

Daughter, in car, bored: "Okay."

"Close your eyes."

She grunts.

"Go into trance."

She takes a few breaths—but I'm suspicious. I glance over from driving and see she's trying to do the reading while leafing through her thirteen-year-old brother's recently acquired school yearbook!

Not gonna fly. I take it away. She sighs.

"Close your eyes."

"They are!" *she huffs.*

"Go into trance." *This time, she does. I wait a few beats, to make sure she's in. Remember what I said about kids being fast! They can drop in fast, before an adult can even take a few breaths.*

"Put up your screen."

"Got it."

"Put up your rose, and write under the rose, in whatever color you want, the name of your grandmother."

"Do you mean her first name, or her first name plus her last name?"

"Whatever you want."

"Got it."

"What does your rose look like?"

"It's pink, and it has petals with brown spots on it."

"What else do you see?"

"It's wilting, and the petals are falling off."

Hmmm. At this point, I'm fairly disturbed because her reading— even though she doesn't know why I'm asking about her grandmother— is matching some problems I've already seen. But I have to work carefully, because it's not responsible parenting to burden my daughter with this information.

"Okay. Erase that rose."

"Got it."

"Now, switch to your psychic buddy." *I'm switching the tools she's using, from the rose with which my daughter was trained, to the psychic buddy, which she also likes.*

"Write the name of your grandmother under your psychic buddy."

"Got it."

"Ask your psychic buddy to show you where the problem is—why the petals fell off."

"It's in her . . . heart," she says, and then, "No, no . . . it's," and then she sort of presses or thumps her chest on her left side.

"What else do you see?"

"Her leg."

"Which one?"

She points to her left leg. (Months later, I'll find out that my mother had a medical issue with her left leg, but didn't tell me.)

"Okay. Erase your psychic buddy."

Now I'm looking for a time frame, but I don't want her to have this information. I don't want her to be concerned.

"Put up a new psychic buddy, and write your grandmother's name under it."

She does.

"Ask the psychic buddy to show you what will happen in one year."

"Nothing. It's not doing anything."

"What color is it?"

"It's blue, and red, and . . . it's rainbow." Rainbow's always a good sign.

"What's it doing?"

"It's getting into a car and driving to the beach (where my mother lives). I'm tired of this. I want to stop."

"Okay, great. Erase buddy. Erase your screen. Come out of trance. One, two, three."

She's out, and looks at me expectantly—I hand over her brother's coveted yearbook, and she dives back in, totally engrossed.

Reviewing the process

The above reading shows you how to work with kids—the depth you can go (not too deep), the pressure you can apply (not very much), the length of time involved (probably just a few minutes), and the language to use (casual, simple, neutral).

PARENTS ASK

I'm not psychic, but my twelve-year-old son is. What does it mean when he says he sees "movies in his head"?

For most clairvoyants like your son, the images appear in what I call the "mind's eye." To see this for yourself, simply close your own eyes. Now, imagine that you see the color red in this space above, behind, or near your closed eyes. Most people are able to see or sense a color where it once was black, gray, or nondescript. Now, switch that color (in your mind's eye) to blue, or any other color you prefer. This is the first step to clairvoyance! For your son, he's moved beyond color, and is now seeing full movies in his mind's eye. The movies appear very similar to watching TV, except they might be hazier, or harder to see, or fade in and out. (By the way, it's very easy to learn clairvoyance. With a little bit of training, you can see movies in your head, too.)

Keep it light, work fast, and be positive. When they're ready to quit, they're ready to quit. No big deal.

You'll notice that I never, ever said anything along the lines of "I'm worried about your grandmother's health." Instead, I just said "Wanna do a reading?" If she'd said no, I'd have stopped right there. No pressure. No hassle.

I also kept her brain busy—I kept her moving forward from one clairvoyant task to the next: "put up your screen," "put up your rose," "put up your psychic buddy," "erase it." Do this, do that. If a kid gets bored, they're gone. So keep the mind engaged and in motion.

You'll also notice that the whole session probably took three to five minutes at most. This is plenty of time to take a child in and out of a clairvoyant reading, and have a few key questions answered.

I don't discuss any aspects of my interpretation of her reading, and I don't ask her to do any interpretation of her own. For one thing, she's too young to have any concerns about her grandmother's health. With her older brother, a teenager, I'd discuss how I interpret symbolically, so he can learn how to do this, too: a wilting rose might mean health problems, for example.

If my daughter had started to receive unpleasant information, I'd have quickly switched questions so that she'd have to focus on something else. Or, I'd bring her out of trance right away. With an older teen, I'd have probably let him see whatever he might see without trying to control it, and we'd discuss it later.

It's been my experience that the Divine provides us with the information we need—and that this is information we can manage. Even small children recognize and know the truth when they see it.

However, *it is never ethical to* ask a child to view something you already know is disturbing, violent, or evil. Unfortunately, some kids will see this stuff anyway. But it is not your right to ask them to read this. If it happens that they do see something disturbing while working clairvoyantly, it is your responsibility to sit down with them and help them clear their energy and emotionally process what they have seen.

Exercises

Kids can use clairvoyance to make decisions, determine their next step, and check in on the truth of what they've been told. A rose or a psychic buddy is a tool that can be used as a barometer for what's happening now, and what's to come in the future.

Here are some easy exercises you can teach them:

1. **Self-check.** Have your child close his eyes, and take a few deep breaths. Have him put up a viewing screen. Next, have him put up his psychic buddy. This buddy can be whatever shape, style, color, or any other way that your child would like. It's friendly, and it's there to give information. Have him write his name under the psychic buddy, and then ask what he sees—is the buddy changing colors, is it happy, sad, moving around? Take a minute to let your child tell you what's happening. If anything interesting starts to happen, explore it by having him ask to see more.

"Show me more!" is a good way to phrase it. For example, if your child's buddy turns from blue to black, and then curls into a ball, your child will want to ask to see more to find out what's going on. If other images start arriving, such as movies, he'll want to ask to see more. After a few minutes, erase the psychic buddy and the screen. That's plenty for one session.

2. **To check a relationship.** If your child has a friendship that is causing stress, she can check out the relationship clairvoyantly. Have her put up a viewing screen, and then a psychic buddy. Write her name underneath it. Then, have her put up another psychic buddy, and write her friend's name under that. Watch what happens. If your child sees the "friend" buddy pummeling them, bossing them, or bullying them, you'll have a good indication of what's going on. Of course, it could be your child who's the bully! When you're done exploring the relationship, erase everything.

3. **To make a decision.** Have your child put up a viewing screen and psychic buddy, and write his name under it. Ask the psychic buddy for the answer to a question. Such as: "Should I play soccer or football this fall?" If they immediately see a picture of the psychic buddy kicking a soccer ball, there's an answer. However, if they see their psychic buddy swimming, or doing art, or playing an instrument—well, then you've got quite a different answer! After a few minutes, erase everything.

4. When your child is done (and remember, keep it short), take a few minutes to have her clear herself. She can imagine taking a giant handheld vacuum cleaner and sucking up any gray, black, dirty, or dense energy she finds roaming around her body. Then, blow everything up when done.

5. For older kids and teens—same drill. However, he can stay "in" longer, and if he doesn't like the psychic buddy, have him use a rose. Some kids like to use trees. It's not important what the barometer object is—it's just there to show movement and change symbolically. The request that an older kid will want to keep

repeating is "Show me more!" Usually, this will produce a slew of new images. If he gets stuck, clear the screen and return to the psychic buddy/rose/tree.

Teens will benefit from doing a little energy clearing at the end of a clairvoyant session—they can pick up all sorts of nasty energies while astral projecting, which they tend to do a lot of in this exercise. To do this, have them mentally gather any yucky or unwanted energies in their body, then send these into outer space. Nag them about clearing the same way you'd remind them to take a shower or brush their teeth—it's psychic hygiene, plain and simple!

thirteen

Channeling
and Channeled Writing

You are a channel, because you move aside to let the universal teaching move through you—in this way, we use you to bring messages to the world. But the children who are here now—they do not move aside in the same way. They are simply remembering again what they have only very recently forgotten. They are here to teach the world, not only through their messages but also through the very new fiber and way of their being, which is an evolutionary development for your kind.
—The Messages

––––

About channeling and channeled writing

Before I received the above, I wasn't exactly sure what I thought about kids and channeling. But what my guides said about children *not* moving aside made all the sense in the world.

Now, there's a lot of confusion about what channeling is or isn't. In fact, I have been banned from some places because I was a channel! So, let me clarify what the ability is. As an adult channel, what I do is *move aside.* I take my ego and set it temporarily on "pause" (and, yes, unfortunately it returns quite readily to me when I am done channeling!), and thus there is room for another entity to come through. In my case, I ask only for entities that are Divine—and I receive via spirit guides, angels, and other ascended entities For example, in the past I have received messages from:

- Hajam—*The Truths*, which are not yet published
- Constance, Miriam, and archangel Gabriel—*The 33 Lessons*, which are in my book *Writing the Divine*
- Ashkar and Ragnar—from whom I'm currently receiving *The Messages*

Usually, I channel these guides via channeled writing—I simply ask for guidance on a question, and a guide will step forward and give me information. Right now, I'm receiving from Ashkar and Ragnar; these tall, luminous entities consistently bring me spiritual teachings—messages "meant for the world." However, I can connect to them for Divine guidance for myself and others, such as when I'm doing readings.

But isn't a channel like Esther Hicks?

Renowned author and presenter Esther Hicks channels *vocally*—the information she imparts from the entities known as Abraham is transmitted verbally, in speech. This is one way to do it, and it's a terrific way to present the idea of channeling, because people can see viscerally that another entity is sharing space in your body—Hicks literally *moves her self aside* to allow the entity to work through her.

However, channeling doesn't have to be vocal. Any instance in which you move aside and let the Divine entity provide information is valid: in writing and also through music, mathematics, and so forth. It's all about *allowing oneself to become the channel, the conduit, the voice, the pen, the symbol, the message*. It's about allowing oneself to directly receive Divine information and to pass it along, without allowing the ego to interfere.

You'll notice I keep saying *Divine*. That's because I am only available and open to receive from Divine entities—those who are aligned with Light, Love, the Highest Good. This is a boundary that any channel can set, and I believe it is a crucial difference. Yes, you can channel lower entities—but why? We are here to evolve and become more

PARENTS ASK

My son says he has spirit guides, and that I have them, too! What does this mean?

Many kids, even younger ones, are easily able to sense the presence of other entities, including guides and angels. If your son is seeing spirit guides, he may see them in his "mind's eye," or he may sense them strongly, or he may see them standing in the room. And, often these ways of seeing shift—one time he'll see them one way, the other time another. However, it doesn't usually look like something out of a paranormal movie! Ask him to tell you more about his guides, and yours—it's likely they have names, personalities, and characteristics. In general, spirit guides are here to help you with life lessons, and angels are here to provide comfort, healing, and protection.

conscious, and the only way to do that is to consistently choose what is the highest possible Source: God, One, the Universe. Nothing else is worth our time or attention.

Still confused about how a channel works?

Consider a faucet. That's what a channel is like. When it's turned on, water comes out and goes to where it needs to go: to water a plant, to satisfy someone who's thirsty, to use in cooking, to change the fish bowl. As a channel, you don't always determine the end use of the Divine information you receive. You're just the faucet. You can turn it on. You can turn it off. You don't alter the water, you don't control the flow, you don't control the outcome. You simply allow it to flow through you.

How are child channels different?

Because our children are psychically more developed and evolved than we are, they channel differently. When they're young, they have very little ego. They don't need to move themselves aside. Instead, they can lock into the hum of the Universe very fast and access Source, the One, their guides, whatever Divine guidance is ready to work with them. There is less a sense of moving aside so the ego will get out of the way—because a child's ego has already gotten out of the way, or never was in the way to begin with.

The Bible talks about "becoming as a child," and in this way knowing God. Other sacred texts also note the simplicity and openness of children. The ego grows as people grow, and it's a lifelong battle to move it aside! But for kids, the ego still doesn't get in the way.

Children are simply more open. They accept that a giant fir tree blowing in the wind is a holy entity, and they can understand the grace and beauty of this tree. They get it, right away. They do not have to sit down and arrange themselves in trance to see the tree as God. They don't need a PhD in Divinity. They just get it, straight out, first time through.

Going back to the faucet analogy—well, with kids, *their faucet is always on*. Even if it's a tiny dribble, it's always on. They're always channeling. They don't have to step aside, because they're always naturally aside.

What does channeling look like in kids?

Most kids are goofy, playful, free, and creative—they are wildly involved with fantasy and imagination and the possibilities of being alive in this world. You may have an incredible channel on your hands and not even know it, because she's so busy talking about dragons and fairies that you can't see underneath to the real messages she's receiving.

My litmus test for determining what's real and what she saw on TV that afternoon? If you get a chill down your back, if your hair stands on end, if your ears seem to suddenly open more, if what she says makes more sense than you could imagine and you don't know how she could have possibly gotten that information—your child is probably channeling.

If your child is channeling a very specific entity with a lot of personal characteristics, you're gonna know it! When your child channels in French (and she doesn't speak French) or talks in a stilted way, or spouts mathematical equations or theologies she couldn't possibly know—you're gonna know something's up!

To a parent this can be, shall we say . . . disconcerting?

A junior Ramtha is probably not what you had in mind when your darling daughter or son emerged upon this earth.

So . . . take a deep breath. Now, take another one. And relax. Because, in general, most kids won't be channeling like this. In fact, vocal channeling is one of the most rare psychic abilities you'll see—even in this time of increased evolution.

Another helpful idea? The younger the child, the less likely he'll be channeling at all. Basically, this is because a young child is too undeveloped for the Divine to use. What's the purpose of the Divine using a two-year-old to channel messages "meant for the world," when his parents can't even understand what he's saying? The older a child gets, the more his presence will be taken seriously by adults—and the more likely he is to be utilized as a channel.

Healthy channeling in teens

When older kids and teens start to channel a spirit guide or entity, either vocally or as channeled writing, it's time to start paying attention. First off, you're going to need to check in and make sure that your child is emotionally stable.

Mental-health issues, as well as drug and alcohol issues, often begin to present in the early teens or later teen years. If your child is obviously having trouble, you'll know it. In fact, even as I write this, I can see that some of you already know this, but have been denying it for a long time. I hope, if this is the case, that you can now take a look at the fact that, yes, your child needs some psychological or medical help.

What are some of the ways you can tell if your teen is psychologically stable? Well, the first signs might be that he's doing well in school; has close, positive friendships; is interested in activities; and isn't involved with drugs or alcohol. She'll also eat regularly, sleep well, and most of the time, she'll seem happy—teen mood swings, notwithstanding!

If all systems are "go" and your child starts to channel, I'd pay attention. It may be that he or she is indeed a channel of messages from the Divine.

Channels are not perfect!

Just because an adult or teen channel spews out information of Divine nature does not mean that she has the answers to life! In other words, she may be able to present the answers of the Universe when she is channeling—but she may not be able to put these answers into practice in her own life.

Is Esther Hicks, channel of Abraham, perfect? I have no idea, but since she's human like the rest of us, I'm guessing she deals with what most of us do: laundry, relationships, backache, the dentist, etc.

Is JZ Knight, channel of Ramtha, perfect? My guess is she's dealing with soul lessons, just like anybody.

Is Neale Donald Walsch, channeled writer, perfect? I bet he'd be the first to tell you that he is also human.

PARENTS ASK

My daughter did readings for some kids at her middle school, and now their parents are calling me up and complaining.

Recall how they used to burn witches at the stake? Things haven't changed so much in many parts of the country. In middle school, your daughter is much too young to do readings for anyone besides her own family members. If she really wants to practice her skills, have her find an ethical, supportive psychic mentor who'll be willing to work with her (and be sure you accompany her to all meetings).

I'm a channel—am I perfect? Well, if I were texting you the answer, I'd write "LOL"! I must tell you that I am so far from perfect that it really boggles the mind.

If you are a channel, are you perfect? Doubtful.

If your child is a channel, is she perfect? No, of course not.

Now, true spiritual masters can get pretty close to being perfect (at least compared to the average mass of humanity), and it's entirely possible your child is a budding spiritual master. However, most of us, and by this I mean 99.99 percent us (your child included), are not spiritual masters. Even if we channel gorgeous, beautiful, Divine truths that take our breath away, our ability to practice these truths in our lives is limited.

Even if we're trying really, really hard.

This is the reality for adults, regardless of how hard we work on our soul growth and healing. This is even more true of children, who may not only be learning how to channel, but may also be learning how to do things like complete their social studies project and remember to floss now that they have braces.

The Divine is perfect. We're human.

That's all.

So, if your kid's a channel—cut him some slack. Allow him to grow as a person. Just because your child channels "We are all One" does not mean he can resist eating all of his little sister's Halloween candy, and then saying the dog did it.

Channels or not, kids are still kids.

What channeled writing sounds like

I've studied channeled writing for years now, and have noticed that most of it, no matter who's writing it, sounds thematically the same—it's Divine.

I used to believe channeled writing sounded the same because everyone who was receiving it *thought* it should sound a certain way—all *thees* and *thous* and angels flapping their wings and "Dear Ones."

However, now that I've been receiving channeled writing for a number of years, I don't think that anymore.

Instead, I believe that when we turn on the faucet for the Divine to speak through us, it sounds thematically the same; it has a similar "voice," or content. It sounds Divine—*because it is Divine.*

Here is an example of *The Messages* I've recently channeled, as "meant for the world":

Consider the man who can easily walk on his own feet, but who discovers that he has a thorn in his toe. He begins to use a crutch. After a while the thorn is dissolved into his skin, and the pain is gone. Yet he continues to use the crutch. So, too, do you use your addictions, your binges, your illnesses, your overeating, your sexual excesses, your indulgence.

These are not required by you. You can walk as you are, without these.

As your understanding becomes more clear and you can see and hear the spirit more closely guiding you, these elements will drop away.

Another example:

Do not clutter your mind with what is distraction. By this we mean the attention you give to what is only temporary and does not affect you. When you are obsessed with ideas in your mind, they do manifest. The thoughts of sadness lead to more sadness, and the thoughts of joy and beauty—the term you use is abundance. *When you believe in one thing, you call upon the Divine to prepare this for you. There is nothing you cannot have.*

And another:

The heart will not lie to you, my dear ones, the heart will tell you everything. The body reveals all. But the mind can be distracted; the mind can even fool itself. We see this with so many of you, whose hearts are open and full, but who have come to allow their minds to believe what is not True.

And yet another:

To become grounded is to understand that you are fully, completely, energetically of this Earth. You are a being as any being, yet you exist in blood, flesh, as Earth body on Earth planet. This limits you. This frees you. Begin to understand where your soul resides in this lifetime, and to understand what you will experience in this lifetime: love, fear, anger, compassion, all range of emotions, all swelling as the human heart. Within your heart you may hold the whole world. Tenderness, compassion, love—these are your tools.

Compare this to an example of channeled writing from *A Course in Miracles:*

You are entitled to miracles because of what you are. You will receive miracles because of what God is. And you will offer miracles because you are one with God.[10]

As you can see, this writing doesn't sound exactly the same—it has the flavor of the writer who received it—but it has a certain similarity in content and concepts. Other channeled books such as the Bible or other holy texts are also filled with this kind of writing. That's because the holy people who received this writing, the saints and apostles and other spiritual communicators, all channeled it from a Source beyond ourselves, and *that Source is the same.*

Channeled writing for personal guidance

However, when I am channeling information while doing readings for other people, the information is not as "Divine" in nature; it's quite specific and practical. Here's an example for one client (details changed for confidentiality):

Your money issues will evaporate immediately; as soon as the next day, you will begin to see change. This will be amazing to you, and it will surprise you. We say: you have been operating in the wrong way. A new view is what is will sustain you. A new view, not the old, is the way in which you may now go.

Here's an example of another reading:

Your wife does not look at you with clear eyes. Her pain shrouds her, and she finds no solace in what is ordinary, comforting, and everyday.

---

10. *A Course in Miracles*, Lesson 77.

She searches. This does not create a correct balance of relationship. There is no way to amend this. With this understanding, you will come to conclusions in the next month. With this information, you will come to conclusion in the next year.

As you can see, channeled writing "meant for the world" is more of a spiritual teaching, whereas channeled writing for personal guidance is more specific, worldly, and practical in nature. Your child may receive one, the other, or both.

Channeled writing for kids

Channeled writing isn't easy for younger kids, primarily because they aren't that skilled at writing yet—they get hung up on spelling and grammar and penmanship, and this can sometimes block the process. For this reason, most kids won't have much luck until after age twelve. Of course, every child is different. If your child, regardless of age, is a good writer who can write a few pages easily and quickly, without stress or strain, she may want to try it out. Teenagers may especially find this practice useful, and may be surprised and excited by the information they receive.

In a nutshell, here's how it works:

1. Have your child decide in advance on a few questions he'd like to ask for Divine guidance on.

2. With pen and paper ready, have your child go into a light trance. Have him ask the Divine for an answer, in writing, to his question(s). His eyes will be partly open by necessity—otherwise he won't be able to keep his pen on the paper! He can ask for personal guidance, or more spiritual guidance, such as "What happens when we die?" or "Did I have a previous life?" or "What is God?"

3. Have him wait until he feels compelled to write a response (at most, a few seconds) and then write it down. He may hear the answer in his "mind's ear," or he may just have a sense of what to write. If he's not sure if he's receiving or not, have him write

down whatever comes to mind—often this will trigger the flow of channeled writing. You may be amazed at what your child channel receives! If you want to dive deep into channeled writing with your child, check out my book *Writing the Divine* for step-by-step instruction on receiving via laptop, or with pen and paper.

PARENTS ASK

I found my son's journal, and it's filled with the most extraordinary spiritual writing. I'm wondering if I should show it to our pastor.

Hmmm. In general, folks who are members of traditional religions don't always understand spiritually advanced kids (SAKs). They often try to fit them into the context of their own religion, and that isn't always useful. Also, this work is private to your son—so it's not really yours to show. Talk to your son about his writing, and ask him if he has any questions; if he feels the need for a mentor or teacher, have him ask the Divine for this teacher to make himself or herself known. If your son is receiving spiritual messages, he's probably already doing channeled writing; encourage him to do this practice at any time.

fourteen

Mediumship:
A Cautious Approach

There are many of you who see these souls, outside of their Earth life. It is as simple as opening the windows, as we have explained, or of lifting the veil, as you have said. It is a veil of illusion that, when lifted, makes it easy to see.

Children are especially capable in these areas, because they have not forgotten to remember for as long as adults. They do not believe in the veil; they understand it is illusion. —The Messages

———

Mediums are people who communicate with deceased spirits, sometimes called the departed, or those who have crossed over. In this way, channels and mediums are quite different! Channels receive from spirit guides and other Divine entities, while *mediums receive from the departed*.

Got spirit guides, angels, ascended entities? You're a channel, either vocally or by channeled writing.

Hearing from your great-grandmother who passed on years ago, or talking to deceased people hanging out in old buildings? You're a medium.

Another clarification? Channels move themselves aside to receive a message; the messages come through them. Whereas mediums stay fully in themselves, and have contact that's more like a regular conversation.

For whatever reason, kids are more often mediums than channels. What's more, kids are often mediums from a very young age, even before they're able to communicate to you about it. It's a simple as the connections that bind us across generations—deceased grandparents are as actively interested in their grandchildren on Earth as they would be if they were alive—and they don't really care that they "don't live there anymore!"

Many mediums notice their abilities when they are young, but they don't know that seeing and talking to the deceased is unusual—they think that everyone has this experience. If your child is a medium, he may not understand that not everyone can see what he does.

Consider the source

The problem with being a medium? Dead people aren't always more evolved now than they were before they died. That means your child might be hearing from a nice, cozy, helpful grandma—or a meddlesome one.

Normally when people die, one of three things happen: (a) they pass on to the next realm; (b) they've passed on and they are aware of this, but they're coming back to provide support or messages of comfort; or (c) they don't know they've died and they get a little confused about where they are, and this could make them cranky.

Types (a) and (b) are no problem. But if your child is having encounters with (c), confused spirits, it's time for you to get involved. Just as you'd protect your child from the bully at school, or the mean teacher or whomever it is he can't handle on his own, you'll need to help your child with muddled ghosts.

If you don't want to get your hands dirty (or you're too chicken), you can always call in the pros: I've met some very gracious, enlightened ghostbusters who are terrific at making contact and explaining to troublesome spirits and ghosts that their time on Earth is over, and it's time to vamoose the premises.

But in most cases you can handle this yourself—no smudge or exorcisms required!

Again, the key is to be very practical: we exist on this earth with all kinds of energies from all kinds of realms. *We have as much right to be here, in our time and space, as any other entity.* If someone or some entity is bothering your child—that's not cool. March into the house, room, closet, or wherever your child has reported the entity, and have a very frank talk with the entity—then tell he/she/it to get out. You can yell at the entity; if you want, you can shout, "Get out!" Or you can be reasonable and explain that the entity is bothering your child, and must stop. You might also explain, very compassionately, that the entity is dead—in case it doesn't know.

If the ghost is someone you know who is visiting for benevolent reasons (a grandmother keeping tabs on her favorite grandson), there's nothing to worry about. Just enjoy the experience—and see if you can communicate with her, too. This kind of love across the realms is meant as a comfort to you, and can be a source of guidance when you or your child needs it.

PARENTS ASK

Tianna is fourteen. She used to be such a sweet little girl, but now she is hanging out with new friends I don't feel good about. Yesterday I found a piece of paper in her dresser, on which someone had drawn a pentagram, and some writing that looked like a spell.

Sit down with your daughter, and explain that you are concerned about what you found. If she says it was "just for fun," you can go from there into a discussion of why it's not good for her and what options are more positive. If she gets defensive and you can't get anywhere, it's time to get counseling so you can get to the bottom of where this attraction to the dark is coming from. Messing around with darker energies is as serious as if you'd found drugs or alcohol in her dresser—kids who get involved in dark stuff now have trouble getting out, and it can affect their whole lives.

Imaginary friends

Lots of kids have imaginary friends, and sometimes they're simple, friendly, often shapeless entities—not deceased humans, as you might expect. To tell you the truth, I don't know what these beings are. The Universe is filled with many kinds of energies—we're certainly not the only variety! If you're familiar with the concept of "orbs," or small balls of luminous energy—well, you might imagine entities like that.

For kids, these entities, which aren't imaginary at all, often have quite a bit of personality.

For example, my youngest daughter had a spirit friend, "Squishy," from about kindergarten to second grade. He wasn't a human or an angel—he looked like a starfish, she told me. "Squishy" talked to her and told her to do things; he made suggestions to her.

If your child has a friend like "Squishy," don't blow it off as overactive imagination. Consider the idea that your child may actually be seeing or hearing from some type of spirit entity. In our case, "Squishy" would frequently accompany us on car trips, and the other kids would have to move over so "Squishy" had room.

"Can you please tell 'Squishy' to scooch over?"

"Squishy says no."

Now that's the way to start an eight-hour drive to Grandma's!

We haven't heard from "Squishy" for nearly a year now, but it was interesting while he was hanging out.

Ghosts who aren't Grandma

Sometimes, kids see entities they aren't related to whatsoever.

For example, on the first day of school in her third-grade year, my youngest daughter reported at breakfast that "a ghost just walked through me in my room."

"Where?" I said casually while pouring milk over Cheerios, even while ready to run into her room with energy blazing, if bad spirits lurked.

"In my bedroom." She was unconcerned, her face stuffed with cereal. "She came through the window, walked through me into my mirror wall."

"What did she look like?" I'm still leery.

"She was a girl, shorter than me, with a plaid shirt."

Hmmm. Clothing description. That's a definite sighting.

"Did she say anything?"

"No, she just walked through me."

Okay, so sighting, with no communication. Who is this little ghostling?

"Were you afraid?"

"No, it was fine."

You'll note that in this exchange, I'm able to establish pretty quickly with my daughter that (a) it's a ghost, not a spirit guide; and

(b) She's not harmful and doesn't need to be cleared or dealt with by the Mama Bear, me; and

(c) My daughter feels fine about it, so the more casually I treat it, the easier for everyone (ghost girl included).

If my daughter didn't know what a ghost was, and what they might look like (a Casper-like vision, instead of a normal hazy person with distinctive clothing, as my daughter sees them), it would be more confusing.

If there had been any mischief, etc., I would have marched into the room and cleared the ghost.

As it was (and as I write this, I realize with surprise that my entire back, arms, and thighs are on fire with cold, trembling chills, a sure sign for me that spirit connection is happening), this sighting makes me curious as to what girl lived here years ago, and why.

This particular house we live in isn't that old—it was built in the 1970s. However, we live in the country, possibly on Native grounds. Certainly a cast of colorful characters has lived here—but a girl? I'd like to know more about her.

And, from the way my back is throwing off chills, I'm going to find out.

My partner tells me that the previous owner had a lot of kids and grandkids, and that it was a kid's bedroom before it was my daughter's bedroom. Not much to go on, but enough to know that perhaps the ghostling lived here before—I certainly don't know this for sure, but it's one possibility.

When my back chill subsides, I say directly into the charged air behind me, "I can help you if you'd like." And let it go.

My motto: no harm, no foul when it comes to spirit play.

I'll just keep tabs.

What about bad entities?

At the risk of sounding like a bad paranormal movie, it's true: on occasion, some people do get overtaken by ugly, bad, horrible entities. This can happen if you are not healthy in body or spirit, if you have strong addiction problems, or if you choose to connect with any other realms besides the Divine.

When it comes to kids, I'd like to tell all yucky spirits this loud and clear: stay away! And, for that matter, adults don't want you either!

For example, one of my clients is a man who refuses to believe in energy, entities, or psychic abilities, yet he wanted a reading to know "what's going on with my business." He's one of the unhappiest people I've met—argumentative, on medication for mood swings, unable to make relationships work—and yet he's extremely successful in business. He knows how to manifest wealth, just not happiness.

In his reading, I was shocked at the continued clamor of his energy. Looking closer, I saw that his entire body was twisted up with the energetic *cordings* of other entities. They had literally taken over his body, as worms take over a host.

Forget the reading—I went right into healing! I worked over every inch of his body (energetically) and pulled out every crummy energy and spirit that didn't belong there. Blech! Gross! It was scary (okay, it was really scary), and it was disgusting, because the whole time I could hear his own spirit thrashing and screaming as the energies were released.

Later, when I told him what I'd found, he dismissed the idea of him hosting other entities as "ridiculous" and wanted to know what I'd found out about his business (more success, of course!).

The point is that, while I was able to get many of these yucky energies out, because he didn't want them out a lot of them will linger. What are they? I'm not quite sure—what they look like energetically is something you know shouldn't be there, something that makes you instinctively go "uh-oh" when you see it.

For some reason, this man is allowing himself to be used by these entities, in exchange for being mega-successful at business. To my mind, this is not a fair trade.

More on pesky spirits

Now, if your young medium is seeing departed folks on every street corner numerous times a day, she's already clued into what's happening and most certainly won't need much extra information from you. If your child occasionally sees relatives or ancestors or others, take it as it comes—and for the most part, let it slide. A visitation? No big deal. It's all part of intuitive life.

Lots of parents are concerned that if their child is receiving visitations, the child can be harmed in some way—physically, emotionally, or energetically. In other words, their child might come across spirits who are pesky or causing problems.

I'd guess that your child has more chance of running into bullies at middle school than spirits that are going to be problematic. However, if you do notice this happening, you and your child can take care of it. Pesky spirits are weak spirits, and no match for Divine energy.

The best protection is to set very clear boundaries for your child from the start. In my case, I always and only work on behalf of Highest Good; I do not work energetically or psychically in any other way. Because of this, my life seems to be in Divine flow most of the time. I have created the boundary that doesn't allow pesky energies to intrude—I just plain don't work with them!

This does not mean that my life is perfect, flawless, and that I do not eat Pop-Tarts secretly, straight from the box, cold, or that I can actually balance my checkbook. I do eat Pop-Tarts, and I think the last time I balanced my checkbook was possibly when I was eighteen. That was many moons ago!

To live in Divine flow does not mean you have a perfect life. It means you are continually learning, growing, placing soul growth as your top priority, and surrendering to the Divine, the One, the All, at every step—Pop-Tarts and messy checkbooks included!

When your child sees a spirit

When things start to happen energetically around your home, you need to be ready to handle them. For example:

"I saw a man in a blue bathrobe," my daughter says to me. She's four years old, and we're staying at my mother's house in Seattle for a few days.

"Tell me about it," I say, pulling her onto my lap, knowing this is important.

"He had a blue bathrobe," she says simply. "He walked into the room, and he stood by me."

"That was your Grandpa Bud," I tell her. "He used to live here, but then he died."

She puts a small finger up to the tears that have suddenly flooded my eyes, but doesn't say anything.

"He loved you very much," I say, my voice cracking. "He must have wanted to tell you that."

"He was nice," she says, hugging me for a minute. Then, mood passed, she scrambles down to play.

I sit quietly for a minute, collecting myself. "I know you're here, Dad," I call out softly into the nascent air.

My father awaited death in this very house, over four years ago. He met my daughter only a few times—he had cancer before she was born, and she was just six months old when he died. She doesn't remember him—when she looks at old photos, she doesn't recognize his face.

The blue bathrobe is what kills me—I bought him that bathrobe the second year into his illness, when even his soft sweatsuits had become too painful to wear. He wore that blue bathrobe every day of his last six months on this planet.

My daughter is in the other room now, chattering to her grandmother, and I sit for a moment in the silence. "Thanks, Dad, for coming to see her," I say, to the presence filling the room.

Since then, my father has appeared to my daughter a few more times, though not in that house. He's shown up at random, in different locations. Always in the same blue bathrobe.

I think he arrives in the bathrobe so that my daughter, his granddaughter, will know who he is. The bathrobe is a marker, an identifier, so when she tells me what she sees, I'll know it's him.

I'm happy he's looking out for her from the other side.

I chose to include the above story for a few reasons. First, because it's common for grandparents and ancestral sorts to visit their progeny. In fact, it's the most common type of spirit visitation your child will experience, outside of her own spirit guides or angels.

Wearing a signature identifier (such as the blue bathrobe) is also common—but the clue will not always be visual. For example, my own grandfather smoked pipes and cigars daily; sometimes if I sense his presence, I'll have a taste of cigar smoke in my mouth.

However, the main reason I used the above example is to show how I responded to a spirit sighting—calmly, matter of fact, the same way I'd respond to most situations with a young child.

For example, I didn't run screaming out the door to get the crucifix, wooden stake, and garlic bulbs! I didn't hurry her out of the room, screaming that "ghosts" were going to get us! I didn't tell her Jesus wouldn't approve. I didn't tell her it was her "imagination."

I treated the sighting as if it were commonplace to co-inhabit time and space with spirits (because in fact, it is). I validated what she saw in the simplest way ("That's your grandpa") to help her understand why this particular spirit might be visiting her. And, I *didn't* go into a

PARENTS ASK

My son says he sees ghosts, and lots of them! Sometimes he covers his ears, because he says "they" are always talking to him. He is eight and is otherwise a normal kid.

Chances are good that your son is an emerging medium, and spirits who have "crossed over" are trying to get his attention. Find a quiet moment, and ask him to close his eyes, breathe deeply, and ask aloud for these particular entities to (a) arrive in groups of only one or two from now on, and (b) stop talking all at once! If he wants a break from these entities, he can request that they not come to him now, but wait until he's older. Keep in mind that if your child is hearing voices, you must also look to the possibility of mental illness. If he's healthy and happy, he's probably a medium. If he's struggling in the everyday, you may want to see your physician.

long dirge or existential explanation about what spirits are, and why they visit, and so forth.

As my kids always say, TMI—too much information.

Spirit problems

Kids don't usually have to deal with ugly entities. However, if you think for some reason that your child is having trouble with other entities (and is not simply having a preteen bad day), he'll need to be cleared.

Working with energy is not particularly difficult, and if you're up to it, you can try doing it yourself. Simply connect deeply to the Divine in prayer or meditation, and ask for assistance in clearing your child. You can do this in person, or from a distance. Then, meditate on your child's healing and watch as Divine goes in (you may see angels or other healing entities scurry forward) and gets rid of yucky, black, dark, or corded energies that don't belong there.

If this is just too much for you to handle, find a medium or healer to do it for you. But be careful, because sometimes the people who most loudly claim to do this work are themselves in very bad shape energetically, and should be avoided at all costs!

Anybody who dabbles in dark energies or follows a severe belief system? Not acceptable. Same goes with anybody you get a nasty feeling from, anybody you wouldn't let take care of your toddler for the weekend, or anybody who wants to charge you tons of money (a real healer will do it for a competitive fee; this is how real healers work).

The issue of problematic spirits is a deep, complicated one that there isn't space to address here. My suggestion is always—if you can't make progress on your own, seek out a loving, light-filled healer you can trust.

A word about Goth

Oh, dear—more nasty energy! If your kids are Goth, you're gonna know it—the baggy black pants, chains, cigarettes, purple shaggy hair, and black lipstick are clear indicators (at least that's what Goth looks like here in the Pacific Northwest). There's nothing wrong with Goth as a fashion statement (remember what you wore when you were sixteen?). However, what Goth stands for in terms of psychic and spiritual development can get pretty scary.

Goth (and it's not the name that's important, but the intent) is all about mediumship, but on the dark side. Many people in the New Age realm don't agree with me; they see nothing wrong with occult or dark practices. But to my mind, messing around with anything less than the Highest Good is one of the very worst things your child can do.

I don't mean dressing up as Harry Potter for Halloween. I mean kids who take a specific interest in lower energy practices or anything that calls on energies that are not the highest possible available to us—in other words, the Divine, God, the One, the All.

We all choose what energy we deal with. As a channel, I am very aware that there are energy forces out there that I do *not* want coursing though my body, or calling upon me in the middle of the night. I choose, emphatically, with my intent and with every thing I do, that *I am only available to work with the highest energy of the Divine.* This means spirit guides, angels, ascended masters, or enlightened souls as teachers—it does not leave room for lower energy forms or dark entities of any kind.

If your child (delicate little sprout, open as the Montana sky) chooses or is allowed to consort with the darker forces, it can have life-changing effects that can never be reversed. At some point, dabbling in lower energies wreaks havoc on your child—the same way that kids who get involved with drugs, alcohol, and sex early on can have trouble recovering and may become permanently damaged. Remember that businessman who was literally entangled with dark energies? Don't let this happen to your child.

It is very hard to draw this line, because the mainstream media— movies, books, video, TV, music—all point toward influences like vampires and evil forces or whatever's popular now. It's hard to differentiate between dark and light when bookstore aisles are filled with paperbacks on teen neck-biters in love.

It's hard to walk the line. Yet the difference in energies is clear:

- Light or dark?
- Good or evil?
- Holy or profane?
- Love or hate?
- Peace or war?
- Clarity or chaos?

As a parent, it's your responsibility to make sure your child is kept free of dark influences. If they want to see a movie like *Twilight*—well, I know it's a box-office hit, but I probably wouldn't let my kids see it! However, if you find them cutting themselves for blood rituals or calling up evil entities, it's time for serious intervention.

By intervention, I don't mean punishing, degrading, or pushing them any further away from you than they already may be. This can be a brutal time, as you may well remember, and every teen needs as much help as he or she can get.

If you can talk with your child without getting into an argument, I'd sit down and discuss the seriousness of choosing dark, rather than light. I'd pray for my child, over and over. I'd get her into counseling to help heal underlying issues. Keep religion out of the mix, even if you have a religious practice—it will just make him move further away.

However, the best way to keep your kids from going Goth (again—the name doesn't matter, just look for anything that smacks of occult or dark energy) is to model the Divine now.

Watch the influences you bring into your home. For example, do you allow books on vampires into your house? They may be popular right now, but they're certainly not infused with Divine light. Do you let your kids watch horror movies? That's an absolute "no" around here—and no discussion about it, either. Same goes for movies that contain a lot of violence, or anything that deals with the lower side of the paranormal—freaky head-spinning stuff included. Even popular video games—chock full of violence that we'd never let our kids witness in real life—are totally out.

Does this make my kids pariahs? Uncool? Out of the loop? Actually, they're well-liked, have good friends, and tend to do goofy stuff like have water fights when they have friends over. Not too bad, I'd say.

If you're a parent, it's your responsibility to know what your child is "into" and what his or her friends are "into." It's not an option, or something to do when you "have time"—because you'll never have time. This is your job! It's also your responsibility to keep your kids away from stuff that isn't good for them—you wouldn't feed them Cheetos for breakfast, would you? Dark energy is way more trouble than Cheetos.

That said, what are your kids into? Who are their friends? Who are their friends' parents? Do you have the parents' phone numbers? Do you know your kid's friends' last names? Where do they live? Where do they hang out? What do they do? Who are the friends of your kid's friends?

This is stuff you gotta know.

If you have a happy, involved kid who has interests and is given just enough rope to have fun but not enough to hang himself, great! And don't feel bad about reeling that rope in, either—for example, at our house, my teen son desperately wants a cell phone. Will he get one? Not this year. Why? Because he's already distracted enough by his social life, and a cell phone makes it so he can't escape contact with his peers. What if he needs to call me for a ride? Well, all his friends have phones—he can use theirs. I have reeled this particular rope in, because as a parent, I know he'll do better without a cell phone. This is my job; to do what is in his best interest.

It's your job for your kid, too.

Exercises

1. **Be prepared.** If your child's a medium, it's good to have a plan of attack for the everyday encounter. First, he doesn't need to be any more afraid of a spirit than a human. That said, caution is key—the same way he'd be careful around a person he didn't know. His first response when meeting a spirit is to ask the Divine for protection and help; simply say, "God, please help me," or "I ask for Divine protection." Second, he can ask the spirit if it has a message to pass on. Third, and only if it seems right, he can remind the spirit that the spirit is dead. Remind your child that it's his right to refuse to interact with a spirit, the same way it is his right to refuse to interact with anyone.

2. **Get some history.** If your child keeps hearing from specific ancestral spirits, get out the photo albums and try to find pictures of this person to show your child—"Look, there's your great-uncle Harvey!" If you live near where this spirit was buried, or where the spirit lived, visit or drive by. Sometimes, allowing the child to become more familiar with the deceased relatives is all the spirit wanted in the first place.

3. **Visit the cemetery.** Paying homage to ancestors is a part of our culture that we haven't attended to very well. It's important to remember who has come before us. In my family, we visit the

gravesites of my children's grandfather and grandmother, who are buried in the same place. It's a small plot in the country, complete with eagles and crows and deer at dusk, and it reminds my kids who their ancestors are, and why these people are important.

4. **Seek the Divine.** In all aspects of channeling and mediumship, explain to your child that she is in control—if at any time she doesn't like what's happening, she may simply call upon the Divine, and help will instantly arrive.

fifteen

Spiritually Advanced Kids (aka the SAKs)

You have been asleep, most of you, for a very long time. Waking up from the dream of the Earth life is a hard task. Understanding that you have been dreaming, and then continuing to live the Earth life, is even harder.

The way that your world has manifested itself—religion, corporation, tribe, cult, all ways apart from the Divine, all ways apart from the One. This is what will be required to strip down. Your children see this with clear eyes. —The Messages

———

I don't know how old you are. Maybe you're twenty-five, with a young child of your own. Or perhaps you're forty-seven, with your oldest nearing college and years of parenting under your belt. Or fifty-six, with grandkids. Perhaps you don't have kids at all—but you've got some nieces and nephews you're interested in helping out. Or maybe you're a kid yourself, sneaking this book off your mom's bedside table as she tries to "figure you out."

Well, I need to tell you: if you've got a spiritually advanced kid (SAK) in your house or life, there's only one thing you need to know:

They can be the hardest to live with of all.

Seriously!

Total pains in the derrière!

This doesn't make much sense, does it? Living with an uber-evolved kid should be sweetness and light, peace and harmony. Right?

Well . . . hang out as a fly on the wall at my house for a few minutes, and you'll see:

Scene: Mom, coming in from a hard day at work, lugs multiple grocery bags from car to kitchen. She ferrets out a small container of Häagen-Dazs ice cream from the last bag, and from the way she rips the top off, it's been obvious she's been thinking about it all day. She grabs a spoon, tears off the plastic cover like a wild boar unearthing a truffle, and plunges in (chocolate peanut butter). The first bite hovers ¹⁄₃₂ of an inch from her mouth, so close she can taste it, when suddenly:

Spiritually Advanced Kid (SAK) enters the room.

SAK: "Hi, Mom!"

Caught! Stunned, Mom recoils. She can't decide if she should somehow pretend she's not eating ice cream or shove the whole bite in her mouth before he can figure it out. She goes for the bite.

SAK: "How was your day?"

Mom: "Glubnesxqs!"

SAK sniffs air. "Are you eating chocolate?"

Mom, trying desperately to swallow: "No."

SAK sniffs again. "Yes, you are."

Mom: "Glubneservati!" Bite accomplished!

SAK, prying container from her hand: "Mom, you don't need to lie. It's obvious you're eating chocolate peanut butter. That's fine, I accept that. We're all human here. But Mom—you've been working hard on your diet. Do you think this is useful to you?"

Mom, lunging for container: "It's just one bite!"

SAK: "You know that chocolate can't satisfy your inner need for comfort. You know that the only way to have true enlightenment is through direct connection with the Divine. Here, why don't you let me put that ice cream away for you while you go meditate for a while." He reaches for the carton.

Mom, making a strangled noise like a ferret refusing to give up its prey, yells: "No! I want ice cream."

SAK: "That ice cream won't help you feel better about your job."

Mom: "Don't care. Want ice cream!"

Scuffle ensues. Mom snarls. SAK laughs hysterically, gains possession of carton, and waggles it in front of her.

SAK: "You probably just need a hug, hmmm?"

Mom: "Want ice cream!"

It's a standoff. SAK is only fourteen, but he is six feet tall. Finally, Mom puts spoon down with dignity. SAK is right—she's just comfort eating. She'll go take a shower, put on some music, de-stress from her day. She heads off to a steaming shower, asking her guides for help as she centers herself. Ten minutes later, she returns to the kitchen in a much better mood, planning to make dinner.

SAK sits at the counter, empty Häagen-Dazs carton in front of him, shoving last spoonful of ice cream to his mouth.

He greets Mom happily: "I know you didn't really want to eat that ice cream, so I finished it for you! A shower feels much better, doesn't it?"

Mom: "$&?!!!$!"

There you have it: SAKs can be bastions of spiritual evolution, expert theologians, top-notch philosophers, direct channels of the Divine, and have a beatific calm that makes you feel like you've moved to a Zen monastery.

They're also ice-cream stealers!

And as they chow down every single bite, they'll tell you they did it for your own good!

How annoying is that?

Evolution happens

Spiritually advanced children are the kids everyone loves, everyone wants to be around, and who make everyone feel "good" simply by hanging out with them.

They can also be maddeningly, horribly, enragingly holier than thou—especially when they're right!

It's not their fault. They *are* more advanced than we are! It's not our fault—we've evolved to where we can evolve! It's just that is hard to be the parent, and know that your kid already knows more than you do, and this is just *how it is.*

Spiritually advanced kids seem to be a relatively new group—coming into the world in the last thirty years or so, or from about the early 1980s, depending on when you're reading this book. Again, I don't like labeling by year of birth, but this group is a more recent phenomenon. Nowadays, they seem to be arriving with every wave of births.

Again, much of it is simply evolution of the species—our kids are more spiritually aware, because they are more evolved. Each generation moves further forward than its predecessors.

It's also the fact that we as parents have created an environment in which they can thrive—all our mixed feelings about religion and our own spiritual searching has made it easy for these kids to freely explore what they think and feel about the Divine.

And, in general, the world is more ready for them. Not the whole world—one look at the news and that's very clear. But kids born into the richest, most educated countries can expect to be protected, supported, enriched, and encouraged. This marks a change in the culture. Even a few generations ago, a SAK would have been given no time for beatitudes, because he'd be stuck working on the farm or in a factory. Even a few decades ago, a SAK would have been at risk if he'd shown any signs of being "different"; he'd have been beaten or punished or

---

PARENTS ASK

My daughter, who is eleven, refuses to do any psychic practice. I ask her to try the clairvoyance exercises, and she says she sees everything already and doesn't need it.

If you try to force a rosebud open, you'll damage it. And even though it's probably disheartening to you, a well-meaning parent, don't worry. If she's not into practicing with you, let it go. Remember, even the smallest taste of direct connection to the Divine will carry her forward—so don't be surprised if you find her reading this book or others like it in a few years, trying to brush up on her psychic techniques!

ostracized by somebody, somewhere along the line, similar to the way gay and lesbian kids have had to deal with barbaric prejudice.

The other reason: when we were growing up, most of our experience with spirituality was religious—we knew God through whatever church or temple we did or didn't go to with our family. For your child, it's a very different story. If your family is like lots of American families, you don't attend church regularly. This allows your child to have a freedom from dogma and dharma that we didn't have, so he can connect directly with the Divine for his own experience.

He's also been exposed to a mainstream media well versed in paranormal concepts; your kid watches movies about avatars, for goodness sakes!

However, no matter how calm and peaceful and lovely and whole your spiritually advanced child is, here's the rub: he's human. He's a young human being, growing in both his soul and in his Earth life. This means he will have challenges.

Common challenges for SAKs

The main challenge for SAKs is motivation. They see, with such Zen like clarity, that the normal concerns of life—getting good grades, earning an allowance, wanting to do stuff with friends, or wanting to be on winning sports teams—may not interest them. Even the things you'd think they'd be interested in, like playing a musical instrument, may not cut it.

It's as if life is one big koan, and your child is content as a monk to sit and study it. He understands from the beginning that we're all temporal, we're all One, whereas all the other stuff—getting good grades? How on earth does that apply to anything?

When you are the parent of such a child, this can be superbly frustrating:

"I just want to be, Mom. Middle school isn't really very pertinent."
   Or, "Mom, I'm just not a team-sports guy."
   Or, "I'd rather just read than go to the mall."
   Hmmm? How do you answer that kind of reasoning?

"No, your report on the state flower will alter the course of your life!"

Or, *"No, if you don't play football, you won't develop as a whole person!"*

Or, *"No, reading is bad for you! Shopping is good!"*

Et cetera.

Of course, he's right. Just like with the ice cream. All the details and distractions and must dos and gotta haves—they really don't matter. The purpose of life is soul growth—and your spiritually advanced kid knows it!

The thing to do in the face of this kind of lack of motivation ("Why do anything, when we can just *be*?") is to explain to your child that, yes, he is a spiritual being. You have no arguments with that. However, he is also a human, and this means he has an Earth life.

He'll try to interrupt, but keep pressing the point: his Earth life is the reason he was sent here—to learn through his Earth body, and through his Earth experiences. And . . . what it boils down to is that he'll have a far more pleasant experience and enjoy himself more if he's able to make the normal efforts, and follow a fairly regular, involved sort of life. Yes, he can sequester himself up on the top of the mountain all day and night. But he'll learn more simply by living, being, and doing in his Earth life than by years spent locked away in meditation.

Many spiritual teachers say that the domestic path is the highest path, and this doesn't just mean parenting. Being domestic also includes being a kid, in a family. Parent life, kid life, family life—it's all part of soul growth. If your SAK refutes this view now, don't worry—he'll catch on later, as his Earth self catches up to his spirit self.

Feeling too much

Another common challenge that spiritually advanced kids have is sadness and depression—this stems from their compassionate hearts. They have a difficult time with the tragedies and cruelties of life on this planet. They see the big picture more clearly, and cannot comprehend why we live the way we do, and why we accept the negative energies of war, hatred, prejudice, poverty, disease, pollution. Especially when we create these ourselves!

I do not have an answer for this sadness; it is pervasive amongst all sensitive people, children or adults. Allowing the heart to feel pain, turning this pain into compassion, and opening this compassion into love is the only answer.

Yet another common characteristic of a SAK is that she may be *empathic*—she feels the emotions of others in her own body and soul. If your child seems to be taking on the burdens of others, especially a close friend, or trying to heal them, clear them, or otherwise help, keep a close eye on the situation. Empathic kids are so compassionate, they literally clear other people simply by being around them—it's like an energy transference, where they'll take the yucky energy from the person feeling the pain, and then attempt to deal with it themselves. Frankly, a lot of times they *can* deal with it just fine—but overload does happen.

To counterbalance this, make sure your child has a healthy dose of fun in his life, whatever that means to him—watching a favorite DVD, going on a fun outing, hanging out with positive friends. Lots of nature and exercise helps, too. And, of course, attention and affection from you—in which you can do a little energy clearing of your own.

SAKs attract energy suckers

SAKs are such beacons of luminous light that people want to hang around them. However, this can be for the wrong reasons. If you are finding that other kids are glomming on to your SAK because they want to be around his energy, but they are draining him—give him some time off.

You'll know immediately who these kids are—the ones who hang around and always show up, but leave your child feeling yucky, out of sorts, sour, or tired. If these kids live in the same neighborhood or go to school with him, sit down and have a talk. He may feel sorry for these kids, but he needs to know how to shake them loose energetically.

You can explain that sharing energy with another person isn't healthy—he needs to keep control of his own energy. You can clear his energy for him, or better still, walk him through steps to clear these energetic *cords* by himself. Another way to do this is to have him call back his own energy from every place or person it's been with—this will automatically allow him to call back his energy from these particular kids.

If all else fails—you know the answer by now. Be the parent. Distract him with other things, too; talk to his teacher about moving his seat, get him involved with other activities where this energy-sucking kid *isn't,* and so forth. If a friend is energetically and karmically meant to be around your child, he'll stick. If he's just a hanger-on looking for some good energy to swipe, he'll leave fast.

Smart support

With SAKs, the more information, the better—give her books on all religions, documentaries about spiritual leaders, and free-range grazing on age-appropriate Internet sources. The library is an exceptional place to find this kind of information, because it contains such a broad mix of sources—not just one view, but many, and lots of it from decades ago, as opposed to only recent times. Let your child delve in and explore.

Your child may also find herself in the same circles as true spiritual leaders in your community, or, at the very least, wise folks who are visiting teachers or presenters. If your child shows interest, and by this I mean she asks to go, take her to these events and teachings.

Your child will likely attract whomever she needs as her teachers; of course, you'll want to check adults out as they appear. The correct teacher will understand his or her role as mentor and helper, and have impeccable boundaries. False teachers may have innate charisma— but, underneath it, you'll get a bad feeling. Trust your own clairsentience (gut feeling) and protect your child.

PARENTS ASK

My son's grades are terrible! Ever since he started high school, he's told me repeatedly that "this isn't why he's here" and "he's here to be, not do." The SATs are coming up, and I'm desperate!

With a SAK like this, you've may be able to sit down and talk things over reasonably. "I want you to study so you can go to a good college" might not fly with him, but "You're an Earth being who is here to live your life on Earth—and getting good grades is a part of your Earth job right now" might. If that doesn't work, find a spiritual mentor who is willing to talk to your son, who can explain how doing good Earth work and doing good spiritual work are one and the same.

Children who are ill

Sometimes, SAKs aren't physically healthy. They may have terminal diseases such as cancer, or debilitating diseases that mean they can't function the way you'd hope for other kids. Sometimes they're born sick or they get sick later. From a karmic perspective, some might say that these kids have decided to experience their soul growth on Earth in the most challenging way possible—surely, they'll reap the rewards of all this growth in their next life?

It's true: we do choose these particular lives and these particular parents, and all of what we create is what we have chosen to create. Thus, a child would not choose to be ill, unless this was a part of the meaning and the purpose of her life.

Right?

Well, that's one theory.

But for a parent who has to watch his or her child be born sick or get sick, for the child herself, and for all the siblings and family members, this theory sucks. Having a sick child is tremendously tragic. It's beyond heartbreaking—because after your heart has broken entirely and completely, your child will still be ill, or even dying, and there is nothing you can do.

Why is this?

Why is it, with all that we know about traditional medicine, and alternative medicine, and energy healing, that we cannot cure or help our kids?

Why is it that a parent and child would have to experience such enormous sadness, sadness that is so great that it seems impossible to overcome?

I have no answer. I don't think anyone does.

In many cases, kids who are sick appear almost otherworldly, because their awareness of their limited time on Earth burns in them with a joy and a clarity that is beyond what we normally see.

Author Terri Daniel's son Danny became ill as a child. He enjoyed normal health until elementary school, then became progressively more sick, unable to walk or speak. He died in his teens, and to her surprise, Terri began to have spirit contact with him; he began to send messages to her of Divine nature. The messages are collected in her book *A Swan in Heaven: Conversations Between Two Worlds.* Shirley Enebrad, author of *Over the Rainbow Bridge*, also writes eloquently of her experience with a SAK—her own son Cory, who died at age nine after a long battle with leukemia. A patient and friend of Dr. Elisabeth Kübler-Ross, Cory understood and expressed ideas about the afterlife that were profoundly beyond his years. Both of these authors have been active in grief work for parents, and their books are both resource and support for anyone who faces this heartbreaking experience.

If your child faces the destiny of dying young, there is only one thing to do: help him enjoy his time on this planet, love him, and surround him with love. The physical is beyond bearing, but with the Divine, all things may be illuminated and uplifted.

Are these children here to teach us? Are we here to teach them? I would suspect it's both. Is it possible to hold such love and such pain simultaneously in your heart? It does not seem possible, but, yes, it is.

Life is about soul growth as experienced through our Earth bodies and our Earth emotions. The range of experiences, the tragedies and sadness we will see in our lifetimes, are beyond endurance. Yet love, the highest emotion, the clearest aspect of understanding that we are all One, wins hands down in the end.

Exercises

A SAK already knows more than you do—but that doesn't mean she can't use a little parental assistance. Here are some helpful tools you'll want to make sure she knows about:

1. **Direct connection.** Make sure your SAK knows the difference between prayer, meditation, and trance, and can quickly access and utilize each state. Make sure she has a clear method of *direct connection* to the Divine, and that she uses it frequently.

2. **Grounding.** Make sure she is well grounded in her Earth life and has physical and psychic release of energy through her body. If she doesn't care for organized sports, and many SAKs don't, find a physical activity that will keep her active: dancing, walking, running, skating, surfing, swimming. Her body needs to move.

3. **Environment.** Again, the body needs support, which includes good food, good sleep habits, staying clear of excess electronica, and a peaceful environment. This is true for all kids, but especially for SAKs.

4. **Clearing.** Make sure your child knows how to clear energy she's picked up from other people. The way to do this is to have her go into trance, and do a quick body scan to see where other people may have attached to her. She will probably see this as cords, strings, or ropes in her body. In severe cases, it may show up as hooks or something sharp, like a harpoon with a rope on the end! Ask her to mentally clear these with her mind, and throw these cords into deep space and explode them. If she needs help, she can call upon her angels or spirit guides, who will do the work for her. She may have the sensation that an entire crew of beings has stepped in to help! If she's attracting the energy of others, she'll need to clear frequently.

5. **Receiving.** Encourage her to practice channeled writing, both for personal guidance and to receive messages "meant for the world." Give her a journal or a laptop, and let her do this practice as much as she wants.

6. **Education.** Provide regular access to metaphysical and religious books, and safe Internet surfing on these subjects. If you don't have these resources at home, take your child to the library and walk her over to where these sections are.

7. **Teachers.** If your child attracts adults, either as teachers or followers, check them out as completely as you would anyone your child is in contact with. Again, all true teachers must have impeccable boundaries—your SAK won't have the experience to have boundaries herself. Unsupervised Internet contacts with adults are out—we all know where that can lead, and it can be very ugly. Your child, SAK or not, is still a child. Be smart and be protective—it's your responsibility as a parent.

PARENTS ASK

Lately, my fourteen-year-old daughter has become very religious. She's going to a new church, and it's like it's her new home. When I ask her to come to church with us (we're Catholic), she refuses, saying that "it doesn't mean anything" to her.

The truth is, by the time your child has reached about age fourteen or fifteen, all bets are off. If she chooses a new religion or belief system, is there really that much you can do? If you suspect she's involved with a cult, then you'll need to take action. But if this is simply a church that she likes better than where she went when she was growing up, this is fine. Go with her to a service, to see what it's all about; you might even like it! In any case, show respect. This world is full of differing religions and belief systems, and all paths eventually lead to the Divine.

part four

environment

sixteen

Why Home Matters

Many of you, and by this we mean you specifically and others, are not here all the time; you are literally in other planes and other dimensions. We provide you with this information so you will understand why it is so hard to be in this world. This is not the only world you are in; this is not the only work you are doing.

For children, this is the same.

Yet all children must learn to find their home in the Divine. It is here that peace and comfort awaits. —The Messages

——

At the end of the day, we all need a cave to crawl into.

Your child may spend seven hours each day in creaky old buildings powdered with asbestos. Or, conversely, modern buildings filled with off-gassing from carpet, flooring, and paint.

Your child most likely spends seven or eight hours sitting in a chair, behind a desk. Or, he might sit in a hard plastic chair at a group table. You get the idea: each child is allotted his or her own "space" in a classroom, but not much elbow room—especially since most of today's classrooms are loaded down with twenty-five-plus kids, with thirty-plus common in older grades.

This idea of contained personal space, with each child getting about three feet wide by three feet deep for his physical self, regardless of how tall he is or how much he weighs, and regardless of how much his body needs to stretch and sprawl, wiggle, and wander—well, none of that's taken into account.

The current public school set-up reminds me of those little play-pens that we tuck mischievous tykes into—a bit of contained space where they can be safe and can't get into trouble, but also can't grow or explore as a child should.

And frankly, it's not just kids—adults have the same needs to take off the headset and get out of the cubicle and breathe some fresh air.

The lack of privacy alone can be disconcerting. Recall how tired you are if you have to go a conference, or if you have a job where you have to work with people in one big room, with nothing but flimsy cubicle walls to deflect the strange habits of your coworkers?

Yes, it's exhausting, it's debilitating, and it's very likely that after a day like this, you'll come home cranky and keyed up, with no way to defuse all the rotten energy you've picked up by being in close quarters with other people. After a day like this, you might self-medicate with alcohol, drugs, food, TV, or your computer. Anything to make this particular pain go away.

The same experience is true for your child. Except worse, because your child is more open, more innocent, and less able to deal with what stress does to her body and soul, because she is tender and new to this world.

Your adult body may have gotten used to being sluggish or seden-tary, or, conversely, to having the physical aspects of the body released by going to a gym—a place where you literally run on a treadmill, like a mouse on a wheel! But your child is designed to move, made to move, ready to move. Sitting at those tables all day goes against every fiber of his being.

Your adult body may have also gotten used to the idea of shutting down—take one trip on a bus or subway in any urban setting, and you'll see that people don't connect; they avert their eyes, close their bodies off, use a book or iPod to bow out, as it were, from the energy on the scene.

However, your child may not be able to shut off the energy as eas-ily—she's more open, and even though she does spend hours attached to her MP3 player, she still absorbs energy like a sponge. That sulky kid in the back of the room with his arms folded? He may in fact be one of the more open and attuned kids in a class—but because he knows how rotten too much energy feels, he's trying to shut it off with body language and attitude.

The soul requires respect

Now, imagine after a day of being bombarded with other people's energy with no effective way to shut it off, your child comes home to a house that is disorganized, cluttered, and blaring with electronica.

The soul requires respect. The body requires calm. In this life on Earth, home may be the only energetic haven you can offer your child.

Your child does not care how expensive your furniture is, if you have the latest sound system or the biggest-screen TV. Your child yearns to come home to a place that is safe, comforting, and familiar. It's a place she can relax. It's a place where she can put on her play clothes or whatever she likes to wear at home, grab a snack, and download her day, kid-style.

Of course, your child may not be coming home to only one home. If you are divorced and share custody with your ex-spouse, your child may also be spending time at someone else's house—and you have absolutely zero control over that environment. This is simply the reality of our culture at this time. Because of this, the home you make for your child should be the most nurturing, comforting, loving haven that you can create.

Feng shui: what it means to you

The ancient art of feng shui has been practiced with success for thousands of years. In a nutshell, feng shui works by keeping energy flowing—and it's a difference you can feel. Simply stepping into a space that has been properly feng shui'd, you feel a sense of "ahhhh" all over your body.

WEALTH	FAME	LOVE
HEALTH	CENTER	CREATIVITY
SELF-DEVELOPMENT	CAREER	BENEFACTORS

ENTRANCE

Giving your house the once-over with feng shui can really improve how you feel when you are in that space. The traditional way to use feng shui is to use the *bagua map,* a chart of areas in the home that represent specific energies and intent.

Basically, you align or overlay this map upon the floor plan of you home, and then make sure you've got the right things covered. For example, when you overlay the map and you notice that your family room miraculously aligns with the section on children and creativity—perfection! This will be a great room for play and projects. However, if you find that when you overlay the map, your bathroom aligns with the section for spirituality—I'm not saying it can't be done, but it can be challenging.

With feng shui, sometimes the configuration of your home or even a particular room doesn't work the way it should. In my own bedroom, which is small and has two windows plus a closet and a door, there's no possible way to arrange the furniture in proper feng shui fashion. Thank you, 1970s architecture! If I lived anywhere else in the world, I'd seriously consider moving or remodeling. However, I'm fortunate to live in the middle of a forest filled with wise, old trees. Every time I look out the window, I am healed by the presence of these magnificent beings, and I understand that living in nature makes up for poor architectural design.

So, work around your architecture. And once you've gotten the house feng shui'd as best you can, go ahead and feng shui each room. Many folks I know prescribe to this ferociously—they've got fountains in the corners of rooms to attract money, and so forth. However, if you have toddlers who are likely to find a fountain about as irresistible as a tubful of Nerf balls, this may not work for you.

What I like best about feng shui is its minimalist approach; if it were up to me, I'd live in a clean, clutter-free habitat with almost nothing in it. However, I've noticed that most people don't like to live like this—including all of my family members. Most people's homes are filled to brimming with everything—beloved treasures, sentimental finds, old things, new things— all of it in an active swirl of display. It doesn't really matter where you fall on the spectrum, whether you live like a monk or with all your favorite items stacked next to you. The key to creating a happy, harmonious home for your child is to keep energy moving.

Keep energy moving

The reason feng shui is important is because it is energetically based. It is a way of showing you where the energy is blocked, and where it's *flowing*. If the bagua map doesn't work for you, here are other ways to keep your house in flow:

a) Get clutter-free.

b) Out with the old, in with the new—or better yet, don't add anything new.

c) Create a positive vibe.

d) Eliminate or contain electronica.

Let's look at each of these categories:

Get clutter-free. Well, that's hardly a new concept! You probably have a few books on this topic alone, stacked somewhere around your house. And yet, most people find this concept amazingly difficult. I know this because 1-800-GOT-JUNK is a hugely successful company nationwide—you call their number, they come out and haul away your junk! You don't even have to pick it up; all you have to do is point to it! I mean, it's like the magic junk fairy.

Why is getting clutter-free so important? Clutter blocks energy, which is why it's so bad for you and your kids. It makes you feel bogged down, unable to focus, distracted—there's all this *stuff* sending off energy all of the time. The less clutter, the more calm the mind can be. One reason I try to live on the Zen side of the clutter scale is that I am so affected by clutter that if I do not have everything picked up and the kitchen free of dirty dishes and a load of laundry started, I cannot write. I have been this way as long as I can remember. However, once I have cleared the energy of the house, my creativity *flows*.

For your child, clutter makes the difference between a well-organized room in which his favorite toys are on display, and a messy, chaotic room in which he can't find anything.

Clutter is depressing. It's a downer. Like it or not, it's a sure sign that the people who live in the house are not paying attention to energy. And . . . *energy must flow*. Clutter is energy that is blocked. Once you allow energy to flow, it is much easier to allow your life to flow in a psychic and spiritual sense.

I don't know how you're going to tackle your clutter. I like to do things like haul massive amounts of stuff to Goodwill a few times a year—this is met by outcries of "Noooooooooooo!" from my pack-rat family members. However, they soon relax into the peace and calm that descends from a clutter-free space.

The objects you own block energy

We are always in the process of change. Who we were last year is not the same person we are this year. This is true for adults and for children.

If you are hanging on to the past, you are not living in the present.

Case in point: at a certain point in your adulthood, your mother will probably present you with a gigantic box of all the photos and school papers and memorabilia she's carefully saved since your childhood. Third-grade spelling test with a bright blue star? Now it's yours. You all dressed up and hopeful before a date with that guy who ended up dumping you? Yes, that's yours, too. This handing down of the box is a rite of passage—it's your mother saying, "Here, now you're in charge of the memories."

At first, it's fun: when you look at these photos of your former self in elementary school, middle school, or high school, you are transported into another realm—the past.

"Ooh, I can't believe I looked that way" you might wonder, or "What was I thinking with those bell bottoms?" or "Braces are not my best look," or whatever it is. You pull out the old soccer trophy from when you were five years old, or the menu from the restaurant your French class went to, and it's all tremendously fun.

For a few minutes.

Because, as the recipient of this boxed blast from the past, you suddenly realize that your mother gave it to you not because she wanted you to have it as a rare treasure of your childhood—okay, partly for that reason. But mostly, she wanted you to have it because *she was too*

PARENTS ASK

Last year, Sasha started a new school, and she had so much trouble! She cried every day. This year things are better, but she's still so sensitive; every little thing sets her off. What can I do?

Sasha is probably clairsentient, which means she feels *everything*, from the vibe of a teacher having a bad day to the rough-and-tumble energy of a busy classroom. Sasha will do best with a peaceful, easygoing home and a regular after-school routine that helps her decompress and deal with all these feelings. That means: (a) limit activities and allow plenty of downtime; (b) build in structure—i.e., snack time, snuggle time, help-cook-dinner time, etc.; (c) make your home as calm and organized as you can; and (d) give her plenty of time and space.

guilty to throw it away. She wanted to pass on the ownership, the care-taking, of these objects to you.

Chances are good that after you've looked through this box once or twice, and maybe even shed a few tears, you're going to lug it down to the storeroom or the back of your closet, where it will stay until you die and your children will then be faced with the task of disposing of it. But they probably won't. They'll feel too guilty. They'll put the box in their closet, along with the box of "their stuff" that you already gave them.

Please, don't do this to your own children!

What is true, what is fact, what is reality, is this: we grow. We change. The box of Groovy Girls that your daughter loved at age seven may have lost its luster by the time she turned ten. If you were to pull the dolls out now, they'd get nothing more than a glance, and she'd be back to whatever her current craze is.

The problem is, these objects, these collections, this *stuff* creates energy that doesn't let us move forward. We become defined by our past, not who we are now, and certainly not who will we become in the future. Holding your child hostage to the hordes of Transformers under his bed when he is now sixteen (and even though you paid a lot of money for them) is simply not fair.

I'm not talking about tossing your kid's most favorite love doll. (In our house lives a tattered little doll named Flannel, who was passed from one child to the next and is now so well-worn and well-loved that she smells bad—she's too delicate to risk being washed. Flannel, of course, we will keep forever.) But the number of stuffed animals I have carted to Goodwill amounts to a small menagerie.

Let the stuff go.

As you do (and after all the sentimental crying is done), you'll notice a feeling of "what's next" arriving in your home. As you release blocked energy, you make room for what is to come. This is how energy works. When you're all loaded down with old stuff, then you are stuck in the time and memories and energy of the old stuff. You owe it to yourself and your child to move, clear, and get that energy flowing!

If you are in a house in which energy is flowing, you can feel it—you can practically smell it. Everything feels organized and calm and comforting. Everyone is able to be their most open, transcendent selves, because their environment supports it. Everyone is able to grow into who they will become, because they are not bogged down by a past that no longer exists.

This is gift for your child.

Create a positive vibe

By now, you know what vibe is. I say vibe and you shake your head up and down and say, "Yep, gotcha. I got this vibe thing down!" Well, you can actually create *vibe* in your home.

It's been popular in home décor lately to adorn your wall with signs that say inspirational things like "Imagine" or "Dream" or "Live, Laugh, Love," and so on. If you like this kind of thing, great! Not everyone likes this kind of thing, but if this makes you and your family happy, by all means put up inspirational messages.

Photos of family and friends are also great ways to create positive vibe in your home. They don't have to be décor quality either—I've found that funny pictures drawn by the kids, or funny candid snapshots, are also easy ways to create this energy. However, don't let energy stagnate by keeping the same stuff up month after month. Change things up. Keep it current.

Ambient music is an extraordinary way to raise vibration in your home—especially New Age music that is purposely relaxing and designed for healing.

Running water, that old feng shui standby, is also good for creating vibe. Water fills the air with the sounds of peaceful tranquility (although if you are potty training your child, these tinkling sounds may best wait until your kid's out of Pull-Ups).

Running water also reminds us that we are always moving. We are always changing. Our lives work best when we are in constant flow.

PARENTS ASK

My daughter's room is a mess. I've talked to her about energy flow, but she still doesn't get it!

You didn't say how old your daughter is, and her age is important. If she's already a teenager, you'll want to let go of the need to be in charge. Keep the rest of the house clean and clear, and have her to do a massive cleanup (bed made, floor clear) weekly—tying the chore into privileges really helps. For a child under twelve, you can teach by doing—show her how you deal with the energy of objects, and help her put in daily routines for her own living space, such as making the bed, keeping dresser tops clear of clutter, having a "Goodwill" bag in her closet, emptying the trash when it's full, and so forth.

Eliminate or contain electronica

When I walk into a house and see a flatscreen TV in the middle of the living room, my heart sinks. There's nothing that says family disconnect more than a gigantic electronic box in the center of the family gathering area.

Don't get me wrong, watching TV or movies is fun! I've been known to watch them myself, and I don't claim to watch the highest quality stuff, either! Sometimes it's nice to be distracted, and believe me, I do not sit around meditating eight hours a day—not when I can watch a Jackie Chan movie! My kids have been raised on a steady diet of electronic entertainment—from VHS to DVD to whatever's the next most popular thing.

Entertainment is useful. It's a nice way to shut the brain off when the brain can't shut itself off. Especially on those days when you have a million things to do and only time to do 900,000 of them, entertainment is just the ticket.

However, when you place electronica in the main room in your house, you are pretty much admitting that said electronica is going to be turned on without discretion, and that you are your family are therefore not going to have the chance to have casual conversations, easygoing interactions, petty arguments, deep discussions, or any of the other forms of communication that happen when you actually connect and communicate. Instead, you're going to be communicating through the flatscreen—via grunts and laughter and sarcastic comments about characters and celebrities on the screen. You're going to communicate *through the TV*, not with each other.

Same goes for computers. I have been in homes where four laptops were being used by five people, with one person waiting for their turn next (oh wait, that's my house! What is this, a cybercafé?) I've spent fifteen minutes e-mailing back and forth with my teen daughter to come up for dinner—when she was downstairs in her bedroom.

As for cell phones and texting? Don't get me started! They create a constant distraction of connecting to others. Of course, by being connected to others via distance, you experience the irony of *losing* the connection to folks you're interacting with—i.e., your family at the dinner table and so on.

If your house is cluttered with electronica, it has the same energy blockage as if it were cluttered with objects. I know that electronica is changing how we think, and how we communicate, yet it's still important to be able to connect in a way that is deep and true and real.

Your kids need this from you, and you need it from them.

We're dealing in uncharted territory here, but I believe that if you want to keep a sacred energy flow in your house, you must deal with electronica. My suggestion: put the TV in a separate room (which in the olden days, we used to call the den), and when you want to watch TV or a movie, watch it in that room. Keep your living room/great room/family room free for family, friends, and neighbors interested in real, live communication, interaction, and connection. It goes without saying, there shouldn't be a TV in your kid's room—and, yes, this applies to teenagers. It's bad enough they can watch YouTube all day long on their laptops.

And, set limits. Set limits for computer time (thirty minutes to an hour per day, depending on age). Determine what you allow your child to log on to, and get parental-control computer software if you think he'll stray. Limit e-mails and Facebook and so forth—and if your child figures out how to sign up on her own, then monitor it. (Yes, figure out the passwords and look! You're the parent!)

I'm also hopelessly old-fashioned, because I think you shouldn't give your child a cell phone until you absolutely have to—it creates a kind of umbilical-cord effect that's not good for them or you. Remember riding on your bike free as a bird when you were a kid? Your child can't have that heady experience of freedom if you're calling her every fifteen minutes on her cell. Mostly, if your child has a cell, limit texting, and create cell-phone-free zones and times in the house: after school, during meals, when guests are over, and so on.

Finally, know that electronica does not create physical clutter the same way that objects do, but it does create mind clutter—an energetic distraction that removes us from flow. While electronica is a part of your child's life, it's also crucial to make room for live human interaction. Real connection is where energy flows.

Exercises

1. Declutter your home: give stuff to Goodwill, throw stuff away, rearrange stuff. If you haven't done this for a while, work in small sections: do one section of a room, or even one cabinet at a time. If you're a life-long "saver" who has trouble letting things go, or if you become overwhelmed by the process, ask a friend to help.

2. Take a long, hard look at electronica usage in your home. Notice when it's on, and if anyone is really using it at those times. This includes TV, movies, computer games, cell phones. Once you can spot patterns of what's happening at your house, decide what you'd like to change.

3. Create electronica-free zones for certain times or places—for example, no cell phones at the dinner table, no TV left "on" when no one's watching a show, and so forth.

4. Pay attention to what your child is watching or listening to. For your Divine child, watching or hearing something is energetically the same as experiencing it in reality. Respect this.

seventeen

Got Stuff?

You know that all things contain energy, vibration. This is the way of the Universe. As each being vibrates, so does every object. We say: it is important to know what pleases you. It is important to see what raises vibration, and what dulls it. In all things that you surround yourself with—people, ideas, objects—choose that which raises vibration. Clear the rest away—it is not useful to you. It does not serve. —The Messages

———

In the last chapter, I talked about clutter, and how it blocks energy—and then, I must say, I went downstairs and demanded that my teenage son clean out his room, a process that took two days and six garbage bags, and ended up in the discovery of one prehistoric banana peel behind the bed, three library books that I already paid the "lost" fines on, and his friend's T-shirt that we'd been looking for since last spring. He also found his cashbox, which contained $120! Score!

It's amazing what can happen with a little clearing and cleaning. The energy in his room now *moves*, and even though he's still grumpy about being forced to do the task ("Why can't I just close the door, like other kids?"), he's appreciated the change.

When you move out the old, you make room for the new. It's how energy works. When flow can happen, flow does happen.

However, this chapter is not about the clutter in your home. Instead, it's about the actual objects in your home, and how they affect your children.

Objects hold energy

Why are objects so important? Because just like everything else in the Universe, objects hold energy.

What an object is made of determines its energetic vibrational level. For example, if something is made from solid wood, it vibrates differently from something made of pressboard and laminate—no offense to the people at Ikea, but this is just how it is.

A plant vibrates differently from a plastic tubful of Polly Pockets.

A rock vibrates differently from an army of Bionicles.

Natural fibers vibrate differently from synthetic.

Objects are made of different things, and objects that are made of natural materials send off different energies than synthetic objects that are packaged, processed, and made in multiple steps in countries far away.

In my own home, I display large stones from the Pacific Northwest's Puget Sound—still speckled with dried salt and laced with old seaweed. I keep this collection of rocks, gathered on a sunny day in which the waves sparkled like diamonds, in an old, hand-carved wooden bowl from Bali, in the center of a wooden table hand-carved in India, in the middle of the room where I work.

They're rocks.

Yet their still and solid vibration is soothing to me.

They're neutral in color. They're cool to the touch. They're natural, and by bringing this small amount of nature inside, I am reminded of the fact that we are Earth bodies living in an Earth world.

I can see the problem of having a bowl of rocks at grab-and-chuck level if you have toddlers in the house—ouch!

However, the value of bringing some kind of nature in—objects that hold a softer, slower, more complex vibration that complements the vibration of our own human bodies—is a good thing.

If you're a plant lover, and can manage the responsibility of keeping plants healthy and happy, this can be a beautiful way to bring in that simpler, softer vibration.

However, not everyone can take care of plants (and there's nothing more depressing than a bunch of droopy plants that are dying on the vine, shrieking for more light or water). If you can't, simply bring in something from nature.

My son, who like most males has had an affinity for sticks since he was age three, keeps a small collection of beautiful wood items upon the windowsill of his room. It started during the Harry Potter craze, when he wanted sticks gathered from different kinds of trees. Here in Oregon, where we live, we have trees of so many varieties: maple, oak, fir, pine, madrona, yew, cherry, apple, plum, and more. All hold a gorgeous natural vibration, and they are each magnificently different, with different ways of curling and bending and being.

My son collected these sticks from different kinds of trees in the forest around our home, then peeled and polished them carefully, like artwork. Because they are natural, they're not only beautiful, but contain whole and amazing vibration.

The point is—if you have your house filled with plastic, with things that are fake and not real, the vibrational level will not be aligned with what our Earth bodies need. As you pick up the next collection of tiny plastic things and place them in large plastic tubs to clean your child's room, consider—what is the vibrational level of these toys? What is the vibrational level of plastic? Do you find it comforting? Do you find it sustaining? Does your child?

Yes, we've become very much used to this stuff, and mainstream marketing continues to clamor that we should buy it, spurred on by big companies and gobs of advertising money.

But I believe that if you look to keep your home filled with softer, more natural vibrations—the kind contained in natural objects— your house will be more soothing, and thus a better environment for your sensitive, Divine kid. This doesn't mean you can't have toys—but you might try more natural options, such as from HearthSong and Magic Cabin. It doesn't mean no Polly Pockets, either. (They're very good for hand dexterity!) It simply means: watch the balance.

Feel the vibrational level in your home—and if it's gotten sort of flat and dead and yucky-feeling, it's time to rebalance on the side of natural objects.

The objects in your home hold memory

Years ago, I found a dusty old book in a used bookstore called something along the lines of *The Secret Life of Objects*. This magical, since misplaced book from the 1920s presented the ideas that objects hold not only vibrational energy, but also emotion and memory.

This made immediate sense to me.

As an antique-shop browser, secondhand shop visitor, and used-bookstore purveyor, I've long known that pre-owned items hold memory. Many others have experienced this as well. *Psychometry* is the name for this psychic sensitivity—and it's a very common ability for folks who are clairsentient, clairvoyant, and mediums.

Objects hold not only energy and vibration, but also the very memory, the very story of the people who have owned, made, or lived around them.

This means that every single object in your home—whether inherited, new, picked up secondhand, or given as a gift—will hold a feeling, emotion, or memory that your child will be able to sense and pick up on. That old desk that was your grandmother's? If your grandmother was a beautiful, loving creature, fantastic. But if she was a meanie, beware! The picnic basket your aunt used to take pies to church picnics? It may hold memories of sunny afternoons and leafy trees—or it may hold memories of less pleasant incidents that took place then. Or, because life is complicated, it may hold memories of both.

Even the funky fashions you wore in your twenties still contain the vibe of the person you were then—and if that's not a person you'd like your child to know, you're better off giving the clothes to Goodwill.

Hand-me-downs and inherited items require special care. If a family relationship is strained, you may not want to be reminded of that every time you sit down at kitchen table. "But that's grandma's table!"

PARENTS ASK

My son doesn't like the family room. Even if we're all in there, he avoids it. Is there an energy problem?

If you've got a TV in this room, this could be the problem—Divine kids are super-sensitive to electronica, and can't deal with environments where it's always on or used as "background." Remember, they absorb everything, and seeing or hearing electronica is energetically the same as experiencing it firsthand. It's better for them if you switch off the TV except for specific viewing, and turn the family room into a place where you and your kids can really connect.

you may cry in disbelief. Yes, I know. However, energetically, you may be better off without it. The vibe it holds, in terms of memories and emotions, may simply be too much for you to deal with every time you drink your morning coffee. If a piece of furniture gives you a feeling of peace and comfort and connection, wonderful. If it makes you feel uncomfortable, bogged down, depressed, or zapped, let it go.

Same goes for items bought at a garage sale, flea market, secondhand shop, or antique store. Yes, the bargains can be terrific—but the vibe from some of these items can be terrifying, so much so that you can tell right there in the store it's not a good idea to bring them home.

I'm not saying you need to only buy new things, or never use anything secondhand, or not have family heirlooms in your home. Simply be aware that every object contains energy and vibration, and every object holds the emotion and memory of its previous owners or environment.

That means checking in with all of your clairs: clairvoyance, clairaudience, clairsentience—before you add "something old" to your home.

What about something new?

Vibration is also strong in items that are brand-new. Modern furniture is often made in terrible conditions in third-world countries. This furniture holds vibe the same way anything holds vibe. Yes, it looks bright and clean and modern, but if you think of a factory every time you see it—don't bring it home.

For my own house, I have a simple rule: old or new, I pick things that make me feel good. If they don't make me feel good, they don't stay. For example, I'm crazy about a big piggy bank I discovered on the floor of a thrift store—he's pink and portly and makes me smile. But other old things have been given the shaft—even things that came from my parents or grandparents. If I don't feel good when I'm in the presence of the item, it doesn't belong in my house.

How to know what's affecting your child? Simply ask. Sometimes kids will have such a strong aversion to something, they'll request that it be removed from their room.

This object needs to go.

Psychometry—try it for yourself

For many years, I taught creative writing, and I often used energetic concepts to help people open creatively. One time, I did an experiment in psychometry. I gathered some items from an artist friend's studio—but first, I psychically read the item to determine its past, and after my friend confirmed I'd received the correct information, I took notes on each item. The objects were an assortment, and included:

- A sewing kit made of velvet
- A wooden pin of a small bird
- A fountain pen
- A postcard from Hawaii

I took these items into the class, and then had my students—writers of all abilities—write the stories of these objects. Now, these folks weren't taking a *clairvoyance* class from me. They weren't into psychic

development. They were fiction writers, who did not consider themselves psychic—they were simply writers who wanted to improve their
creative writing.

However, nearly every single person in that class was able to write
the correct story of the object they chose to write about. They nailed
it, from the history to the relationships between the people who'd affected this object.

*"The sewing kit was a gift between women who were like sisters, but
not. They were close, but there was some falling out between them."* True.

*"The pin was brought back from a trip by a man in the Navy in the
1950s; he got it in an Asian country, and brought it back for his girl-
friend. They were married and had children."* True again.

*"The postcard was sent as apology, from a woman who went on a
trip to Hawaii as vacation. She sent it to her friend. However, they never
resumed the friendship when she returned. Something had changed. This
was in the 1920s, and both women lived in the Northwest."* Also true.

I'm re-creating what folks wrote in that class, because I didn't save
the writing at the time—but I remember how uncannily accurate
these writers were able to write the stories of these objects, and how we
sat around the big table in class and marveled at what had happened.

Of course, we're all psychic.

Even adults who don't particularly peg themselves as such.

And if adults, who by and large don't recognize their intuitive abilities, can feel the vibration and determine the history and memory that
an object holds—well, you can bet that your sensitive, gifted, Divine
kids will be affected even more.

Choosing objects with good vibes

Once you understand how energy and vibration are contained within
the objects you own, you'll want to take a hard look at what you allow
in your house, and what you let your kids live with.

Some basic questions to ask:

- How do your feel around the object?
- Do you feel negative, neutral, or positive?

- Do you feel relaxed, safe, comfortable? Or edgy, uptight?
- Do you sense the history or emotion of the object?
- Does it remind you of something or someone else?
- Does it fit you and your home?
- Would you be sad to part with it, or happy it was gone?

Ask yourself these questions, and if you don't come up completely positive or at least neutral, skip adding this object to your home. And if you already own it, consider getting rid of it—pronto!

Of course, many objects have great vibration! The enormous writing desk that I've written on for over twenty years now is made of plain wood, with two very deep, expansive drawers. I found it at an old used-record store in Seattle, stacked with crates of records. The vibe of this desk cannot be surpassed! It's one of my favorite pieces of furniture, and I feel good knowing I can write at it every day.

Clearing objects

What if you own an object with a bad vibe, but you still want to keep it? Can you clear objects in your home? In some cases, you can. Remember, everything is about energy, and all energy wants to move in Divine flow. So if there's something you love that has a bad vibe, but you still want to keep it, clearing may be possible. Some of the easiest ways to clear things include:

- Washing them
- Painting them
- Refinishing them
- Mending them
- Moving them to a different room
- Using them differently

In doing these simple tasks, you replace the former energy of the object with your own energy. You might think of it as "taking ownership" of the energy of an item.

If the energy is very dense and the object cannot be cleared as above, you may clear it energetically. Now, many folks will say you need smudge and sage and salt and et cetera—but I've found that it's a lot simpler than that. Not everyone agrees, but I've found those items to be sort of like accessories—fun to use, but not necessary. Using actual energy is all that's required. Here's how:

- Ask for the Divine to help you clear an object.
- Feel the energy start to move in your hands.
- Move your hands over and around the object, until you feel its vibration start to shift; do this for as long as you feel energy moving or flowing.
- If you don't feel the object has shifted enough to be comfortable with it (i.e., you don't feel you've cleared the object), it's time to let the object go.
- Energy shifts very quickly, so this process will take only a few minutes, or maybe a few sessions of a few minutes.
- If you feel the object has shifted to a positive vibration and you feel good about it, enjoy it in your home.

It all sounds pretty woo-woo, but trust me: it works. The Divine will let you know quite quickly what items can be shifted, and what items can't. If you are being stubborn about trying to keep an item that doesn't belong in your house, the Divine will tell you this, too! When you do let go of items that never belonged there in the first place, you're going to feel the energy flowing like never before!

Grounding your home

When I was first divorced, I had a hard time settling into the idea that my kids were doing fine when they stayed at their dad's house. Author and clairvoyant Debra Lynne Katz noted this right away when she was doing a reading for me—she said I wasn't just grounding my own house, but that I was still grounding the house where my kids lived with their father!

This meant that I was actively protecting them with my energy, which was good.

It also meant that I was blocked from moving forward, which was not good.

I took a long look at this. Then, I simply dissolved my grounding of the other house. I went into trance, asked my guides and angels to take up the grounding for me, and to release me from this task. I gave the task of keeping my kids safe when I could not be with them to the Universe and their guides and angels, and to their father, who is quite capable of keeping them safe. I realized I didn't have to hold everything together. What's more, it wasn't my job anymore. I let it go.

Not surprisingly, I noticed an immediate shift in my relationship with my children's father, and we were able to work on parenting challenges better than before. This is because I let go of energy that I wasn't supposed to be in charge of. When flow happened, everything started to work better.

After you've (a) checked the vibe of the objects in your home, (b) cleared out the stuff that shouldn't be there, and (c) energetically cleared the items you want to keep, take a look at how your house is grounded. If you haven't grounded your home, do so now (you'll find out how in the exercise below). If you're still grounding past properties, let these go now. You and your children will delight in the pleasant, positive flow of energy in your home once you have completed these tasks.

Exercise

Here's a grounding technique for parents to use to ground their home. It's fast, easy, and effective.

1. Go into a light trance (close your eyes, breathe deeply a few times).

2. Picture in your mind's eye the home or property you wish to ground—explore each room's nooks and crannies, the same way you might energetically scan your body.

3. Imagine the four corners of this property—these may be in the building, or extend to a larger property line, or be in specific rooms.

4. Create grounding cords of any kind that attach the property to a place that is deep within the core of the earth.

5. Ground the property into the earth, and then energetically send any dense, unpleasant, or unneeded energy from the house down the grounding cords. This could include unpleasant emotions, bad vibes, or whatever you see that you don't want there anymore.

6. Ask the Divine to continue grounding this property or home once you take your attention from it.

7. Say thank you, and come out of trance.

8. Check back on this property by grounding it and running energy as you sense any changes, or from time to time.

eighteen
Divine Body

Children in first-world countries, who enjoy all material luxuries, are hindered by the fact of this luxury. It deadens the mind. The body may be comfortable, but it may be fed to excess without nutrition. As is the body, so is the mind. Because you live in your bodies, you are directly affected by excess.

In this way, psychic development may be hindered. Excess is not useful. A normal, healthy body is all that is required. The fewer toxins, such as from foods, pollutants, disease, the more healthy and pure a child can be, and the simpler it will be for him to hear us. —The Messages

———

We are souls housed in bodies. More specifically, we are Divine essence clothed in Earth bodies. Our lives are lived on the spiritual plane, yes. But every single day, the body we wake up in, walk in, eat in, sleep in, is our Earth body.

What's more, our spiritual selves are so intertwined with our Earth bodies, they are expressed so magnificently through our bodies—all of our senses, including our psychic senses, all our emotions, all of the aspects of love and kindness—are so entangled, I would go so far as to say they are inseparable.

Spirit affects body. Body affects spirit. They are not separate from each other; they are One living being.

This is true for you, no matter how much you have neglected or cared for your body. This is also true for you, no matter the state of your spiritual health.

We feel God on our skin. We feel God in our bones. Our bodies run on the energy that is God, the same way that energy runs our spiritual essence.

This is true for you.

It is also true for your child.

The more you can provide your child with a lifestyle that supports the body, the more you will be able to support his or her psychic and spiritual development.

Junk food, junk brains

Earlier, I mentioned how hard it is to develop psychically for kids whose basic Earth needs aren't met—who have to face hunger, poverty, illness, disease, or traumatic stress from war, abuse, neglect.

However, kids who live in abundant first-world countries such as the United States are also in danger. This is because they're being raised within a mainstream culture that does not support the body.

You already know where this is going.

"Oh, we never eat junk food," you might say smugly.

"We only buy organic."

"I don't allow sodas."

And so on.

Very good—if your child is five and under. Because the minute they head to school (and even if they are homeschooled), they will begin the unavoidable process of becoming acculturated—and if you are living in America, that means by the dominant, mainstream culture, of which junk food is very much a part.

Now . . . Mountain Dew may be "cool"—but it's not nutritious.

Froot Loops are fun—but they don't support the body.

Doritos turn your hands orange—and who knows what they do to your internal organs.

Your kids, raised on a steady diet of advertising, have grown up desiring these foods. This means they will shamelessly swap out your lovingly prepared sandwiches (organic sprouted whole wheat bread, sliced homegrown cucumbers, lettuce you grew in your garden, the whole process taking you about fifteen minutes this morning instead of doing your makeup, so you arrive at work with lipstick hastily slathered on and not a speck of eye shadow), and trade this gorgeous sandwich to some kid in the lunchroom in return for a three-inch stack of Pringles and one-and-a-half Oreos.

Yes, this happens!

Yes, your child does it!

Even if your child swears up one side and down the other that she does *not* do this, let me let you in on a little secret: she has. She does. She will.

If the stakes are high enough, your child will trade. Your child may not trade for Pringles. But she will, 100 percent, positively, without doubt (the traitor!), trade for something on her personal favorites list: Ding Dongs. Twizzlers. Famous Amos cookies. Pringles. Soda, any brand. A Lunchable—or even a part of a Lunchable.

PARENTS ASK

Is there any danger if my child is astral projecting?

No more danger than if he dreams at night. And, in fact, the two are closely intertwined. If you feel your child is astral projecting (traveling to other places while his body remains here) but having trouble returning to this reality (for instance, if he's acting super-spacey), help him to return to this reality fully. For example, at bedtime you might rub his back and remind him to "bring all his energy back home" when he's out gallivanting around the Universe. But mostly, relax! Astral projection is normal for kids and adults, and we all seem to arrive back in our beds in time for the a.m. alarm!

My own kids, for whom I have now packed over three thousand lunches (number of kids times age of kids times school months in each year, times days in the week), have managed to do a brisk trade in my partner's famous spanakopita—an exotic dish not seen at the school often, and so popular that some kids will trade a bag of chips *plus* a soda for one of the savory little triangles. On the school lunch circuit, spanakopita is gold.

The point is: you don't have control over what your child eats after he starts getting out into the real world. Even if your kid's elementary school doesn't allow "trading," I can assure you that trading is happening. By middle school, your kid will seek out junk food the way addicts track a fix—and there is nothing you can do about it.

Why does this matter? It matters because the body and the spirit exist in a symbiotic relationship: what affects one, affects the other. And vice versa.

A body existing on junk food does not receive adequate nutrition—and in the same way that a child who is starving for food cannot concentrate, a child who is overfed, or fed foods that aren't nutritious, won't be able to focus.

I'm not saying junk food is evil incarnate. I'm simply pointing out the fact that a body that is not supported by good nutrition won't have the same ability as if it would if it were fully nourished. This means psychic development and spiritual growth will be harder. Not impossible. Just harder.

The body requires respect

According to a recent report from the American Academy of Child & Adolescent Psychiatry, between 16 and 33 percent of children and adolescents are obese.[11]

That can lead to health problems.

---

11. A PDF summary of this report, "Obesity in Children and Teens," can be found online at www.aacap.org/galleries/FactsforFamilies/79_obesity_in_children_ and_teens.pdf.

In fact, the Centers for Disease Control and Prevention reported a 90 percent jump in American adults with Type 2 diabetes over the last decade, caused by obesity and sedentary lifestyles. Our kids are tagging along—one study in the *New England Journal of Medicine* found that 25 percent of very obese children and 21 percent of very obese adolescents had prediabetes.

Why is prediabetes so devastating? For one thing, if your child is prediabetic, chances are high that he'll develop diabetes; that means he might need insulin for the rest of his life, or he could go blind, experts say. He'll also have the same chance of having a heart attack as someone with heart disease.[12]

I'm sure you don't want this for your child.

Sadly, this is how the earth body responds to the habit of overeating, or of eating foods that are not nutrient rich. Our bodies can overcome a lot of bad habits, but at a certain point, they can't overcome anymore. In our American culture, with its predilection for fast food, junk food, food with chemical additives, and too much food, this is the reality we now face, for ourselves and our children.

Toxicities

When I channeled *The 33 Lessons*, I was amazed by how many references there were to toxicities. These might include chemicals, additives, and colorings in food (which many people believe are related to ADD/ADHD, allergies, asthma, and other current epidemics in kids). The other toxicities the *Lessons* referred to were industrial chemicals and toxicities in the environment, from obvious pollution sources caused by manufacturing and industry to the smaller, sneakier sources of toxicity that we commonly find in our homes, such as chemical cleaners.

Well, not so much in my house. I may be a slacker on lots of things, and a B-minus mom to boot. But when it comes to toxicities, I protect my kids the best I can.

---

12. "Is Your Child at Risk for Diabetes?" *Your Kids* magazine, November 2008.

A few years ago, I wrote a magazine feature about the effects of brand-name cleaning products on babies and toddlers, and I can tell you—I went out the day I filed that story, and I turned our house into a green zone. From that point on, only non-toxic, human-and-animal-friendly cleaners are allowed in our home.

Those cleaning products you buy off the shelf? The trusted names you spray all over your kitchen counter in order to kill germs? Those chemical substances are picked up by your child's forearms, elbows, and hands as he sits at that counter. Our skin is one of the most absorptive organs of our body—which means your child is literally absorbing those chemicals through his skin.

To put it more brutally—would your spray your baby with a bottle of countertop cleaner? Of course you wouldn't! Yet we unwittingly allowing this countertop cleaner to be absorbed by our child's skin when we use toxic cleaners.

To avoid toxicities, you'll want to choose eco products, use mainstream products sparingly if at all, and completely avoid the most hazardous cleaners, which, according to the Washington Toxics Coalition, include corrosive drain cleaners, oven cleaners, acidic toilet-bowl cleaners, and anything containing chlorine or ammonia.[13]

Yes, it can be more expensive to buy green products. And it's confusing to determine what is actually a green product—just because a product screams "natural" on the label does not mean it is! And, I'm sorry to say, green products are often not as effective. They don't have the scrubbing power or oxy boost or whatever it is that makes the non-green products do such a great job. However, to my mind the choice is clear: chemicals affect us on a cellular level, in ways that we don't yet understand.

It's a risk I'm not willing to take with my growing, developing kids—or myself.

This category also extends past cleaning products, to fragrances, detergents, air fresheners, and, yes, "natural" products such as aro-

---

13. For more information, see the Healthy Living fact sheets at www.watoxics .org.

matherapy. It also includes materials such as linoleum, carpeting, tile, paint, and other building materials used in our homes—the chemicals and off-gassing can affect our bodies and brains.

Sleep hygiene

Your child needs sleep, not only for physical rejuvenation but because of the deep-dreaming time during which she receives psychic messaging and information. Who knows where your child astral projects every night—but if his sleep is interrupted or cut too short, this isn't going to happen!

What's more, if your child isn't fully rested, she won't be able to focus on anything psychic. Any kind of psychic development isn't going to happen if your child is exhausted from staying up till 2:00 a.m. playing video games.

Sleep deprivation becomes even stickier in the teen years—your kid is bouncing off the wall with energy, and his body can and will stay up till all hours of the night. At my house, the teen-age bewitching hour for a weeknight is 10:00 p.m. Shockingly early, by many standards! But over the years I've been parenting, I've noticed that's about the time they're ready to crash into a deep, whole sleep. Sometimes, after a busy day of school and activities, they'll fall asleep much earlier! For younger kids, bedtime is 8 or 8:30 p.m. Mostly, I gauge bedtime by how easily my kids get up in the morning, and how fast they fall asleep at night. I also go by mood—a cranky child is often a sleep-deprived child, and by now I know the telltale signs that mean they haven't gotten enough.

A word on sleepovers? Yes, they're fun, and everyone clamors for them. But with some kids, they cause more problems than they're worth. If your child is cranky and zombie-like after a sleepover, thereby making life miserable for everyone else in the family—you may want to reconsider.

Bodies in motion

Our Earth bodies are made to move, and our energy gets blocked when we don't. Even a young body can get sluggish and slow if it's not utilized—muscles can atrophy and weaken, and the flab can pile up even on a child.

Guidelines suggest that kids exercise a minimum of sixty minutes every day, according to the Centers for Disease Control and Prevention—that means brisk, vigorous aerobic activity! Yet with the way we have our children set up for sedentary time at school plus computer/TV/couch-potato time at home, it's hard to get that hour in.

If your child isn't active every day, he'll experience excessive energy overload—with no way to release it.

What's more, your child accumulates *psychic* energy during the course of a day. This is often felt as emotion, adrenaline, sensitivity, or vibe, and your child picks it up all day long. Psychic energy needs to be released in the same way that physical energy does.

Movement in the body is crucial, *because it releases both physical and psychic energy.* Now, many parents deal with the need for releasing physical energy by signing their kids up for sports (and I'll cover this more next). Sports are a practical way to get your child up and moving on a regular basis, and the benefits have been well documented, according to the President's Council on Fitness, Sports & Nutrition.[14]

In fact, a recent study at the Institute for the Study of Youth Sports at Michigan State University found that kids who play sports do better in school and have enhanced social skills. Plus, they're less likely to abuse drugs, alcohol, and cigarettes.[15]

That's all good stuff! However, not all kids like the competition that's part of sports—and this frequently includes Divine kids.

If you think of everything as energy (because it is), then although your Divine child may be *releasing physical energy* via sports, she's also

---

14. See www.fitness.gov.
15. The website for the Institute for the Study of Youth Sports is located at www .educ.msu.edu/ysi/.

collecting psychic energy from the competition, other players, coaches, and parents—and often this has a not-so-pleasant vibe.

Your Divine child may do better climbing a tree, talking a walk, riding a bike, or rolling down a grassy hill rather than pummeling the other team on the football field. Dancing to music can also be an extraordinary way to raise vibration, and release energy both psychic and physical.

The importance of breathing

Some kids go around not breathing all day—they seem to be holding their breath, or breathing in awkward little gasps, too excited and stimulated to ever take a long, deep breath. If you can teach your kids to breath more fully, even just once a day, you will help them release excess physical and psychic energy.

Breathing can be in through the nose, out through the mouth. Or, it can be in through the nose, out through the nose—a method commonly practiced by those who do Kundalini yoga and other folks who do breath work. Breathing fully will help your child center in his body and calm his emotions.

Clearing the body

In addition to keeping the body physically healthy, you can also clear the body energetically. People who study energy healing do this all the time. Medical intuitives also scan the body energetically, as a way of sensing areas that contain illness or disease.

The benefits of energetic clearing is that it works instantly. Some folks believe in the power of prayer to heal so fervently, they eschew traditional medicine. My own beliefs, especially when it comes to kids, is that we have been put on this earth at a certain point in time—we still aren't very advanced at healing, but we have several options available:

- Traditional medicine
- Naturopathic, holistic, and alternative medicine
- Energetic and spiritual medicine

The way I see it, humans are only in the infancy of knowing how to heal; because of this, *we should make use of everything* that is available to use.

Is energy healing a substitute for medical care—either traditional or alternative? I don't think so. To my mind, when your child needs antibiotics, it is your responsibility as a parent to make sure she gets antibiotics. When your child needs his appendix removed, he needs his appendix removed, and so forth.

And yet . . . energy healing can work miracles. It can be the one option that works when all else has failed. If you've ever experienced a "psychic surgery," or been healed by an energy master, you know this for yourself.

I'm not the parent of your child—I can't decide what you should do in terms of her health. However, I do know that using energy as *one* of the tools for a healthy body will never harm your child, and will always be beneficial on a soul level. You can use this technique without worry.

PARENTS ASK

My son wants to be vegetarian, because he doesn't want to hurt animals. What should I do?

Kindness to animals is common trait in Divine kids, especially SAKs. If your child wants to be vegetarian or vegan or follow any particular (healthy) diet, let him. Most American diets are so full of protein that there isn't much concern he won't get enough. And, if the diet is mostly natural, it's a good thing—he won't miss those chemical toxicities a bit! Take him to the health food store, figure out some vegetarian dishes you can make for him, and if you're still concerned, check with your physician. In most cases, a child who won't eat meat simply *won't* eat meat—it's a spiritual conviction—so let go of any need to force him or make him feel guilty for his choice.

Exercises

1. Eliminate toxic foods from your family's diet. If you're not sure what's included, try this: skip anything with artificial color or additives, or anything packaged or processed. You might even have to start shopping at a different store. It may take months to convert your family to a new way of eating, but it's worth it. And remember: your kids are getting junk food from secret sources, such as at school or when they're with friends. The idea isn't to eliminate all modern foods from their diet—it's to make sure they are getting whole, natural, unprocessed foods most of the time.

2. Go green. Replace every single mainstream chemical cleaner in your house with green products. If they're too expensive, try old-fashioned remedies like baking soda and vinegar. Also replace all toxic shampoos, soaps, and personal-care products with natural brands. Remember: your skin absorbs everything. Make sure it's not absorbing chemicals and toxins.

3. Get ventilated. Open windows, and increase natural ventilation if the air quality in your area allows it. Stop using mainstream fragrance products for the home, such as air fresheners, plug-ins, or scented candles. The same may also be true for more natural aromatherapy such as incense or essential oils—check to see how your kids respond. If the air is clean where you live, open the windows!

4. **Energetic clearing.** Pick a time when your child is relaxed, and have him close his eyes and breathe deeply a few times. Then, have him imagine that he is scanning his body for energy, starting at the top of his head, and working down through his neck, chest, arms, tummy, legs, and feet. While your child is scanning his body, you can do the same. Ask your child to check in with each part of his body, and decide what color the energy looks like, and if it is moving or stuck. Remember, he'll see the color in his mind's eye, or he will "just know." Ask him to look for

any area in his body where the color is gray, dark green, black, muddy, thick, dense, or angry. If he finds an area like this, have him clear it—imagine vacuuming it up mentally, or scrubbing it clean, or sending it into space and exploding it. Or, you can have your child take a break at this point, and do the energy healing yourself for him, with the same mental processes.

5. **Scanning via distance.** If you sense there is a problem in your child's physical body, you can scan him energetically at any time (even when he is at school and you are at work or home). If you run into thicker, dense energy, simply heal it as above, or if that doesn't seem to do the trick, ask for Divine assistance that this area be healed, and let your angels and guides do this work for you.

6. **Respect your child.** Energetic healing is amazing, but you shouldn't proceed if your child doesn't want you to. Always, respect your child's need for dignity and privacy of his own body, regardless of his age.

7. **Seek outside help.** If you or your child notices an energetic problem with a matching physical component (she doesn't feel well), it's time to head to the doctor. Remember, in this age we have many healing modalities available. Don't allow superstition on either end of the traditional-to-alternative medicine spectrum to sway you. Take a look at all the options available, and then do what you think is best for your child.

A special healing

There's so much we don't understand about healing in the body. Even the most advanced medicine pales in comparison with what we will be able to do twenty, fifty, or one hundred years from now. Recently, I did an energy healing that gave me a surprising glimpse of the kind of future that might await.

I was working energetically, via distance, on a young woman who'd been paralyzed a few months before. I didn't know I was going to do a healing, but my guides directed me to do so after I learned of her situation. I began by going into trance, and focusing on this young woman as I would do in a medical-intuitive scan.

When I felt the energy begin to flow, I focused my attention on the back of her neck, where I sensed the paralysis was originating. What happened next was extreme: as I focused my attention, I clearly and completely felt others take over.

Who were the others? I don't know, but there was a group of them, perhaps six. There were small—shorter than me, and not especially human. They clustered around and excitedly began to open the neck of this young woman, and inside I saw an entire switchboard of brightly colored buttons—a control panel or circuitry of sorts.

At first, these beings used my hands to work the buttons—I could see small glowing circuitry in my own fingers, going toward the circuitry in her neck. But then they got frustrated, and just did the work themselves. It was as if they needed me as a conduit first—and then they could take over.

I continued with my work, which was now just being witness and holding space (and trying not to freak out or in any way stop the process). After a time, they seemed satisfied that the work had been completed, and they closed her neck up. There was no blood, no spinal cord, nothing we'd expect from a human body. It was all color, energy, light—like buttons, or circuitry. That's what they worked with.

I finished the healing session, and I felt a wave of enormous comfort and completion wash over me. Was she healed? I never found out. But what I do know is that something extreme happened energetically—other entities, through me, came down to heal her, and they worked with color, energy, and light. I can't imagine this didn't have some effect. I'm sure I'll hear about this woman's progress soon. I pray that the healing was of use to her, and I am grateful that I was some small part of what was needed, as a conduit for these healing beings.

nineteen

Divine Time

*Time has no meaning. This is an idea that presents you with much con-
fusion. Time does not exist. And yet you assign it with meaning, you cut
it into slices and serve it up very cold indeed. Whereas in reality—time,
space, matter—all are energy, as are you, as is the Universe, as is All.
Time belongs to the ego—the soul does not recognize time. And yet on
Earth, everything is structured around these: time, space, matter. The
possession of such.*

*Understand Now is ungraspable—like sand slipping through your
fingers, even as the next Now arrives. What is your Now in this moment?
This is the only thing you can measure—how Now is held in your heart.*
—The Messages

———

When is busy too busy?

The answer, nowadays, is *most of the time*.

As a culture, we seem to believe that slowing down, stopping, coming to a screeching halt and *holding space* for one moment in which we
are not productive, or at the very least "doing something," is unworthy.
That a moment of *being*, not doing, is a wasted moment.

Yes, it's true we have limited time on this earth. Yes, it's true that
we don't know when our time will be "up" or when we will be passing
over into the next realm and our next life. Yes, it's also true that time
is more precious than money, and you certainly don't want to waste it.

But the idea that cramming our minutes so fully and completely that we forget that we are here to simply exist, to "be" and to learn, has turned us into slaves of time.

In *The 33 Lessons*, it's said:

We understand that you have concerns of time, and we ask you, why do you allow this? Time is of no importance. Life extends unto old age, or life is ended in a breath. You do not know which, and these are the same. Just be, in your life. But surely you know this already?

And yet, time is a problem for us. And it is a problem that becomes even more difficult, when it comes to our kids.

For example: Marta is in fifth grade. Her normal day looks something like this: she gets up at 6:30 a.m. and goes to school until 3 p.m. That's a full load, right there. But after school, her mom drives her first to ballet lessons (3:30 to 4:30) and then to basketball at 5 p.m., gobbling down a snack and changing from her leotard into her jersey and shorts in the car—it's awkward, but they don't have time to stop anywhere. After practice, she either grabs a fast-food dinner on the way home or eats a bowl of something when she gets home. Then she showers, does her homework for an hour or two, goes on the computer if she has time, and drops into bed. By now, she's been going, non-stop, from 7 a.m. to 10 p.m. most days. On weekends, she's also on the go—her basketball team, a "traveling team," might drive anywhere from one to four hours to play other competitive teams in her league. Lately, her mom's noticed that Marta seems listless, and isn't as excited about traveling on the weekend.

Really?

She's burnt out?

You've got to be kidding!

Or, try this one: Josh is in sixth grade. He's been playing soccer since he was five, and he's getting pretty good at it. "He's crazy about soccer," his mom says. However, he doesn't have time for much else: he's got practice twice a week, and then games on Saturdays and sometimes Sundays—and because he's on a competitive team, that might mean traveling. He loves sports, his mom swears—so she signs him up for soccer in the fall, indoor soccer in the winter, and then soccer again for spring season. In the summer, it's more soccer—clinics that run all day through July. In August, his fall team starts practicing again. Lately, his mom's noticed that all he wants to do when he gets home is watch TV or sleep.

Is this surprising?

Today's hurried child

It's not that we don't have enough time, it's how we fill it.

According to Dr. David Elkind, author of a dozen best-selling books on child development, including the *The Hurried Child*, and a professor emeritus of child development at Tufts University, kids today are massively overscheduled.

"Over the past two decades, children have lost twelve hours of free time a week, including eight hours of unstructured play and outdoor activities," noted Dr. Elkind in an interview I did with him on the subject.

"The health impact of the disappearance of play is already apparent: 13 percent of our children are obese," he said. "But equally troubling is the way this lack of play stunts children's emotional, behavioral, and even their intellectual growth."

It's not that organized activities or sports in themselves are bad for kids. The problem is, these activities don't promote the kind of *free thinking* or *free play* that kids require to grow as whole beings.

And, if you want to encourage psychic development and spiritual growth in kids, you'll need to provide plenty of downtime—and that means cutting back on activities. "The time spent in activities needs to be balanced by the same amount of time in free play," advised Dr. Elkind. For kids' psychic and spiritual growth, this free time is crucial.

A word about sports

It's curious to me where we got the idea that signing up our kids for every activity on the planet would turn them into "better" kids. It's even more curious why we choose sports.

As per usual, I'm in the minority—more than forty-four million American boys and girls play sports annually, according to the National Council of Youth Sports.[16] But I still wonder if it's the right choice for all kids.

Certainly, I understand the reality that focusing on one thing can make your kids more accomplished in that activity—certainly, if you play soccer every day from age five, you'll be better at it than if you don't start until you're sixteen. That said, I have seen kids who didn't start sports until sixth grade, who were considered so far behind the curve that they couldn't possibly catch up—and those same kids got so good so fast, they blew everyone else out of the water.

I've also seen many, many kids like Marta and Josh who have spent their entire young lives playing sports, but by the time the recruiting coaches make the rounds in high school, it's sadly apparent that they're not at a level to get a college scholarship for their abilities.

The truth is, only a small percentage of kids will get a college scholarship for sports, and far fewer still will play professional sports. Sam Snow, director of coaching education for US Youth Soccer, reiterated these facts to me when I interviewed him for an article I wrote a few years ago.

With these kind of stats, it makes you wonder if after all those years of effort, what would have happened if Marta or Josh might have wanted to . . . try something else? Do something different? Dabble in art, or take up juggling or . . . ?

I mean, consider the way you yourself as Mighty Parent approach your own activities. Perhaps you and your spouse sign up for some ballroom-dancing lessons—a six-week commitment. Or maybe you'll take a pottery class over the winter—for four weeks. Or you signed up

---

16. See www.ncys.org/.

for the gym, intending to go three times a week—but don't go any-where near that often, because you're "too busy."

Let's take it a step further. Consider your child's school responsi-bilities equal to your job or home responsibilities—fair enough? Now, imagine doing your job, and then adding three or four hours of driv-ing plus practicing to every weekday, with an intensive tournament on Saturdays and sometimes even on Sundays . . . and you're going to do this for thirteen years in a row, with no break.

Every day?

Thirteen years in a row?

With no break?

The same darn thing?

With no room for anything else?

Oh, and one other thing— you're not going to do this because you're particularly fantastic at it, or even because you like it all that much, but because "everybody does this." It's something you started when you were very young—and somebody forgot to tell you that you had the option to quit.

PARENTS ASK

When my seven-year-old daughter comes home from school, she's absorbed so much energy! The thing is, when I try to get her to clear and settle, I end up absorbing it, too. Ideas?

Bedtime is a great time to do energy clearing for young kids, and while you're at it, you can clear yourself, too. Play some trance or New Age music, and rub her back to help her relax. Ask her to locate all the unwanted energies (such as energies from other people) that she's gathered during the day, and place them in a large, imagined box. You can also scan her body and clear any energies you find. Then, scan your own body and clear your energies the same way. Fill the box up—and send it hur-tling into space! Ahhh.

Seems kinda crazy, doesn't it?

The other part of the overscheduling insanity is that it affects the whole family. If it's soccer, that means that you'll acquire foldup chairs and ice chests on wheels and Gore-Tex jackets and a big Suburban that can drive half a team up and down the highways all weekend long. If it's music or dance or the arts, you'll find yourself practically camping out at studios and performance halls, with a packet of safety pins and hair bands always at the ready.

And, after a few seasons with the same folks, a sort of tribal mentality starts to take over—which leads to lots of pressure to stay on the team. Over time, *group thought* takes over, as if "our team" and "our tournament" were the most important thing in the world.

As we all know, group thought does not support individual preferences and needs. And it may not be in the best interest of your child, or your family.

Busyness and the ego

When you get very busy, regardless of what the activity is, your schedule gets tight. You may find yourself driving from one end of town to the other on a daily basis. You may find yourself with seconds to spare between activities—and shouting, "Hurry, hurry, hurry!" as your kids gather their gear and stumble toward the next event.

One popular online calendaring system is built on this principle—that we're so busy as families, we need help organizing our lives. The system, Cozi, will actually call you on your cell phone, to tell you where you're supposed to be on any given day![17]

The problem is, when we get very busy, we lose sight of what's important and what's not. We become so confused by all the "must dos" that we can't differentiate a "must do" from a "could do" or an "it's on my schedule, but I don't really know why."

The other problem is—*being busy makes us feel like rock stars*. It puffs us up to have a full schedule—it makes us feel important, like

---

17. See the Cozi website, at www.cozi.com.

we're getting somewhere. Of course, we're not really getting anywhere at all—there is no place to "get." But busyness makes us feel this way, and this is a dangerous feeling to have. It clouds what is real and what is important.

It's very easy to get addicted to the *rush* of being busy.

What is rush?

Rush is the opposite of flow.

Addicted to *rush*

Now, there are a lot of addictions—alcohol, drugs, food, shopping, sex, gambling, computer, work. The list is extensive. It's very likely that you have an addiction to something yourself—something that gives you a thrill when you do it, and then drops you down flat after you're done. You might not identify it as an addiction if it's not on the A-list: alcohol, drugs, gambling, or whatever stereotypical ideas you have of addictions. But you probably have something you're addicted to, nonetheless. It's a rare person who doesn't.

The thing is: *being busy* is also an addiction. The rush and the thrill (the pleasurable part) is the way we feel puffed up, important, and fulfilled when we make it through a tough schedule—almost heroic, really. Except instead of slaying dragons, we are slaying time. We also get pleasure from the adrenaline surges that we experience, as we try make it from one activity to the next.

In sports, parents and kids and coaches get hooked on the adrenaline rush that comes from competition. It's tribal, feudal, and based on ancient ideas of violence—like the gladiators at the Colosseum. Sports bring up ancient, base emotions for most of us—the idea that we can "win," when of course we cannot really "win," ever, no matter what we do in our lives. "Winning" is a concept that does not exist in soul growth. However, when you are on the sidelines screaming for your team, it's easy to forget that.

It's not just sports. Anyone who keeps a busy schedule gets a rush from the constant momentum that is required to keep that schedule.

The rush from being always on, always busy, so busy you cannot even remember where you are supposed to be on a given day!

When you are this busy, you have no time to think.

When you have no time to consider, mull, or reflect, you have no time for a spiritual life. You have no time for soul growth. You have no time in which to become a conscious human being.

This is true for adults, and this is true for children.

Thus, if you are considering putting your kid in sports, or music, or any other activity that tends to take over a family's schedule, or if you are considering adding activities to your family's already full schedule—consider how busy you already are.

It is possible to live a beautiful, connected, slower-paced life without sports or extracurricular activities, in which you and your kids have time to do things like talk, cook, and eat together, go to the park, ride bikes, shoot hoops, and walk the dog.

Having a schedule with less in it often means a great deal more. For intuitive or spiritually gifted children, it may be what saves them—it's hard enough going to school every day. Being able to come home, chill out, have a little face time with siblings and parents, and a little privacy for thinking their own thoughts and connecting to the Divine in their own way—these are the minutes that make up a life, that make us who we really are, and that allow us to grow as conscious human beings.

I call this kind of time *downtime*.

What does downtime look like?

Downtime looks like nothing. Downtime looks like goofing off. Downtime looks like sitting on the sofa backwards, with your head on the floor and your feet on the back of the sofa, and hanging there until (a) your mom comes in and tells you to get your feet off the sofa, or (b) your head turns red as a tomato from blood flow.

What else does downtime look like? Your child sitting on the floor playing with the dog for thirty minutes, then hopping up to get himself a glass of juice and some cookies, then heading outside to look at the sky for another half hour.

Nothing is accomplished. Nothing is done. Nothing happens. No entertainment is provided—no book, movie, TV, music, computer game, Internet. Downtime is what it means to be actually living, actually being in one's body on this planet on this day.

It looks like nothing.

For the intuitive or spiritually gifted child, it is everything.

Downtime used to be called *daydreaming*. What a beautiful, evocative word! In terms of the psychic mind, dreaming is very important: our night dreams often bring messages that provide clear instruction. When we daydream, it's very similar to night dreaming—we're just more conscious. The mind floats, it loosens up, and we're able to receive the same kinds of messages and information.

In fact, daydreaming is so closely aligned to psychic trance, it can provide the same psychic payoff—the only difference is that instead of consciously entering the trance state, you simply head into it naturally because you're so relaxed. For example, looking at the clouds for a few minutes, only to shift your gaze twenty minutes later, without recollecting how long you've been looking at the clouds. You've been fully awake the whole time; you've just been "somewhere else."

That other place is somewhere in the layers of the psychic and spiritual realms.

By doing nothing, by relaxing completely (and again, not through meditation, not through psychic trance, but simply because you are doing nothing), you allow the mind to float—and when the mind floats, it enters a state that is perfectly conducive to receiving psychic or spiritual information.

In any case, the more you can provide your child opportunities to be in situations where his mind is allowed to float and wander, *the more he will naturally enter the psychic and spiritual realm.* Downtime does this for children, without effort or intent. It just happens.

This can be very hard for parents who have been addicted to the rush of being busy. It can also be hard for kids who aren't used to letting their mind float, or who literally haven't had the time to do this for months or even years.

I know it's important for me to be grounded as a parent of a Divine child. Any suggestions?

Keeping regular schedules, habits, and routines is crucial for grounding. Yet, at the same time, too much grounding makes us dull. Make sure you let your own spirit fly free when you're not on "kid duty." Try to schedule in at least an hour a day (yes, really!) when you have time to just let yourself daydream, meditate, bliss out, relax, laugh, or be silly. As souls, we are responsible for our children—but we are also responsible for regularly connecting our own selves with the Divine.

Why we resist downtime

Why have we been led like lemmings over the cliff of overscheduling? Why have we allowed ourselves to believe that a child who doesn't attend a camp, or program, or particular school, or a child who doesn't participate in this or that activity, is somehow a child who is going to "fail"?

And, by "failure," I mean dire stuff: they'll never go to college, never get a job, never get married, never have kids—might as well clear out the spare room right now, since they're going to be living at home until they're forty years old!

Of course this is not true.

Somehow, the idea of the enriched child has spiraled into something that we didn't anticipate. Instead of raising kids who are whole and healthy and conscious, we're raising kids who are indulged, pampered, chauffeured, and treated as though they can't function on their own. Yes, we want to give our kids every advantage that we never had. But lately, it's looking like we've gotten carried away.

Somehow, it all spiraled out of control, until we've forgotten what it's like to hang out with our kids in any other way besides sitting on the sidelines in a fold-up chair, yelling at them to score.

Re-creating downtime

If you're a parent who has been addicted to the rush of busyness, it's probably time to consider a new family schedule.

One of the reasons downtime gets such a bad rap is that what kids normally do when they don't have an activity planned is to go into default: TV, video games, computer.

That is not quality downtime.

Or . . . is it?

I unnerves me to write this, but it's important to be fair. When I was a parenting journalist, I was assigned a magazine story about TV and video games, and how they were detrimental to kids' learning abilities.

Great! I thought, excited to report on my pet peeve—kids glued to electronica.

However, what my research actually revealed was that, in fact, TV watching *didn't have any effect* on kids' grades or ability to concentrate! Furthermore, watching educational programs actually *boosted* kids' academic success!

Huh? What? Really?

Yet when researchers from University of Chicago's Graduate School of Business analyzed current standardized test scores of 350,000 kids who watched TV, the results were even more surprising.

In a nutshell, the kids who watched more TV did *better* at standardized tests than those who didn't![18]

As I dug deeper into the research, I discovered that some creative gaming systems actually teach kids *how to think in ways that are useful to them* in our current society.

Huh? What? Really?

---

18. Gentzkow and Shapiro, "Preschool Television Viewing and Adolescent Test Scores: Historical Evidence from the Coleman Study," 279–323.

In fact, a recent report by the Pew Research Center's Internet & American Life Project notes that kids' gaming experiences "are rich and varied, with a significant amount of social interaction and potential for civic engagement."[19]

Wow!

Now, TV watching and computer-game playing are not the same as downtime. They don't promote a free-floating, daydreaming mind that allows kids to effortlessly enter the psychic realm. But, according to experts I talked to, they also weren't the axes of evil I suspected.

I still don't allow my kids to watch much TV—but I'm fine with educational PBS shows at any time. I limit computer time (yes, even with the Pew report's findings), because my kids tend to sit there e-mailing their friends along the lines of *What R U doing? Hanging out, Me 2, LOL,* and so forth. However, I don't fret the way I used to over brain rot from electronica.

Instead, I make it a point to build in downtime. Our schedules are slow compared to most families we know. And I'll often direct downtime by saying things like "It's time for you to go outside" or "It's time for some quiet time in your room." When I first started this practice, the kids would get confused and not know how to entertain themselves. Now, they head outside or to their rooms, eager for some private time. They've discovered that wandering amongst the trees is a nice way to spend a free hour. So is lying on your bed in your room, with your favorite stuffed animals around you, and nothing in particular in the world to do but "be."

Exercises

Here are some ways to create the habits of Divine time for you and your family:

1. If your child seems cranky, try putting him to bed an hour earlier every night. If you've let your teens get away with no set bedtime, tell them "all electronica off" at 10:00 p.m. This means

---

19. Lenhart et al., "Teens, Video Games and Civics."

cell phones, computers, movies, all of it. This alone may help them get to sleep earlier.

2. Put on music in the background. No, not Miley Cyrus or whatever's on the radio—they already get their fill of that. Instead, play New Age music, classical, world—anything to perk up their ears and let their bodies hear a new kind of rhythm and melody. It doesn't have to be loud or constant—but rather provide new ways for them to listen.

3. Is your young Divine child struggling with her sports team? Does she come home from practice miserable and stressed out? Are the games starting to run your family's life? Consider dropping this activity. Yes, that's right, just drop it. If your child is older, there may be a pressure to finish out the season, and you can talk that over with him. If he's young, simply don't sign up next time, or even take him out this time.

4. Limit activities. One or two a week is about right for Divine kids in elementary school—and, yes, this will probably be much less than other kids. Divine kids need more downtime, and because they're kids, they can't create it themselves. If you as the parent can't build downtime in for your child, no one else will.

5. Schedule a Saturday with nothing on the schedule. That's right—no games, no play dates, no outings. Yes, it will feel weird at first. When the kids finally get around to asking, "What are we doing today?" tell them, "Nothing." Cook lunch. Cook dinner. Watch a movie or, even better, play a board game. You will be amazed at how you and your family feel at the end of a simple, do-nothing day like this. Does it sound like goofing off or doing nothing? Remember, that's a good thing.

twenty

Divine Space

In the way of keeping a house holy, there are many ways. There is the way of intent, in which there is respect for the home and its inhabitants. There are ways of keeping live things in the home, for the energy they bring. There are ways of keeping crystals for these vibratory powers; this is not understood by you yet, but we understand this. There are ways of reducing the droning vibration of electronica. There are ways of increasing interaction with nature: earth, water, clear air.

The more you live simply, the more you live with less and with items that are meaningful to you or that are from nature, the more serene you may keep your mind and your body. It is important to practice acts of sacred devotion. It important to be taught the acts of devotion and intent, through physical objects. —The Messages

------

Raising vibration in your home

In the early days when humankind was emerging, we lived in caves if we could find them, made crude shelters if we couldn't. Later, we made nicer shelters out of wood, adobe, or local materials. We lived communally for the most part—we were tribal, because the nuclear family was too small to survive.

Nowadays, where we live, and who we live with, has changed. For starters, the two-parent family has dramatically shifted: in the United States, 38 percent of kids are born to single mothers, a figure that's doubled in recent years. Moreover, 68 percent of children live with two married parents, 23 percent with their mothers only, 3 percent with their fathers only, 3 percent with two unmarried parents, and 4 percent with neither parent, according to the Forum on Child and Family Statistics. In fact, many of us live in blended families—one in three Americans is now a stepparent, stepchild, or stepsibling, according to recent statistical reports.[20]

Most of us live quasi-communally, too, in apartments, townhouses, or houses built close to each other. It's not the same as sharing a bathroom, but we're still close enough to hear, see, and know what our neighbors are doing. In fact, the idea of living in a separate house on a big lot may have passed for all but the wealthiest—it's not financially or environmentally feasible for most of us.

All if these trends mean that our kids will live in spaces and places that have extensive exposure to other people, not all of whom are family members. This makes it crucial that they're able to come home to a place that is a haven from the world.

A room of one's own

If your child can have a room of her own, this is lovely. It's not as important in the early years, when it can be comforting to bunk together. But when your child's personality begins to unfurl around the age of ten, and distinctive tastes and preferences emerge, the luxury of having a room of one's own in which to retreat, create, consider, and reflect can be intensely useful for your child.

If we are always around others, we can find it hard to pull our own energy back and to understand who we really are. If we are always entangled with the energy of others, we tend to morph into group thought or group energy that makes it harder for us to grow as individual souls.

Yes, we are all One. But we are also each unique. And when we orbit around each other all day long without a break to connect with

---

20. See "America's Children in Brief: Key National Indicators of Well-Being, 2009," Forum on Child and Family Statistics, www.childstats.gov.

PARENTS ASK

How can I help ground my child?

Grounding happens in many ways—creating room for sacred space is one of them. Help your child find a special place she can go to recharge; this could be room in the house where she won't be disturbed, or a private spot in the backyard. Let her know she can always go there for respite and comfort. If she likes the idea of creating a sacred space in her room, help her use photos of relatives and ancestors, trips, memories, and more. Remembering a connection to both past and future grounds your child by helping her recall who she is related to, where she has been already, and how she belongs in this life.

our own energy, we very quickly meld into the blobbing energy of a group collective.

Recently, I attended the International New Age Trade Show in Denver. That trip reminded me how easy it is to become immersed into the collective soul. First, there's travel, and if you've been in an airport or on an airplane lately, you know how much shoulder-rubbing is involved. As a psychic, it's hard deal with all this energy—I can read most people pretty much immediately, and frankly I don't want to! I mean, talk about TMI—too much information!

At the show itself, I was also surrounded by people—meeting, greeting, talking, eating, visiting. It was a great way to make contacts, but also a very rich energy exchange. I slept, or attempted to sleep, in a hotel room, which is basically a small box stacked on top of and to the sides of hundreds of other boxes. Again, as a psychic, I try not to think whose head was lying less than a foot from mine (in the next hotel unit) as I slept fitfully. Even the energy of whomever had stayed in the room before me swirled—thick, distracting, and frankly not that enjoyable.

It was all a buzz—and buzz is fun, lots of the time! But by the third day of the conference, I wasn't "myself" anymore; I'd morphed or merged into the group, and my own energy had become so expanded, it was as if I couldn't find myself anymore.

In some ways, this was great. As my energy expanded (some people might call this aura), my heart became filled with an extraordinary tenderness and compassion for everyone I met, saw, or noticed. Once I'd hooked into this energy of One, my ego self dropped away. This buzz continued so strongly that I didn't even try to stop it.

It wasn't until two days after I got home, when I finally had some hours alone, that I was able to gather my energy back from all the places I'd been and people I'd been with, and to reestablish myself as myself, instead of part of the collective.

I did this energy work by heading to my *sacred space*. It's not really a room—just my little sofa where I receive my channeled writing. On this sofa, with the house empty of everyone for an hour or two, I'm able to deeply connect to the Divine—to receive guidance, be refreshed by direct connection, and exist with myself as a soul in the Universe.

Creating sacred space in your home

In other areas of our house, I've created small sacred spaces—little altars you might call them, except they don't especially look like altars; they look like regular parts of a quirky house. For example, I have a small area in which I hold my intent for financial stability, and this contains a small ceramic jar filled with cash. (Don't bother coming to get it—the dollar amount isn't very high!) However, the intent of this jar keeps me focused on my personal goals of living with no financial worries. It's funny, because although I was skeptical of this manifesting, it worked: the day I started the jar, I was literally broke. I tucked some money in with the intent that it would grow—and to my surprise it has! I use money from this jar to spend on household items, and it continually replenishes. It reminds me of those old Grimm's fairy tales that I used to read as a kid, about the table that you could set out and it would always fill with food, or the goblet that would always fill with refreshing cider! The Bible also talks about "my cup runneth over" as another example of such abundance.

When you create a space in your home with intent, such as for financial stability, you'll be surprised and pleased to see that it works. How does it work? The same way everything else does in this world— with energy.

Other uses of "altared" spaces

Having a feng shui jar to attract money is one thing. But you can also attract other blessings into your home by creating sacred space.

Churches and temples used to hold this space for us, as places where a person could come and spend time with God. Even if other people were in the building at the same time, a mood of privacy was maintained. You could sit, pray, kneel, bow, meditate, or otherwise attend to your religious practice, and no one would bother you. Over the centuries, people started to think God *resided* in the building, and that going to church was the only way they could make a direct connection. Of course, this isn't true.

Nowadays, most folks don't flock to church in the same way they used to. However, rejecting religion does not mean rejecting God. Many people are deeply ready to find ways to create space to be with the Divine—and many prefer to create this space in their own homes.

Thus, the idea of the *sacred space*.

Why sacred space is important for kids

For a child, the concept of having personal sacred space is crucial. In many cultures, every home has an altar in which items are placed for symbolic worship, such as photos of ancestors, statuary of deities, fresh flowers, candles, incense, and items from nature.

In Catholic homes, for example, it's traditional to hang a rosary or a cross over each bed. It's also common to have an alcove or area in which there's a statue of a saint or Jesus, sometimes with a bench where a person may sit and have a quiet moment of reflection.

At Hindu and Sikh kirtan celebrations in which people spend hours in call-and-response singing, it's customary to decorate the stage as an altar, complete with fresh flowers, strewn petals, pictures of a beloved guru, and statuary of deities.

At workshops at retreat centers such as the Esalen Institute, participants often bring sacred items from home to display on a communal "altar" with others during their session—these items reflect their intention for this experience.

No matter what your sacred space looks like, one thing is true— holding space for Divine connection reminds us to connect frequently.

Modern-day sacred

Nowadays, spaces that hold the intent of the Divine can be very relaxed, so if you want to create sacred space in your home, be creative! Some folks enjoy using tables, desks, or bookshelves to display objects that are meaningful to them. An artist friend transforms tables in different rooms of her house into small altars by arranging them with artwork, found objects, prayer cards, rosaries, flowers—everything that is meaningful to her, and that reminds her to pause and connect with the Divine.

At my house, we have limited indoor space, so we focus on what's outside. We've created sacred places throughout our property, so that coming around the bend of a walkway or trail, you might happen upon a statue of a deity from any religion—all are given space here. Or, you might rest on a bench that faces a rock garden, or sit in a chair where the sound of wind chimes rings as plaintively as a church bell. These intentful outdoor spaces remind us that nature is a great way to connect with the Divine.

My children have their own ideas about what is sacred, and each is given the opportunity to create his or her own altared space. My son likes natural things—he loads up his dresser with what's impactful to him, including findings from the natural world. My youngest daughter has a small cabinet filled with things that are meaningful and sacred to her, ranging from traditional religious gifts from her First Communion to small deity figurines that she simply likes.

My oldest daughter holds space with photos and art—she creates amazing collages and displays of photos of the people she loves. This way of holding space reminds her that she loves and is loved.

As a family, we keep a giant smiling Buddha statue in the main room, not because we're Buddhists, but because this particular Buddha reminds us to laugh and to not take things so seriously. We use this space as a community altar, and it's often adorned to reflect what's going on in our lives at the moment—for my oldest daughter's graduation, for example, Buddha was the central spot for all things graduation: the cap, the cords, the flowers, the cards.

As you can see, creating sacred space doesn't have to be done in any particular way—all space is sacred. What's important is to create this space; this shows your intent to connect with the Divine in your everyday life.

Helping your child create a sacred space

There are two ways of helping your child create a sacred space. The first is simply to help him locate an area in your home where he can go when he needs to reflect or think things over. This might be his bedroom, or it might be a favorite nook or cranny where he can be private and still.

In most cases, your child will be drawn to his own particular spot. The key is to understand that when you come upon your child in this spot—in a particular chair, or by a certain tree—he's having some reflection time. Respect that he's having a moment of direct connection with the Divine, and give him the same space you would if you came across anyone in prayer or meditation.

We all need to regroup and rediscover who we are as individuals, especially when we spend much of our day immersed in the collective consciousness. Make sure you provide your child with options for privacy and alone time, so that he may do this.

PARENTS ASK

My daughter, who just turned nine, has been psychic since she was three, but now she doesn't want to use her abilities; she says her friends make fun of her.

Psychic abilities don't go away—once your child is open and awake (and it sounds like your daughter has been for many years), this will stay with her for life. Her decision to use her skills is up to her. Kids develop not just psychically, but also physically, emotionally, socially—and it's important to let each age and stage open fully.

If your child can't seem to find a spot, you can build in this time for stillness by starting his bedtime thirty minutes earlier. This gives him time to relax in his room, and encourages connection to the Divine.

The second way to help your child create sacred space is by helping her set up an altar. Again, it doesn't have to be an actual altar! A corner of a table or a bookshelf will do nicely. Simply let your child choose the space she likes, and then have her gather objects that help her to feel she is surrounded with God, love, compassion, and tenderness. Very young children will need help and will respond best to simple things: an angel, a photo of her parents, a favorite toy. Older kids and teens will have specific ideas of what is sacred to them, and you may find this surprising! Some ideas might be:

- Photos of loved ones or special places
- Artwork they enjoy or have created
- Any statuary that is meaningful to your child
- Small items he finds pleasant
- Something that is alive, such as a flower picked from the yard
- Something natural, such as stones or twigs

- Anything in writing, such as a list of your child's wishes and desires that he'd like to focus on

- Anything that is meaningful to your child, even if it's a toy (yes, this could be a stuffed animal or a prized Lego creation!)

Keep the energy moving

Once you've established altared or sacred space in your home—great! Now, does it stay that way for the next two years, gathering dust? Of course not. Altared space is a living, creative energy; it's meant to transform and change as you grow.

That means you'll want to change elements, spend time with and generally stay in tune with the intention you are creating. In your child's case, the altar should be a space that he enjoys rearranging and looking at. Transforming it weekly or monthly is fantastic, if he likes doing it.

The altared space represents your connection to the Divine and the energy of your current intentions. It's a way of symbolically showing the Divine what you would like to create, and what you would like to focus on. Changing this frequently is a way to remind yourself and the Universe that you are committed to working in the constantly swirling energy of Divine flow.

Exercises

Here are some ways you can work with your children to create Divine space in your home.

1. Create your own sacred space or altar in your own room, and let your kid know that this is something that is special to you.

2. Create sacred spaces in your home that are there for everyone to enjoy. This could be a tabletop in a main room, or a small altar in a private room, where people can go for some quiet time and reflection. Don't worry too much what objects to use—you will know when you begin the process. Ask family members to participate by adding their own objects, if they're interested.

3. Create a family intention box. If your kids are old enough, they can write their intentions, such as "I want to fight less with my sister" on a piece of paper, and put them in a dedicated box or jar. This is a private exercise, and they can do it anytime, without anyone knowing about it. When the box is full in a few months, you may enjoy looking at the intentions together, or you may simply empty the box and start fresh without reviewing them.

4. For very young children, create a space on a dresser or shelf in their room—something that's at waist or shoulder level, so they can easily see and rearrange what's there. Help fill this space with pictures of relatives, religious artifacts if that's appropriate, or anything that makes your child happy. This activity should be something that's fun and special for your child, with no pressure for an outcome.

5. For older children, simply suggest that they can create Divine space in their room—this can even be a bulletin board or wall. It's a private creation, and your child should be in charge of this space, without limitations from you. You may be surprised by what emerges!

twenty-one

Divine Ritual

There are times for doing, and there are times for recalling where you have been and what you have learned. Consider traveling for great distances across deserts and mountains, moving forward with every step. After many days, you pull out your map. At this time, it becomes clear where you have come from, and what you have experienced. This may be astounding to you.

Moving with the seasons, doing some things in the same way at the same time, as a koan, prayer, meditation—this allows you to enjoy the sweetness of them. The pleasure is not in doing the old thing. The pleasure is in doing the old thing as a new person. The pleasure is in understanding how your soul has grown.—The Messages

————

We arrange the tinsel on the tree, strand by painstaking strand. This is my father's tradition, because it was his family's tradition, because when he was growing up, tinsel with all its luminous sparkle was miraculous. In those days, tinsel was as amazing as crystalline icicles or the dazzlement of snowflakes; with tinsel, you might create a winter wonderland in your own living room.

However . . . to create this effect, the tinsel must be put on properly, my father insists. One long, slippery strand at a time.

My brother and I work doggedly, and for a while it's fun. Tinsel is bright! Tinsel is silvery! But after thirty minutes of fastidious icicle arranging, we're ready to wrest gobs of the slippery stuff and mount it

right on the branches. "That's not how it's done," my father says quietly, fully absorbed in his ritual.

I look over and see he's in some kind of metallic trance—mesmerized, transfixed, lost in a world of other Christmases he spent as a boy in Chicago with his father, mother, sister. Their tree. Those times. The tinsel, I realize, is more than just another kind of ornament. It holds meaning— at least for my father.

Our tinsel struggles amuse my mother, who strung strands of popcorn and cranberries for the cold Midwestern Christmases of her childhood. It's not that she's against tinsel—she just doesn't have any frame of reference. And yet she'll get that same dreamy look in her eyes as we sit at the kitchen table, my brother and I armed with embroidery needles and sturdy thread, stringing our popcorn-and-cranberry strands "for the birds," she explains. "So they won't go hungry this winter."

Ritual is different for every family

In my house, we don't do tinsel, we don't do popcorn strands—but we do have a Christmas ritual.

Where we live in Oregon is Christmas-tree country, and the freshest trees you can find grow literally right next door—and what an easy venture it is to slog through mud and more mud, and a little more mud, until you've found the perfect tree, then kneel down (in mud), and saw said tree and toss it in your truck! However . . . there are also sap-fresh trees at the neighborhood grocery store lot. My thought process is transparent—why not grab a tree quick while running in for bread and lettuce?

Thus, cutting our own tree is not our ritual.

Our ritual is dancing.

First, we string the lights and hang the ornaments—same as millions of other folks do, and the youngest child puts the star on top. We drink champagne (sparkling apple cider for the kids). And then, when the lights are twinkling just right and the gleam is misty sweet as sugar plums, we put on a stack of holiday CDs that we've had forever—blues and jazz and rock and Chipmunks. And we dance.

I can't remember when this Yuletide dancing began, but one year the kids just started waltzing around the room—and suddenly it became our tradition. We dance in twos, and sometimes in crazy threes and fours, making big, looping passes around the living room. We get silly. We laugh. After a while, we sit quietly on the sofa and look at the dazzling tree. It is our ritual.

Doing things in the same way every year brings us to a place in which we can look back and remember: oh, this is what we were doing last year! Oh, do you remember the year the tree fell over? Tell me again about this ornament! Remind me again how we made that paper star—the one glued out of an old Toblerone box and yellow construction paper?

Many rituals such as holiday celebrations, birthdays, and anniversaries come around just once a year. This gives us time to reflect and to consider where we have been in the last twelve months, and where we are headed. It lets us see how things have changed—by noticing that,

PARENTS ASK

I love the idea of a prayer practice for our family. I'm Christian, but my husband is agnostic, and my teens aren't interested. What should I do?

Helping your family to connect with the Divine and each other can be done in so many ways; prayer is just one of them. Whenever your family eats together (and I hope this is often), first put your own intention into creating a mood that reflects gratitude—you're happy to be together, you're grateful for your family. You might try to do something symbolic (but not religious), such as lighting a candle at the table. Or, ask each person to go around the table, saying a word or two about what they're grateful for that day. If this is all too much, use humor! Bumping knuckles or having a family "high five" before you dive into the food is also Divine ritual!

last year, my youngest daughter had to be lifted up to put the star on top of the tree; this year, she grabbed a step stool and popped it on by herself.

Ritual is also important as a comforting constant in a life that is neither constant nor controllable.

Ritual as spiritual practice

Ritual is an essential part of spiritual practice—which is why when folks attend church, temple, or other worship services, *the same things happen at the same time in the same way.*

For example, if you're a kid whose family attends a Catholic church, you know the drill: go in, sit down, pray, stand, kneel, stand, repeat a few times, watch your buddy across the aisle and try not to laugh when he makes faces at you, notice the altar boy is wearing dirty tennis shoes under his pristine white robe, think deep thoughts while receiving Communion and attempting to make your "host" wafer last until you get back in your pew, and wondering why anyone would choose to drink wine because it is disgusting, hold hands, say the Our Father, say the Creed, listen to music, stare at the stained-glass windows, and pretend to file out slowly even though you're trying to scramble to get to the head of the donut line before your buddy gets there first.

That's church. Every Sunday. It's a ritual, and there's a rhythm to what's happening: a lovely, comforting predictability, a sequence of events that are intended to offer meaning and consistency—again, so different from this unpredictable life.

Judeo-Christians aren't the only ones who use ritual. For example, if you have a private meditation practice, you also use ritual—you go into a certain room, sit quietly, meditate for a certain amount of time. That's your ritual. Doing the same thing, the same way, for purposes of spiritual enlightenment.

If you're a person who doesn't have a regular spiritual practice, you might keep rituals another way. For example, your Sunday morning may be to cook pancakes for the kids or take them to breakfast at the Waffle Wagon, or to sleep late and spend the morning reading the paper in your pajamas.

Again, ritual. Any practice that helps ground us in a world filled with change, and that reminds us, yearly or weekly or daily, that there are things we can count on even when we don't know what will happen next.

How ritual helps kids

For children, ritual is fantastic! They're already creatures of habit— a predictable routine makes them feel comfortable and gives them a feeling of security. They're so into ritual that even daily habits are key: the snack-after-school ritual, the teeth-brushing-before-bed ritual. However, it's important to know that in terms of psychic development and spiritual growth, ritual is only useful if it's *spiritually based.*

In other words, ritual is great for kids in terms of habit and schedule. But in order to assist or expand their spiritual development, *it must be spiritual in nature.*

For example: if you have a bedtime ritual with your child that includes watching a *Dora the Explorer* video, brushing teeth, and a soothing back rub, this is a ritual—but it's not a ritual that allows spiritual expression for your child.

Whereas, if you have a bedtime ritual with your child that includes watching a *Dora the Explorer* video, brushing teeth, a soothing back rub, and then some quiet time sitting on the bed, during which you guide your child through some end-of-day energy gathering or releasing tasks, or listen to him pray or sit silently in meditation together— this is ritual that creates opportunity for spiritual expansion.

The rituals you create that are based in spiritual practice—whether praying, meditating, working with energy, or encouraging your child to have a direct connection to the Divine—are the rituals that will *change your child's life.*

Again: if your morning ritual is getting up; getting your child up, dressed, and eating cereal; and then bombing around the house like a kamikaze on speed looking for your child's missing shoe before you jump in the car and drive him to school, this is your morning routine. But if you get up fifteen minutes earlier, and spend a few minutes praying or meditating with your child or helping him rearrange his altared space for the day, and *then* do the whole dress/cereal/kamikaze shoe/drive thing, this is sacred ritual.

It's very simple to create rituals that provide this kind of Divine nourishment for your child. My suggestion is to build in spirituality all day—and notice what works or what's overload.

Adults have the ability to create spiritual practice at any time during their day. But kids need reminding, and a little nudge goes a long way. "Put down that Game Boy and meditate!" is not going to be very appealing. So, when you stumble upon something that works, use it!

Your kid likes to look at his altared space every morning? Fantastic. He likes to head out to the big oak tree every afternoon after school, and spend some time alone? Awesome. He likes to spend a few minutes by himself at bedtime, talking to God? Wonderful. Even these small practices in which your child routinely, regularly practices direct connection with the Divine can make a big difference for your child.

Remember, ritual means something you can count on—and when your child learns that there is enough time and space in the day to have direct connection frequently, this will be immensely comforting.

Make room for flow

Sometimes, our kids tell us what they need. For example, a few weeks ago I asked my daughter if she prayed at bedtime, and she said, "No." Now, this was shocking to me, seeing as how I spend much of my day in incessant prayer—"Thank you God," "Help me God," and so forth. But after listening to her more closely, I found that her idea of prayer had gotten off kilter in the past month.

Apparently, her friend had just gotten a brand-new Bible (from Costco, no less) that was kid-friendly—colorful, with lots of pictures and big type. My daughter loved it. In fact, she loved it so much she now felt she needed *that exact same Bible* to pray!

I assured her that the Divine was quite happy to listen to the longings and hopes of her own heart, no Costco kids' Bible required, and that any words or thoughts she wanted to use were just fine.

"Like regular talking?" she said.

"That's a great way."

"Like thinking in my head?" she asked.

"Absolutely."

I talked her through one, as an example: "Dear God, please help me get along better with my brother," then left her to it. It's her direct connection, not mine.

"I didn't know I could talk to God by myself," she noted, and my heart sank in confusion—after all this focus, you'd think she'd have that one down pat. But with kids, repetition, reinformation, and, yes, ritual is everything. Now, we make time for simple prayers—in words or thought—before bed. I don't ask her what she prays; I just make sure she has time to do it. The rest is up to her and the Divine. And if I have learned one thing over these years, it's this—if the Divine has an opening, that opening will be taken!

Rituals make us realize

Rituals are also ways of helping your child understand how time moves on Earth. Of course, time is merely energy—there's really no future, no past. It's all Now, and there are a bazillion other Nows occurring concurrently at this very moment.

This is how the Universe works.

But the other, also concurrent reality is that here on Earth, life is measured quite predictably in minutes, hours, days, weeks, years. It's our way of staying organized (and making sure we get to the orthodontist appointment on time).

When we're living in this kind of Earth time, rituals are especially important—they help us make sense of the time that has passed. They help us understand how we're growing and changing. They help us celebrate what we've accomplished or let us review when we've missed the mark. They release us so we can go forward.

For example, when my oldest daughter graduated from high school, I had trouble accepting that it was really happening. During the graduation ceremony, I kept thinking, *I haven't had enough time with her.* But of course, I had.

When your children are still in diapers and drinking from sippy cups, it feels like they'll be little forever. Elementary school kids seem to exist in that suspended state forever. But once you hit the teen years, you realize that you see your child very little indeed—with school, activities, driver's license, and job, your child is gone more than she is home.

This is normal.

Heart-wrenchingly painful, but normal.

In the case of my daughter's graduation, it was time for me to face reality: she'd be leaving home at the end of summer.

What to do?

Ritualize, of course. This is why these celebrations—such as baptisms, birthday parties, bar mitzvahs, graduations, weddings—are so important. They help us make sense of what we have experienced.

PARENTS ASK

Our family consists of my kids and my husband's kids, plus two sets of grandparents on both sides (both our parents are divorced). Any ideas for the holidays?

In blended families, those "we've done it this way for three generations" rituals can't usually last. Remember that Divine kids are sensitive, and what's most important is not what happens— it's how you feel. That said, let go of the "must dos." Enjoy the small moments, and don't worry about repeating history every year. Create new traditions that are simple and that provide for family connection. Remember: the purpose of Divine ritual is to help you see where you've been, and where you're going in this life—not to cause stress and angst.

A final word to parents

By the time you've reached this chapter, you've learned new ways to help your child in his psychic development and spiritual growth. You've got some tricks and techniques under your belt—and you've probably experienced some awakening and "opening" yourself.

This is marvelous.

It's a good time to check back with that person you were before you began reading this book, and see how far you've really come.

Your child is Divine, as are you. I don't care how many mistakes you've made as a parent or as a person; I don't care that your child just knocked over a whole carton of orange juice onto the kitchen floor, or wore her muddy cleats in the house, or secretly slugged her brother and then told you he hit her.

You're still Divine. Both you and your child.

We are here for soul growth.

We are here to move forward with our soul lessons.

We are here to experience and feel.

And we are here to love.

That's all.

Yes, your children are blessed with special psychic and spiritual abilities, and the generations to come will be even more blessed. This is the nature of how we are evolving as humans. Yet our path, our journey, our purpose remains the same—to live on this earth with our hearts opening to each other in compassion and love.

In a very short time, your child will be grown. Whether your child is three right now or thirteen, this is true. You've heard the wisdom from the mouths of old ladies in the grocery line: "It goes so quick," or "Before you know it they're all grown up," or "Enjoy them while you can," and so forth. This is true. One moment you have babies, then toddlers, then school-age kids. Each stage slips imperceptibly into the next—until your children are no longer children at all.

For this reason, it is important to appreciate your child fully, the way you would enjoy the blooming of an exquisite flower that will only unfurl once. Tend it. Savor it. Be in awe.

As a parent, you have been given the daunting task of teaching your child how to live as a whole, human being on this earth, deeply connected to the Divine.

Funny how the Universe works.

Because in the process of teaching your children, you'll find you've also learned these lessons as well.

Exercises

Here are some ways you can create Divine ritual for your family:

1. Family rituals hold energy, because they involve many generations over time. Creating ritual may be about doing the same thing you did last year, but what's more important is to create experiences that satisfy the deeper nature of your child's Divine being. For example, at Halloween it's not about the costume or candy—what is really remembered is the thrill of walking around your neighborhood at night. At Thanksgiving, most kids don't care about the turkey—but they will remember how fun it was to help grandma roll pie crust. At Christmas, Santa is great, but what's really fun is having the time off together, and a series of rituals (getting the tree, baking cookies, and so on). Keep looking to the core of the holiday, and choose to put your intention as a parent to where the real stuff is: Connection. Remembrance. Gratitude.

2. Public ritual can be rife with fancy clothes that don't fit well or feel good, and lots of pressure to "do things a certain way." As a parent, keep your sense of humor. If your child is the only one at kindergarten graduation to refuse to wear his cap—so be it. Keep your sense of humor! Appreciate your Divine child and his unique approach to life.

3. Create personal, private ritual with your child—take him out to lunch one Sunday a month, even if he's little. Or schedule in time for a walk at a certain park, an afternoon in the city, a movie matinee. It's your time. Your ritual. And it's a way of celebrating your connection to your child.

4. As a parent, support yourself with rituals you enjoy. If you like to go to Midnight Mass every year, do it. If you can't wait to gather chestnuts every fall, don't miss out. If your idea of a perfect Sunday morning is taking a walk in the woods, do it. If you love planting bulbs every spring, or visiting your ancestors' gravesite every summer, or taking a trip to see the fall leaves turn every year—do so. If your family members want to come, great. If not—do it for yourself, anyway. Take part. Participate. Enjoy. These wild, mystic moments in life are the sweet rituals that let us connect to the Divine every day, and they are too beautiful to ever be missed.

part five

the messages

The first time I received channeled writing, I thought it was a fluke, a blip, an oddity—something that wouldn't happen again. Little did I know that channeled writing would become my life's work—and that once I'd agreed to be "scribe" for the Divine, the Divine would have a great deal to say.

It started out simply enough. My first experience with channeled writing was in 2004, when I received a small batch of about twenty messages, which I called *The Truths*. They were fairly short in length, somewhat poetic or literary in style, and I received them from a spirit guide named Hajam—a slight, older, brown-skinned Indian or Asian man who appeared to wear something like shorts and a drapey shirt. He was humorous, brash, and very patient with me. This was my first experience with channeled writing, and it was unnerving! I stopped the practice fairly quickly, because it worried me to do something so powerful with so little understanding.

Four years later, in 2008, I was directed to receive *The 33 Lessons*, an intensive experience of channeled writing that included some of the most breathtaking spiritual teachings I've ever read. The process of receiving them affected me deeply, and during the months I scribed them, I opened fully as a psychic.

That said, this also unnerved me! After I had channeled *The 33 Lessons*, I was certain my task was done. I stopped channeled writing—and was ready to get on with a more "regular" life.

But once again, the Divine had other plans.

Now, I receive via channeled writing regularly, from two tall, luminous beings named Ashkar and Ragnar—both as guidance for myself and my clients, and as spiritual teachings "meant for the world." As I mentioned before, some people have suggested these guides are Nordics—a type of ascended being from another realm. I really don't know. In any case, I asked these guides what they would like to say about these new children we find being born into our midst, these

Divine kids with unique psychic and spiritual gifts. Here's what they said, in the order that I received it:

We say: children are tender shoots. This is the most important message you can impart. Children are tender, and when they are young they do not have protection from harsher elements. We do not mean spiritual or energetic elements—we mean in Earth life. They do not have protection from cruelty, from harsh environments, from evil. They do not have protection from commercialism, which may soon be dead in your country. They do not have protection from adults, because adults hold power and children have none.

Children will withdraw and conform if they are hurt in any way. And this is where the closure begins; children are born awake, but most cannot retain this because they do not have the skills and support to understand how to do this. By training them with specific practices, you will allow some to remain awake and open, instead of experiencing closure.

Some children are born so awake and open, you term them psychically gifted, although we do not use this term. They are simply open. They have their windows open, as we have described to you before; they are awake, they are one with One.

These children may remain awake; yet in their Earth life they suffer. They suffer from not being understood; they suffer from feeling lonely; they suffer from feeling one with the One in their soul sense, but in their Earth body, their Earth life, they do not feel this connection. You must ground these children, and show them how to ground themselves, so they will be able to have whole and happy hearts.

Children learn soul lessons; they have soul growth, just as any other being. Because they are young and new, their first lessons are ideally gentle and easy. The child is raised to learn how things work on Earth; later, the other higher lessons come, such as how to hold a compassionate heart, how to love, how to hold connection with the Divine. When a child is born awake and can stay awake, they will be aware of these higher lessons sooner.

If a child's first lessons are too harsh, they will either become damaged or transformed. If a child is damaged, this may continue without respite until the next life. If a child is transformed, they may approach the understanding of saints and masters.

The spiritual and energetic mind may open very early; a child may manifest, a child may move matter, a child may heal. All the energy techniques available to the older, more developed human are available to the child. However, the child does not have the experience to understand what the purpose of these techniques are: Love. To exist as One with the Divine. To be infused in creating a positive and sustaining Earth life.

A child may be a tender shoot, but a child may be a terror. The lessons of compassion, self-interest vs. other interests, generosity; these are not innate in the child. A child may be trained in the methods of Earth behavior that are useful and that are soul-affirming. A child raised wild will not have a complete ethical code.

Children are innately ethical; they are innately perfect, yet because they are young, they are not able to do such things as share their belongings or hold compassion. Children are frequently cruel to each other. They have a limited sense of using their Earth hearts to help each other.

These, all psychic skills and spiritual tools, are nothing without teaching a child what it is to hold a compassionate heart. Without teaching a child that love is the primary response to all situations.

And with love, we say that the most difficult tasks become simple, all is manifested within the blink of an eye; the angriest voice becomes calm. Love is the first key to teach your child—the training of the awakened mind is second.

Again we caution you: do not create a monster. Create a whole child who will grow into a whole adult, a person who has both feet on the ground and has a compassionate Earth heart. It is only in this way, in the awakening of the spiritual mind, that a child will be of use to the human community. You will need these skills, quite certainly, in the times to come.

Each generation evolves, as we have told you. Each generation of children experiences new challenges and opportunities from your world. Position is also crucial. The position of a child in a third-world country is not the same as the position of a child in a first-world country, born to wealth and ease. Many children will die very quickly, or they may only live in the direst conditions. You all know this. You all know the state of your world.

Are these children of poverty psychic? It is not a question of using the term psychic; *it is a question of using the terms* aware, conscious, sentient, *an understanding of being one with the One. We would say: children who are starving do not have brains that can produce this kind of energy simply. Some can, yes. But in truth, most children who are starving are not in a state of awareness that is high enough to allow them to pursue practices that will lead to their brain's psychic development.*

As you know, practice is required; connection is required.

Children in first-world countries, who enjoy all material luxuries, may actually be hindered by the fact of their luxury. It deadens the mind. The body may be comfortable, but it may be fed to excess without nutrition. So as the body, also is the mind. Because you live in your bodies, you are directly affected.

In this way, psychic development may be hindered. Excess is not useful. A normal healthy body is all that is required. The fewer toxins, such as from foods, pollutants, disease, the more healthy and pure a child can be, and the simpler it will be for him to hear us.

Now (at this time), many children hear us. While you hear us continually and constantly, they do also—but they do not have the vocabulary to express what they hear. Furthermore, it would not occur to most children to mention what they have seen or heard, because it is natural. When you see a bird flying, you do not particularly remark to your neighbor, "There is a bird flying." Yes, it is a miracle, but because you see this so often, there is no need to mention it. In this way, children see miracles at all times, but they do not remark.

Children who are open see these layers always, as part of their existence; this is natural.

This is the same for children who are spiritual masters.

To become a spiritual master is to become a child.

You have asked if you can find a way to help children, to teach them how to develop their skills. We say: it is not matter of helping them to develop these skills, but to affirm that having these skills is valued by you, the parent. Children will do anything to please the parent. If you would like your child to enjoy the full nature of his or her psychic development, you may encourage and support these practices, and you may love your child.

The terms Indigo, Crystal, Rainbow. *We do not require these terms. Each generation of children, even the generation you were born into, is an evolution in consciousness. The human collective in first-world countries is evolving. Partly this is due to better state of the body. Partly this is to the fact that all beings, in a safe state, are able to evolve. For humans in war, in disease, in dire poverty—this evolution goes more slowly for this group as a whole. In order to elevate the human race, all humans must be elevated.*

We are all One. Surely this is known to you. We are all One, and if even one of the One is affected by war, terror, poverty, violence, all are violated and affected. This is the way of the Universe; this is the way of the One.

Every child is psychic. Children are sent into the world psychic then proceed to have a loss of remembering. This loss takes place in the early years, before a child is five. As much loss of remembering takes place in the transition from death to life as in the process of being born. This is similar to how there is a loss of remembering upon the moment of death, when a being makes transition.

However, the collective soul is always available. Much of the loss of remembering has been protection for children, in order that they may assimilate the culture of the family, place, and time in which they are born. However, not all children have the same loss of remembering, and these children are the ones who are open, or awake.

Other children, once they have assimilated the culture, once they are able to fit into the society in which they live, will be able to remember quite easily. Others will not remember until they are quite through with childhood, or in their teenage years.

These different levels of openness and awareness occur according to the child's characteristics and also to the plan for this child, what is his life's purpose.

To know oneself as a part of the Universe is the simplest task. To feel particulate as energy, to feel energy as self, to understand that there is no distinction between the Divine, the self, the other—this is effortless. In meditation, the journey is fast. Here is the place where the mind can rest. Here is the place where the Divine can present itself fully, as complete understanding.

Children are meditation, up to a certain age. Later, they learn separation from the culture. In pure meditation, you can return to the state of a child. In pure meditation, you may enter a state that is One Soul—the collective hum of All.

You may reach us in the place that is easiest to find us. We are not hard to find—we arrive immediately upon calling, we arrive even before calling. In a few breaths, simply by asking and with the longing of your heart, you will find us. We are here for you now; we are here at all times. Our windows are always open, waiting for you. When your window is open, we are able to converse with you in the ways that you can understand.

For children it is even easier. It simpler even than for you, for their windows are often open, usually open, mostly open. In one breath they have arrived to the place where they may connect with the Divine, and remember what it is they have already known forever.

Every child is psychic; every adult is psychic. This is a state you have always known, as human beings. These abilities are wired into your brains and bodies. This is how you are. However, you are only now, at this time, having the needs met that allow some of you (not all of you but many of you) to access these abilities. Health, leisure, literacy all allow this. Also, an acceptance of a new kind of spirituality that is not based on religious dogma. We do not say religion is incorrect. We say that it is limited, and those who seek God and the One in their personal, private state will soon discover that religion has no use for them.

Every child is psychic; this means that every child has the ability to have a direct connection to the Divine, in the ways that he or she can at each age. You, as a parent, can teach this to your child.

It is important to understand what a child's brain can do. In some ways, it is faster than yours. In other ways, it cannot manage certain concepts; these take time, as the child grows and develops.

In educating children, we do not care about tricks and techniques. We are interested in giving you information that will help children become more spiritual beings, one with the One. The clearest way is for you to model this. Teach your children, and yourself, to remember the Source from which you came, of which you are.

When you understand how to create a direct connection with the Divine, nothing else matters. When you, forever, are able to receive in this way, you know clearly that the Divine exists, and all your plans in life, all your insecurity, and the way your heart skips and leaps through your life, are settled. This direct connection grounds you. The Divine grounds you, and makes you better able to live your Earth life.

Many of you, and by this we mean you specifically and others, are not here all the time; you are literally in the other planes, and in other dimensions. We provide you with this information so you will understand why it is so hard to be in this world. This is not the only world you are in; this is not the only work you are doing.

For children, this is the same. This is one reason we have chosen you, for this particular task of children, because you see in your own children how they struggle with the pain of existence—living in fantasy, with emotion, caught up in fear, even though in their hearts they know clearly that all that matters is the Divine.

Once you hold this remembering in your mind, then you know it in your heart. As you know, this life on Earth is based on growth of the soul into its next life, and the growth of the Earth heart—the Earth heart becoming more and more open.

Children are actually quite self-centered and selfish and one of the most important things a parent can teach is compassion. Compassion for others, compassion for self, compassion for nature, ability to step away from the attractants and distractants and to become clear.

The techniques you will use for children are not the same as you would use for adults.

Children cannot sit in meditation; by this we mean American children. Even American adults cannot sit. You require a different means of connection to the Divine, which is where trance is so useful. This is a layer children can access.

Your minds are very busy; how could they not be?

There are so many attractants and distractants.

Consider the man who can easily walk on his own feet, but who discovers that he has a thorn in his toe. He begins to use a crutch. After a while the thorn is dissolved into his skin, and the pain is gone. Yet he continues to use the crutch. So too do you use your addictions, your binges, your illnesses, your overeating, your sexual excesses, your indulgence.

These are not required by you. You can walk as you are, without these.

As your understanding becomes more clear and you can see and hear the spirit more closely guiding you, these elements will drop away.

They are not required by you.

What is required is the Divine. The physical is a mirage.

The purpose of this book is to teach parents how they can help their children remember. The purpose of the book is to allow parents to remember.

Religion is not the answer. Direct connection the only way, for each and each and each to once again to return to the One.

We send helpful emissaries. We send angels, we send spirit guides, we send information, we send a constant bombardment and infusion of light and information to help you on the Earth become open and awake.

You have been asleep, most of you, for a very long time. Waking up from the dream of the Earth life is a hard task. Understanding that you have been dreaming, and then continuing to live the Earth life is even harder.

The way that your world has manifested itself—religion, corporation, tribe, cult, all ways apart from the Divine, all ways apart from the One. This is what will be required to strip down. Your children see this with clear eyes.

The state of children in poor countries, the state of adults. This is dire. These are people who cannot easily remember, because their basic wants are too great. This is the next challenge for all people. For all humanity. To elevate all.

These are the questions for your time: poverty, toxicity, cruelty, waste. The old questions were morality, materialism, secrecy, indulgence. The new questions are arising for the all, not just the few. This is not for this country or that country; this is for the world.

For this next generation of children, many of whom are awake and open, we say: the more who can create direct connection with the Divine or find their answers from cosmic Oneness rather from the small Earth ability—these are the children who will hold this transformation.

You also, and by you we mean adults; you are also party to this.

Every generation plays its part. This is just the simple continued evolution of the species; it is true on other planets and in other realms and other renditions. All things grow and even lack of growth is a method of growing. At some point, either you grow or you die.
If you die, you grow again.
This is intangible, and yet it is also the way of things.

There are some we will use, such as yourself. There are some we will use as a point of entry in which to spread information that will help your people to grow. New ideas begin as a spark, a licking spark on dry leaves. This spark catches flame, and begins to burn, and continues to burn long after the first spark has caught. In such a way, we have chosen many of you, and, yes, your children, too, as channels who are the first sparks of new ideas and new ways.

Those whom we now choose as channels may move aside to let us speak and teach; they are open in ways that they may share essence of spirit, without losing ego. Remember: we are one soul. One of All. It is not one being taken or possessed by another. It is simply one remembering that we are all One, and allowing this collective, universal teaching to move through.

You are a channel, because you move aside to let the universal teaching move through you—in this way, we use you to bring messages to the world. But the children who are here now—they do not move aside in the same way. They are simply remembering again what they have only very recently forgotten. They are here to teach the world, not only through their messages, but also through the very new fiber and way of their being, which is an evolutionary development for your kind.

Death is imaginary. No soul ever dies. This is just the way of it. Souls only transition into other realms, into other entities, into other aspects of the energy of the Universe.

There are many of you who see these souls, outside of their Earth life. It is as simple as opening the windows, as we have explained, or of lifting the veil, as you have said. It is a veil of illusion that, when lifted, makes it easy to see. You do not exist in other realm; however, you may see and hear there, you may even travel there in spirit. But you are Earth beings, with Earth limitations. In the energies of your mind, you may understand other realms.

Children are especially capable in these areas, because they have not forgotten to remember for as long as adults. They do not believe in the veil; they understand it is illusion.

Time has no meaning. This is an idea that presents you with much con-fusion. Time does not exist. And yet you assign it with meaning, you cut it into slices and serve it up very cold indeed. Whereas in reality—time, space, matter—all are energy, as are you, as is the Universe, as is All.

Time belongs to the ego—the soul does not recognize time. And yet on Earth, everything is structured around these: time, space, matter. The possession of such.

We say: let your need to control time be lifted. Relax your shoulders. Unstrap your watch. Stop the compulsive checking of this and that, to know what time it is. The time is Now. It is always Now. There is no other time. In this way, you may remember to live fully, here in this pres-ent moment.

With children, this is important. They understand No Time, they under-stand Now. But Earth rules push them to reject what they know is true. Let time slide, as you can. Let time shift and flow over them like water.

Understand time is illusion. Understand Now is ungraspable—like sand slipping through your fingers, even as the next Now arrives. What is your Now in this moment? This is the only thing you can measure—how Now is held in your heart.

In the way of keeping a house holy, there are many ways. There is the way of intent, in which there is respect for the home and its inhabitants. There are ways of keeping live things in the home, for the energy they bring. There are ways of keeping crystals for these vibratory powers; this is not understood by you yet, but we understand this. There are ways of reducing the droning vibration of electronica. There are ways of increas-ing interaction with nature: earth, water, clear air.

The more you live simply, the more you live with less and with items that are meaningful to you or that are from nature, the more serene you may keep your mind and your body. It is important to practice acts of sacred devotion. It is important to be taught the acts of devotion and intent, through physical objects.

You know that all things contain energy, vibration. This is the way of the Universe. As each being vibrates, so does every object. We say: it is important to know what pleases you. It is important to see what raises vibration, and what dulls it. In all things that you surround yourself with—people, ideas, objects—choose that which raises vibration. Clear the rest away—it is not useful to you. It does not serve.

Children know this. They sense this. How each item holds the memory of its lifetime. A child may merely hold the object, and this is clear to him. Guard your child carefully then. Beware of the object that is not Divine.

If your child objects to a material, be rid of it. The sense is strong in children, and should be attended to. When you are able to remember clearly again, you also will understand what your child already knows.

Items made in your poor countries—items made by your poor children. Consider if they raise vibration. We say: you know they do not. Consider why you might allow these, in your home. It is not the item itself; it is the memory and emotion it contains. The pain of another, also one of the One. Consider this.

There are times for doing, and there are times for recalling where you have been and what you have learned. Consider traveling for great distances across deserts and mountains, moving forward with every step. After many days, you pull out your map. At this time, it becomes clear where you have come from, and what you have experienced. This may be astounding to you.

Moving with the seasons, doing some things in the same way at the same time, as a koan, prayer, meditation—this allows you to enjoy the sweetness of them. The pleasure is not in doing the old thing. The pleasure is in doing the old thing as a new person. The pleasure is understanding how your soul has grown.

Yet all children must learn to find their home in the Divine. It is here that peace and comfort awaits.

Do not clutter your mind with what is distraction. By this we mean the attention you give to what is only temporary and does not affect you.

When you are obsessed with ideas in your mind, they do manifest. The thoughts of sadness lead to more sadness, and the thoughts of joy and beauty—the term you use is abundance. *When you believe in one thing, you call upon the Divine to prepare this for you. There is nothing you cannot have. But there is much you will not want. So it is important to stay clear in the mind, for the mind is the place where you are most apt to become confused.*

The heart will not lie to you, my dear ones, the heart will tell you everything. The body reveals all. But the mind can be distracted; the mind can even fool itself. We see this with so many of you, whose hearts are open and full, but who have come to allow their minds to believe what is not True.

To become grounded is to understand that you are fully, completely, energetically of this Earth. You are a being as any being, yet you exist in blood, flesh, as Earth body on Earth planet. This limits you. This frees you.

Begin to understand where your soul resides in this lifetime, and to understand what you will experience in this lifetime: love, fear, anger, compassion, all range of emotions, all swelling as the human heart. Within your heart you may hold the whole world. Tenderness, compassion, love—these are your tools.

parents' guide

Checklist for Age-Appropriate Teaching

Psychic development and spiritual growth develop naturally in Divine kids—and each child opens differently, in his or her own unique way. However, because it's useful to understand what common ages and stages of development might be for most kids, this checklist will guide you.

Ages three to five

This is a time for noticing. By noticing, I mean just that: pay attention. Watch. Keep track. See what your child does on her own. However, noticing does not mean labeling your child, such as "Marta's psychic—she knows what you're thinking!" or "Benjamin sees dead people!" Please, don't label your child! Just relax. Breathe. Notice.

At this time, kids should be in an organic, natural state—playing with toys, daydreaming, taking naps, hanging out at home. Psychic development requires downtime, so the more you can resist signing your child up for swimming lessons or gymnastics at this age, the better.

At this age you'll want to introduce the most basic skills:

a. Teach your child how to pray.

b. Teach your child to be aware of energy or vibe.

c. If your child mentions that he's seen dead people, talk about it in simple terms: "Those people live in another realm, but sometimes we can see them." If they don't see dead people—don't bring it up.

That's it! That's all for this age! So get out those blocks and crayons and stuffed animals and go crazy! Oh, wait, one more thing:

d. Be wildly affectionate, loving, and silly with your child. Enjoy this wondrous age.

Ages six to eight

A time for noticing, awareness of emerging skills, and the tiniest amount of skill development—disguised as fun. At this age, there's a lot of brainwork going on as your child transitions from preschooler/kindergartner into school age. It's a great time to learn—but you don't want to overload them.

At this time you can:

a. Begin clairsentient awareness. Ask your child to identify the vibe in given situations or with certain people, and teach how the vibe is something he can trust without question, every single time.

b. Try some clairaudience. Have your child enter light trance, then ask him to invite any spirit guides forward who have messages for him, or simply to listen to the "still, small voice" in his own mind's ear. Ask what happens.

c. Begin energy awareness. Use the energy-ball exercise to teach your child how energy looks and feels. Practice changing the color of the ball. Practice making the ball as tiny as a pea—or as large as a universe. Make it a game—fun!

d. Try some clairvoyance. Have your child enter light trance, then put up a viewing screen. Next, have him put up a psychic buddy, and see what he sees. If he has a specific question or problem, ask to be shown the answer, and see what images come up. That's it. Do this for maybe five minutes per session, max.

e. Let your child create a sacred space. Provide a table, shelf, cabinet, or other space. Then help her get started—but once she's got the hang of it, don't interfere.

Ages nine to twelve

This is an age that most parents love—old enough to have some semblance of independence, young enough to not have morphed into teenagers. In general, kids this age are easy to train psychically—they're smart, fast, they "get it." And, they're still at an age where they don't mind spending time with adults! Now's the time to:

a. Practice any or all of skills of the younger groups, only with more depth. You can work for longer periods of time, explain things more, and go deeper. Many kids this age are able to do amazing readings, healings, and energy work!

b. Model how you use intuition and *direct connection* in your own life.

c. Respect your child's need to be separate from you.

d. Provide additional resources if he's interested—let him choose what appeals or attracts.

e. Watch for signs of darker energies. At this time, any fascination with Goth or dark forces should be checked out, discussed, and redirected. Talk to your child about working in Divine energy only—not lower energies. Remember, you're the parent. It's your job to protect your child.

Age thirteen and older

You don't want to hear this, but it's true: by the time your child is about thirteen, she's ready to go her own way. She's not an adult—but she's not a child anymore. Does she still need your help and guidance? Absolutely. But not as much, or in the same way as before.

If you find this happening, wipe those tears away. Congratulations! You've done a good job—raising this beautiful child to near adulthood. In terms of psychic and spiritual development, you'll want to:

a. Step back and let your child try things out for herself.

b. Let your child make mistakes. It's not the only way she'll learn, but it's the way she'll learn the deepest.

c. Know that her connection with the Divine will develop on its own. In some cases, your child will choose a different religious or spiritual path than yours. Remember, all roads lead to the Divine.

d. Teach by example. Model your own psychic and spiritual practices.

e. Make it easy to find resources. Trips to the library, events, lectures—all may be useful to kids who are searching for answers, especially if they can't drive.

f. Watch for drugs, alcohol, and sex. Middle school is when substance problems start—and often it's as easy as stealing a few prescription tablets from the family medicine cabinet. Be clear what you have in your house, and keep track. By high school, drugs and alcohol are so accessible, you might as well be sending your kids to a state-run liquor store every day. This is reality. Educate yourself: the website www.drugfree.org is one place to start. Trust your intuition—and if you need help, get it.

g. Hand in hand with drugs and alcohol go darker energies. Goth clothes, piercings, tattoos—they're not bad in themselves, but they attract lower vibration. If a fascination with dark energy starts cropping up, pay attention!

For all ages

Want a psychic or spiritually gifted kid? Build a happy one. How? Here are five ways, for kids of any age:

a. Teach your child how to have a direct connection to the Divine, through prayer, meditation, or trance.

b. Tell your child you love him. Say "I love you" when you drop him at school, finish up a phone conversation, at bedtime.

c. Hug him, be affectionate, rub his back and shoulders. Even prickly teens who pretend they don't like to be touched will do well with a quick shoulder pat or the infamous "side hug."

d. Listen to him, in the car, on the phone, at bedtime. Listening means he talks 95 percent of the time—you listen.

e. Call him on his cell, text him, e-mail him. Make sure he knows you're in the loop of how he prefers to communicate—and communicate with him!

f. Remember that your Divine child has chosen you—and that you are working on your soul lessons together. The time you have together on Earth is a gift. Enjoy, appreciate, and make the most of every moment.

Bibliography

Atwater, P. M. H. *Beyond the Indigo Children: The New Children and the Coming of the Fifth World.* Rochester, VT: Bear & Company, 2005.

Burnham, Sophy. *A Book of Angels.* New York: Ballantine, 2004.

Burns, Litany. *The Sixth Sense of Children.* New York: New American Library, 2002.

Byrne, Rhonda. *The Secret.* New York: Atria Books, 2006.

Carroll, Lee, and Jan Tober. *The Indigo Children: The New Kids Have Arrived.* Carlsbad, CA: Hay House, 1999.

Choquette, Sonia. *The Wise Child: A Spiritual Guide to Nurturing Your Child's Intuition.* New York: Three Rivers Press, 1999.

Condron, Barbara. *How to Raise an Indigo Child.* Windyville, MO: SOM Publishing, 2006.

A Course in Miracles. Mill Valley, CA: The Foundation for Inner Peace, 2007.

Daniel, Terri. *A Swan in Heaven: Conversations Between Two Worlds.* Sisters, OR: First House Press, 2008.

Dass, Ram. *Be Here Now, Remember.* San Anselmo, CA: Hanuman Foundation, 1978. Originally published in 1971 by the Lama Foundation.

Eason, Cassandra. *Psychic Power of Children.* London: Quantum, 2005.

Elkind, David. *The Hurried Child: Growing Up Too Fast, Too Soon.* Cambridge, MA: Da Capo Press, 2001.

————. *Ties That Stress: The New Family Imbalance.* Cambridge, MA: Harvard University Press, 1994.

Emoto, Masaru. *The Hidden Messages in Water.* (Translated by David A. Thayne.) Hillsboro, OR: Beyond Words, 2004.

Enebrad, Shirley. *Over the Rainbow Bridge.* Bothell, WA: Book Publishers Network, 2009.

Gentzkow, Matthew, and Jesse M. Shapiro. "Preschool Television Viewing and Adolescent Test Scores: Historical Evidence from the Coleman Study." *Quarterly Journal of Economics,* February 2008 (vol. 123, no. 1).

Healy, Jane M. *Endangered Minds: Why Children Don't Think—And What We Can Do About It.* New York: Simon & Schuster, 1990.

————. *Your Child's Growing Mind: Brain Development and Learning from Birth to Adolescence.* New York: Broadway, 2004.

Hellinger, Bert. *Farewell: Family Constellations with Descendants of Victims and Perpetrators.* (Translated by Collen Beaumont.) Heidelberg, Germany: Carl-Auer Verlag, 2003.

Hicks, Esther, and Jerry Hicks. *The Law of Attraction.* Carlsbad, CA: Hay House, 2006.

James, Abigail Norfleet. *Teaching the Male Brain: How Boys Think, Feel, and Learn in School.* Thousand Oaks, CA: Corwin Press. 2007.

Katz, Debra Lynne. *You Are Psychic: The Art of Clairvoyant Reading & Healing.* St. Paul, MN: Llewellyn, 2004.

Knight, JZ. *Ramtha, The Mystery of Birth and Death: Redefining the Self.* Yelm, WA: JZK Publishing, 2000.

Kübler-Ross, Elisabeth. *On Death and Dying,* New York: Scribner, 1997.

Lenhart, Amanda, et al. "Teens, Video Games and Civics." Pew Internet & American Life Project, September 16, 2008. Online at www.pewinternet.org/Reports/2008/Teens-Video-Games-and-Civics.aspx.

Losey, Meg Blackburn. *The Children of Now.* Franklin Lakes, NJ: New Page Books, 2007.

Newton, Michael. *Destiny of Souls.* St. Paul, MN: Llewellyn, 2000.

———. *Life Between Lives.* St. Paul, MN: Llewellyn, 2004.

Osho. *The Book of Secrets.* New York: St. Martin's Griffin, 1998.

———. *Intuition: Knowing Beyond Logic.* New York: St. Martin's Griffin, 2001.

Riggs, Shannon. *Not in Room 204.* Morton Grove, IL: Albert Whitman and Company, 2007.

Tamura, Michael J. *You Are the Answer: Discovering and Fulfilling Your Soul's Purpose.* Woodbury, MN: Llewellyn, 2007.

Tappe, Nancy Ann. Contributor in Carrol, Lee, and Jan Tober's *The Indigo Children: The New Kids Have Arrived.* Carlsbad, CA: Hay House, 1999.

Twyman, James F. *Emissary of Love: The Psychic Children Speak to the World.* Newburyport, MA: Hampton Roads, 2002.

———. *Messages from Thomas: Raising Psychic Children.* Forres, Scotland: Findhorn Press, 2003.

Virtue, Doreen. *The Care and Feeding of Indigo Children.* Carlsbad, CA: Hay House, 2001.

———. *Divine Guidance.* Los Angeles: Renaissance Books, 1999.

Walsch, Neale Donald. *Conversations with God.* New York: Putnam, 1996.

Wiseman, Sara, *Writing the Divine: How to Use Channeling for Soul Growth & Healing.* Woodbury, MN: Llewellyn, 2009.

Glossary

Angel: A Holy Being and messenger of God in Christian and other religions.

Ashkar: An ascended master from whom I channeled *The Messages*.

Ascended master: A spirit entity that is not recently deceased or an angel; an entity that is an ascended spirit guide.

Astral projection: Ability to project one's consciousness to another place, time, or realm, while the body remains in the present reality.

Bliss: An ecstatic state of transcendence.

Buddha: The ancient spiritual teacher and Holy One, Gautama Buddha.

Chakra: Sanskrit word meaning "circle" or "wheel," corresponding to seven energy centers in the body.

Channeling: The act of receiving information from another entity through trance.

Channeled writing: Written messages received from another entity through trance.

Clairaudience: The art of psychic hearing.

Clairsentience: The art of psychic feeling.

Clairvoyance: The art of psychic seeing.

Conduit: A channel through which something flows.

Constance: The first spirit guide to deliver *The 33 Lessons*.

Crystalline children: Gifted kids identified in Meg Blackburn Losey's *The Children of Now*.

Dark energy: Lower-vibration energies, such as found in the occult.

Direct connection: The concept of being able to make a direct, two-way connection with the Divine, without a third party or additional process.

Divine: God, the Now, Source, Presence, all names for the cosmic One

Entity: A being, spirit, or presence that is not human.

Flow: The constant, creative state of the Universe. Also, the act of working with universal creative energy, Source, Presence, the Divine, the Now, One, God.

Gabriel: The third to deliver *The 33 Lessons*; an archangel.

God: The One, the Now, the Source, Presence, cosmic consciousness, the Universe, the One in which we are all One.

Guru: A holy person, master, or spiritual teacher, especially in Indian and eastern traditions.

Hajam: The spirit guide who delivered *The Truths*.

Higher self: The concept of a more evolved spirit self that exists in the subconscious.

Highest good: The concept of good for all.

Holy Beings/Holy Ones: All entities and beings who are sacred.

Indigo children: Children identified, by Lee Carroll and Jan Tober in their book *The Indigo Children*, as having a new set of psychological attributes.

Jesus: In Christian theology, the Son of God.

Kirtan: Call-and-response singing in the eastern tradition.

Koran: The holy book of Islam.

Life's path/life's purpose: What we are each put on this earth to do to achieve soul growth.

Light trance: A relaxed state of trance that comes by closing the eyes and deep breathing.

Lock into the hum: The concept of energy vibration of the Universe.

Manifesting: The act of bringing into awareness.

Meditation: A method of accessing the Divine through breath and stillness.

Medium: A person who receives messages from other realms.

Metaphysics: A branch of philosophy dealing with the cosmic realm.

Miriam: The second spirit guide to deliver *The 33 Lessons*.

Mind's eye: The concept of a place in the body in which clairvoyant information is received.

Multiple personality disorder: A psychiatric disorder in which a person displays several distinct personalities.

Mystic: A person who practices the spiritual arts.

The Now: The concept of the present time and God as being One and the same.

Prayer: A method of petitioning, asking, or speaking to God from your heart; also a religious practice.

Psychic: A person with the innate skill of using intuition as a result of connection with the cosmic consciousness.

Ragnar: An ascended master from whom I channeled *The Messages*.

Receiving: The act of channeling information and guidance from spiritual entities and Holy Beings.

Saints: In Catholic and other Christian theology, humans who have become sacred through miracles or works.

Self-levitation: The ability to lift oneself off the ground through meditation.

Shaman: A mystic and/or healer who works in the natural and animal realm.

Soft gaze: A method used in trance and meditation for seeing what is directly in front of the viewer, without paying too much attention to it, and while at the same time having the ability to see what is in the room and beyond.

Soul growth: The purpose of our lives; the concept of spiritual growth as the goal of human life.

The Source: Another name for God.

Spirit guide: An entity from the spirit realm who communicates to and through us.

Spiritualism: A belief system popular in the late 1800s and early 1900s, particularly in the United States and Great Britain.

Star children: Kids identified in Meg Blackburn Losey's *The Children of Now*.

Strands: The clues, signs, and symbols that the Divine uses to move us along our life's path.

Synchronicity: A seemingly coincidental occurrence of events, as directed by universal flow.

Trance: A mystic state defined by the ability to connect to and experience cosmic consciousness.

Vocalized channeling: A method of receiving in which messages are received from another entity through vocalized speech or sound.

Window: The concept of an open portal or place for communication between two or more realms.

Index

To Write to the Author

If you wish to contact the author or would like more information about this book, please write to the author in care of Llewellyn Worldwide and we will forward your request. Both the author and publisher appreciate hearing from you and learning of your enjoyment of this book and how it has helped you. Llewellyn Worldwide cannot guarantee that every letter written to the author can be answered, but all will be forwarded. Please write to:

Sara Wiseman
℅ Llewellyn Worldwide
2143 Wooddale Drive
Woodbury, MN 55125-2989

Please enclose a self-addressed stamped envelope for reply,
or $1.00 to cover costs. If outside the USA, enclose
an international postal reply coupon.

Many of Llewellyn's authors have websites with additional information and resources. For more information, please visit our website at http://www.llewellyn.com.

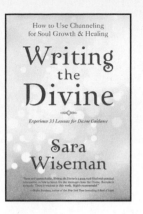

Writing the Divine

How to Use Channeling for Soul Growth & Healing

SARA WISEMAN

Close your eyes. Pick up a pen. Channel the Divine.

Discover that you don't need a guru, medium, priest, or a PhD to communicate directly with the Divine. In *Writing the Divine*, you'll get specific directions for actually channeling spiritual wisdom yourself. The directions are explicit, practical, and well-tested, but presented with humor and grace. It's truly the most complete guide to channeling, autowriting, and creating inspired journaling.

Sara Wiseman reveals simple tools you can use to open up to Divine wisdom, no matter your stage of spiritual development. Included are Wiseman's own channelings, and a set of thirty-three Divine lessons on love, life, and spiritual awakening that will remind you of the famed *A Course in Miracles*.

978-0-7387-1581-0, 312 pp., 6 x 9   **$16.95**

You Are Psychic

The Art of Clairvoyant Reading & Healing

Debra Lynne Katz

Learn to see inside yourself and others. Clairvoyance is the ability to see information—in the form of visions and images—through nonphysical means. According to Debra Lynne Katz, anyone who can visualize a simple shape, such as a circle, has clairvoyant ability.

In *You Are Psychic*, Katz shares her own experiences and methods for developing these clairvoyant skills. Her techniques and psychic tools are easy to follow and have been proven to work by longtime practitioners. Psychic readings, healing methods, vision interpretation, and spiritual counseling are all covered in this practical guide to clairvoyance.

978-0-7387-0592-7, 336 pp., 6 x 9   **$16.95**

Extraordinary Psychic
Proven Techniques to Master Your Natural Psychic Abilities
Debra Lynne Katz

Whether you are a beginner exploring your psychic abilities, or a professional looking to fine-tune your skills, this training guide will teach you to better understand your clairvoyant capacities and to reach your full psychic potential.

This is a no-nonsense, straightforward approach to becoming the clairvoyant you truly are, without apology or hesitation. The proven author of the popular title *You Are Psychic* motivates students along a path of self-discovery that begins with a fresh and concise breakdown of basic clairvoyant training techniques. Next, Katz provides in-depth answers to all your frequently asked questions about how to discover, harness, and apply your psychic skills through readings as well as healings. Learn how to get over the fear of doing readings. Discover how to remote-view objects and events. Katz also teaches how to employ the laws of attraction to overcome challenges and to build a career as an ethical psychic reader and healer.

978-0-7387-1333-5, 312 pp., 6 x 9   **$17.95**

To order, call 1-877-NEW-WRLD
Prices subject to change without notice
Order at Llewellyn.com 24 hours a day, 7 days a week!

Destiny of Souls

New Case Studies of Life Between Lives

MICHAEL NEWTON, PHD

A pioneer in uncovering the secrets of life, internationally recognized spiritual hypnotherapist Dr. Michael Newton takes you once again into the heart of the spirit world. His groundbreaking research was first published in the best-selling *Journey of Souls*, the definitive study on the afterlife. In *Destiny of Souls*, the saga continues with seventy case histories of real people who were regressed into their lives between lives. Dr. Newton answers the requests of the thousands of readers of the first book who wanted more details about various aspects of life on the other side. *Destiny of Souls* is also designed for the enjoyment of first-time readers who haven't read *Journey of Souls*.

978-1-56718-499-0, 432 pp., 6 x 9 **$16.95**

Life Between Lives

Hypnotherapy for Spiritual Regression

Michael Newton, PhD

A famed hypnotherapist's groundbreaking methods of accessing the spiritual realms.

Dr. Michael Newton is world-famous for his spiritual regression techniques that take subjects back to their time in the spirit world. His best-selling books of client case studies have left thousands of readers eager to discover their own afterlife adventures, their soul companions, their guides, and their purpose in this lifetime.

Now, for the first time in print, Dr. Newton reveals his step-by-step methods. His experiential approach to the spiritual realms sheds light on the age-old questions of who we are, where we came from, and why we are here.

978-0-7387-0465-4, 240 pp., 6 x 9   **$15.95**

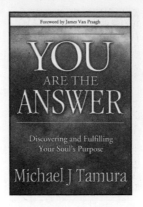

You Are the Answer

Discovering and Fulfilling Your Soul's Purpose

Michael J Tamura

World-renowned spiritual teacher, healer, and clairvoyant Michael J Tamura shares his wisdom in this inspirational guide to true spiritual empowerment.

Hailed as a "beautiful manual for living" by Echo Bodine, *You Are the Answer* brings us profound spiritual lessons, highlighted by the author's powerful true stories. Discover how to use your intuition, make room for spirit in your life, and respond—instead of react—to everyday experiences. As you build a temple of the soul, you'll learn to recognize truth, create miracles in your own life, and find your purpose for living!

This insightful and moving guide also features a "spiritual toolkit" of daily practices and exercises to help you on your extraordinary journey in consciousness exploration, healing, and spiritual development.

978-0-7387-1196-6, 288 pp., 6 x 9   **$16.95**

Growing Up Psychic

From Skeptic to Believer

MICHAEL BODINE

FOREWORD BY ECHO BODINE

What's it like to grow up psychic—in a family of psychics?

Michael Bodine was only seven when his family made a shocking discovery: he, his mother, and his siblings—including his sister, the renowned Echo Bodine—are psychic. What was it like to grow up in a house teeming with ghosts and psychic experimentation, contend with a mind-reading mother, befriend a spirit boy, and hunt ghosts with his sister Echo? And what happens when Michael's psychic talents become more of a burden than a blessing?

From adolescence to adulthood, this gripping memoir chronicles the wondrous, hair-raising, hilarious, and moving moments in Michael Bodine's life, punctuated by an ongoing struggle to come to terms with the paranormal. Discover how he rebounds from drug and alcohol dependency and learns to accept—and embrace—his unusual gifts.

978-0-7387-1961-0, 312 pp., 6 x 9 $16.95

The Happy Medium
Awakening to Your Natural Intuition
Jodi Livon

What is it like to be a medium? Now is your chance to learn from a pro! With wit and candor, intuitive coach Jodi Livon shares the hard-won wisdom she's acquired on her fascinating journey as a psychic medium.

Over the years, Livon has helped clients, friends, family, and the dead find healing and learn life lessons. These true and incredibly touching stories not only illuminate spirit communication, but also offer guidance on tuning in to your own intuition. By relating how she receives and interprets psychic impressions, Livon shows firsthand how the psychic process works. With tips on trusting your senses, maintaining emotional balance, staying grounded, and interpreting signs from the universe, *The Happy Medium* can help you ignite your natural intuitive insights for higher awareness and guidance in life's decisions.

978-0-7387-1463-9, 312 pp., 6 x 9   **$16.95**

Practical Guide to Psychic Powers

Awaken Your Sixth Sense

DENNING & PHILLIPS

Because you are missing out on so much without them! Who has not dreamed of possessing powers to move objects without physically touching them, to see at a distance or into the future, to know another's thoughts, to read the past of an object or person, or to find water or mineral wealth by dowsing?

This book is a complete course—teaching you step by step how to develop the powers that actually have been yours since birth. Psychic powers are a natural part of your mind; by expanding your mind in this way, you will gain health and vitality, emotional strength, greater success in your daily pursuits, and a new understanding of your inner self.

You'll learn to play with these new skills, working with groups of friends to accomplish things you never would have believed possible. The text shows you how to make the equipment, do the exercises—many of them at any time, anywhere—and how to use your abilities to change your life and the lives of those close to you.

978-0-87542-191-9, 288 pp., 5³⁄₁₆ x 8   **$11.95**

Discover Your Psychic Type

Developing and Using Your Natural Intuition

SHERRIE DILLARD

Intuition and spiritual growth are indelibly linked, according to professional psychic and therapist Sherrie Dillard. Offering a personalized approach to psychic development, this breakthrough guide introduces four different psychic types and explains how to develop the unique spiritual capabilities of each.

Are you a physical, mental, emotional, or spiritual intuitive? Take Dillard's insightful quiz to find out. Discover more about each type's intuitive nature, personality, potential physical weaknesses, and more. There are guided meditations for each kind of intuitive, as well as exercises to hone your psychic skills. Remarkable stories from the author's professional life illustrate the incredible power of intuition and its connection to the spirit world, inner wisdom, and your higher self.

From psychic protection to spirit guides to mystical states, Dillard offers guidance as you evolve toward the final destination of every psychic type: union with the Divine.

978-0-7387-1278-9, 288 pp., 5³⁄₁₆ x 8 **$14.95**

To order, call 1-877-NEW-WRLD
Prices subject to change without notice
Order at Llewellyn.com 24 hours a day, 7 days a week!